Foundations in Accountancy/ACCA

Applied Knowledge

Financial Accounting (FFA/FA)

Practice & Revision Kit

For exams from 1 September 2023 to 31 August 2024

BPP

First edition May 2011

Eleventh edition 2023

ISBN: 9781 0355 0101 4

Previous ISBN: 9781 5097 4601 9

e-ISBN: 9781 0355 0066 6

British Library Cataloguing-in-Publication Data

A catalogue record for this book is available from the British Library

Published by

BPP Learning Media Ltd

BPP House, Aldine Place

142–144 Uxbridge Road

London W12 8AA

learningmedia.bpp.com

Printed in the United Kingdom

Your learning materials, published by BPP Learning Media Ltd, are printed on paper obtained from traceable sustainable sources.

The contents of this course material are intended as a guide and not professional advice. Although every effort has been made to ensure that the contents of this course material are correct at the time of going to press, BPP Learning Media makes no warranty that the information in this course material is accurate or complete and accept no liability for any loss or damage suffered by any person acting or refraining from acting as a result of the material in this course material.

We are grateful to the Association of Chartered Certified Accountants for permission to reproduce past examination questions and extracts from the syllabus. The suggested solutions in the further question practice bank have been prepared by BPP Learning Media Ltd, except where otherwise stated.

BPP Learning Media is grateful to the IASB for permission to reproduce extracts from IFRS® Accounting Standards, IAS® Standards, SIC and IFRIC.

A note about copyright

Dear Customer

What does the little © mean and why does it matter?

Your market-leading BPP books, course materials and e-learning materials do not write and update themselves. People write them on their own behalf or as employees of an organisation that invests in this activity. Copyright law protects their livelihoods. It does so by creating rights over the use of the content.

Breach of copyright is a form of theft – as well as being a criminal offence in some jurisdictions, it is potentially a serious breach of professional ethics.

With current technology, things might seem a bit hazy but, basically, without the express permission of BPP Learning Media:

- Photocopying our materials is a breach of copyright
- Printing our digital materials in order to share them with or forward them to a third party or use them in any way other than in connection with your BPP studies is a breach of copyright

You can, of course, sell your books, in the form in which you have bought them – once you have finished with them. (Is this fair to your fellow students? We update for a reason.) Please note the e-products are sold on a single user licence basis: we do not supply 'unlock' codes to people who have bought them secondhand.

And what about outside the UK? BPP Learning Media strives to make our materials available at prices students can afford by local printing arrangements, pricing policies and partnerships which are clearly listed on our website. A tiny minority ignore this and indulge in criminal activity by illegally photocopying our material or supporting organisations that do. If they act illegally and unethically in one area, can you really trust them?

IFRS

Contents

Question index

Helping you with your revision

BPP Learning Media – ACCA Approved Content Provider

As an ACCA Approved Content Provider, BPP Learning Media gives you the **opportunity** to use revision materials reviewed by the ACCA examining team. By incorporating the ACCA examining team's comments and suggestions regarding the depth and breadth of syllabus coverage, the BPP Learning Media Practice & Revision Kit provides excellent, **ACCA-approved** support for your revision.

These materials are reviewed by the ACCA examining team. The objective of the review is to ensure that the material properly covers the syllabus and study guide outcomes, used by the examining team in setting the exams, in the appropriate breadth and depth. The review does not ensure that every eventuality, combination or application of examinable topics is addressed by the ACCA Approved Content. Nor does the review comprise a detailed technical check of the content as the Approved Content Provider has its own quality assurance processes in place in this respect.

BPP Learning Media do everything possible to ensure the material is accurate and up to date when sending to print. In the event that any errors are found after the print date, they are uploaded to the following website: www.bpp.com/learningmedia/Errata.

Selecting questions

We provide signposts to help you plan your revision, including a full **question index**.

Attempting mock exams

There are three mock exams that provide practice at coping with the pressures of the exam day. We strongly recommend that you attempt them under exam conditions. **Mock exam 1** is the ACCA Specimen Exam. **Mock exam 2** and **Mock exam 3** reflect the question styles and syllabus coverage of the exam.

Using your BPP Practice & Revision Kit

Aim of this Practice & Revision Kit

To provide the practice to help you succeed in the examination for Financial Accounting (FFA/FA).

To pass the examination you need a thorough understanding in all areas covered by the syllabus and teaching guide.

Recommended approach

- Make sure you are able to answer questions on **everything** specified by the syllabus and teaching guide. You cannot make any assumptions about what questions may come up in your exam. The examining team aims to discourage 'question spotting'.
- All sections have a selection of **OBJECTIVE QUESTIONS** (including Multiple Choice Questions). Make good use of the **HELPING HANDS** provided to help you answer the questions.
- There is a mark allocation for each question. Each mark carries with it a time allocation of 1.2 minutes. A 2-mark question should therefore be completed in 2.4 minutes.
- 70% of the exam consists of individual **objective test questions**. You should attempt each bank of objective test questions to ensure you are familiar with their styles and to practise your technique. Skills checkpoint 1 Approach to Objective Test Questions will provide useful guidance on how best to approach these questions.
- The remaining 30% of the exam is a multi-task question, which is essentially a range of related objective test questions. Skills checkpoint 2 Approach to Multi-Task Questions will provide guidance on how to tackle these.
- Once you have completed all of the questions in the body of this Practice & Revision Kit, you should attempt the **MOCK EXAMS** under examination conditions. Check your answers against our answers to find out how well you did.

Passing the FFA/FA exam

Financial Accounting aims to develop your knowledge and understanding of the underlying principles, concepts and regulations relating to financial accounting. You will need to demonstrate technical proficiency in the use of double entry techniques, including the preparation of basic financial statements for incorporated and unincorporated entities, as well as simple consolidated financial statements for group entities. You also need to be able to conduct a basic interpretation of financial statements. If you plan to progress through the ACCA qualification, the skills you learn in FFA/FA will be built upon in the exams for Financial Reporting (FR) and SBR Strategic Business Reporting (SBR).

To access the Foundations in Accountancy syllabi, visit the ACCA website: www.accaglobal.com

Computer-based exams

The Financial Accounting exam is a computer-based exam (CBE).

Computer-based examinations (CBEs) are available for the Foundations in Accountancy exams. The CBE exams for the first seven modules can be taken at any time, these are referred to as 'exams on demand'. The Option exams can be sat in June and December of each year, these are referred to as 'exams on sitting'. Financial Accounting is an 'exam on demand'. Computer-based examinations must be taken at an ACCA CBE Licensed Centre.

How do CBEs work?

- Questions are displayed on a monitor.
- Candidates enter their answer directly onto the computer.
- Candidates have two hours to complete the examination.
- Candidates are provided with a Provisional Result Notification showing their results before leaving the examination room.
- The CBE Licensed Centre uploads the results to the ACCA (as proof of the candidate's performance) within 72 hours.
- Candidates sitting the Option exams will receive their results approximately five weeks after the exams sitting once they have been marked by an expert.
- Candidates can check their exam status on the ACCA website by logging into myACCA.

Benefits

- Flexibility as the first seven modules, exams on demand, can be sat at any time.
- Resits for the first seven modules can also be taken at any time and there is no restriction on the number of times a candidate can sit a CBE.
- Instant feedback for the exams on demand as the computer displays the results at the end of the CBE.
- Results are notified to ACCA within 72 hours.

For more information on computer-based exams, visit the ACCA website:

www.accaglobal.com/gb/en/student/exam-entry-and-administration/computer-basedexams.html

Approach to examining the syllabus

The exam is structured as follows:

	No. of marks
Section A – 35 compulsory objective questions of 2 marks each	70
Section B – 2 compulsory multi-task questions of 15 marks each	30
	100

The Financial Accounting syllabus is assessed by a 2 hour exam. The pass mark is 50%. All questions in the exam are compulsory. This means you cannot avoid any topic, but also means that you do not need to dedicate time in the exam deciding which questions to attempt.

Section A consists of 35 objective test (OT) questions worth two marks each and cover a broad range of syllabus topics. The OT questions can take the form of multiple choice, multiple response, number entry or multiple response matching. This means that the examining team is able to test most of the syllabus at each sitting, so you need to have revised right across the syllabus for this exam.

Section B consists of two multi-task questions (15 marks each) testing the candidates' understanding and application of financial accounting skills in more depth. In Section B candidates are required to provide answers which test their understanding and ability to draft financial statements. Candidates may be required to prepare financial statements for a single entity or for a group of companies. There may also be some element of ratio calculation/interpretation. You may not always be required to prepare the full financial statement and may instead be asked to complete a partial statement. In this situation there will be additional elements to the question. Candidates will be required to prepare the financial statements using a variety of number entries, pull down menus and multiple response matching.

Revision

This Practice and Revision kit has been reviewed by the FFA/FA examining team and contains the ACCA Specimen Exam, so if you just work through it to the end you would be very well prepared for the exam. You must also visit the ACCA website (www.accaglobal.com) to familiarise yourself with the CBE software. It is important to tackle questions under exam conditions. Allow yourself just the number of minutes shown next to the questions in the index and don't look at the answers until you have finished. Then correct your answer and go back to the Workbook for any topic you are having trouble with. Try the same questions again a week later – you will be surprised how much better you are getting. Doing the questions like this will really show you what you know, and will make the exam experience less worrying.

Sitting the exam

If you have diligently done your revision you can pass this exam. There are a couple of points to bear in mind:

- Read the question properly.
- Don't spend more than the allotted time on each question. If you are having trouble with a question, use the 'flag for review' function in the exam software and carry on. You can come back to it at the end.

Remote invigilated exams

In certain geographical areas it may be possible for you to take your exam remotely. This option, which is subject to strict conditions, can offer increased flexibility and convenience under certain circumstances. Further guidance, including the detailed requirements and conditions for taking the exam by this method, is contained on ACCA's website at https://www.accaglobal.com/an/en/student/exam-entry-and-administration/about-our-exams/remote-exams/remote-session-exams.html.

Essential skills areas to be successful in the Financial Accounting (FFA/FA) exam

We think there are three areas you should develop in order to achieve exam success in Financial Accounting (FFA/FA):

(a) Knowledge application: You will develop your technical knowledge as you work through the BPP Financial Accounting Workbook and this Practice & Revision Kit.

(b) Specific FFA/FA skills

(c) Exam success skills

These are shown in the diagram below.

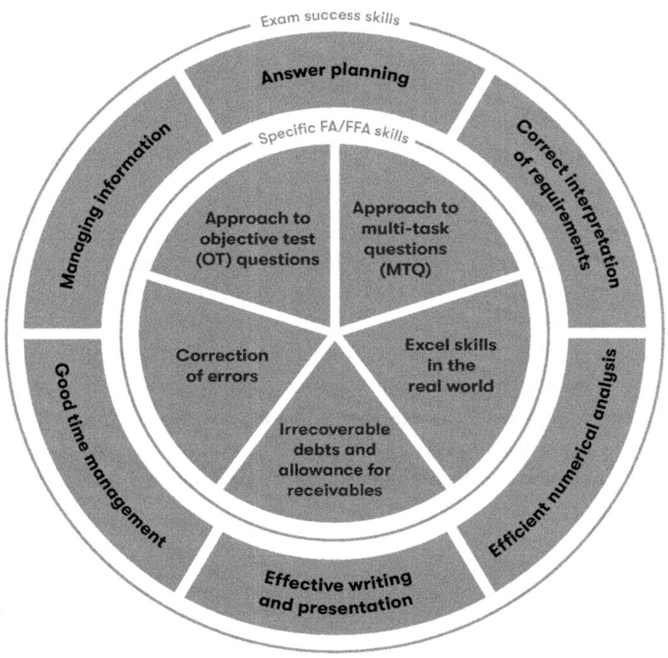

Specific FFA/FA skills

These are the skills specific to FFA/FA that we think you need to develop in order to pass the exam.

In the Workbook, there are five Skills Checkpoints which define each skill and show how it is applied in answering a question. A brief summary of each skill is given below.

Skill 1: Approach to objective test (OT) Questions

The FFA exam contains two sections. Section A consists of 35 objective test (OT) questions worth 2 marks each and Section B contains 2 multi-task questions worth 15 marks each. The multi-task questions are made up of OT questions and therefore being able to answer OT questions effectively is extremely important.

This skills checkpoint will focus on Section A questions, explaining the best way to tackle these questions and illustrating the technique through worked examples.

BPP recommends a step-by-step technique for approaching objective test questions:

Step 1 Read the requirement first!

Step 2 Apply your technical knowledge to the data in the question.

Step 3 Answer the questions you know first – flag the ones you don't know and come back to them later.

Step 4 Answer all questions – there is no penalty for an incorrect answer.

Skill 1 is developed further in Skills Checkpoint 1 which is available in the Financial Accounting Workbook.

Skill 2: Approach to multi-task questions (MTQs)

MTQs in Section B might ask you to prepare financial statements for a single entity or for a group of companies. There may also be some element of ratio calculation/interpretation. You may not always be required to prepare the full financial statement and may instead be asked to complete a partial statement. In this situation there will be additional elements to the question.

In this skills checkpoint, we will focus on the specific skills required in a multi-task question. We take you through the technique you should adopt and illustrate that through the use of questions.

BPP recommends a step-by-step technique for approaching multi-task questions:

Step 1 Read the requirements of all tasks

Step 2 Recall any relevant technical theory

Step 3 Answer the questions you know first

Step 4 Answer all questions

Skill 2 is developed further in Skills Checkpoint 2 which is available in the Financial Accounting Workbook.

Skill 3: Excel skills in the real world

As you move through your ACCA examinations and your accountancy career you will need good spreadsheet skills. It is crucial that you have a good working knowledge of spreadsheets and that you are able to use them quickly and effectively. Many people do not use Excel to its full potential, for example they type in totals rather than asking Excel to sum it for them. This often leads to errors.

This is a practical skill aimed at your working life rather than being directly related to a skill that you need to pass this exam.

Whilst this section is not exam focussed, spreadsheets will be a key part of your accountancy career. Future employers will always look for good core spreadsheet skills when selecting a candidate for a role.

Skill 3 is developed further in Skills Checkpoint 3 which is available in the Financial Accounting Workbook.

Skill 4: Irrecoverable debts and the allowance for receivables

The 2018/2019 examiners' report commented that the topic of 'irrecoverable debts and allowance for receivables' continues to be an area of the syllabus where performance is mixed with many candidates not providing the correct response. There is often a lot of detail in these questions and they need to be read very carefully.

In this skills checkpoint we will recap some of the key areas and identify where students typically struggle with this topic and how to get to grips with it.

Skill 4 is developed further in Skills Checkpoint 4 which is available in the Financial Accounting Workbook.

Skill 5: Correction of errors

The correction of errors area of the examination often causes difficulties for candidates as they are required to think around the subject rather than just rote learning.

A step-by-step technique for attempting these questions is outlined in the checkpoint along with a reminder of the key areas of this topic.

Questions are used to highlight the problems students face and how to address them. It is similar to the structure we have seen for our other skills.

Skill 5 is developed further in Skills Checkpoint 5 which is available in the Financial Accounting Workbook.

Exam success skills

Passing the FFA/FA exam requires more than applying syllabus knowledge and demonstrating the specific FFA/FA skills; it also requires the development of excellent exam technique through question practice.

We consider the following six skills to be vital for exam success. The Skills Checkpoints show how each of these skills can be applied specifically to the FFA/FA exam.

Exam success skill 1

Managing information

You will not have to deal with large amounts of information in each individual question in FFA. Some of the questions in the exam will present you with a short scenario, particularly in the Section B questions. The skill is how you handle this information while working under time pressure.

You must take an active approach to reading each scenario. Focus on the requirement first, underlining/ highlighting key instructions, including words like 'NOT'. Then think about any technical knowledge that is relevant before reading the scenario for the question. Doing this means that your mind will be focussed as you read the scenario, which means you will take in the information better.

Exam success skill 2

Correct interpretation of the requirements

It is important to note the requirement carefully. Look out for the number of options you have to choose, as not all questions require only one option. Also, beware of challenges, such as the information being presented in one particular order in the scenario, but being presented in a different order in the options.

Exam success skill 3

Answer planning: Priorities, structure and logic

This skill is not so relevant for the Applied Knowledge exams.

Exam success skill 4

Efficient numerical analysis

An important tip in numerical questions is not to look at the options until you have completed the calculation as you think it should be done. The reason for this is that the 'wrong answers' are chosen carefully to look very realistic, and you may be tempted to choose one of these if you don't do the calculation first.

Exam success skill 5

Effective writing and presentation

This skill is not relevant for FA/FFA as all the questions are objective test and multi-task questions so you will not have to write.

Exam success skill 6

Good time management

The exam is two hours long. You should therefore spend 1.2 minutes per mark. It is best to work through Section A first, which should take you 84 minutes, before spending the remaining 36 minutes on Section B.

Don't get stuck on difficult questions – if a particular question does appear difficult, move on, and come back to it after you have answered all the easier questions.

Don't time yourself for each question, but do check every half hour that you have answered 25 marks worth of questions.

Two minutes before the end of your time for Section A, go back and answer all outstanding questions, even if you have to guess. There is no harm in guessing as there is no negative marking in ACCA exams, so the worst that can happen is you don't gain two marks for the question.

If you find that this approach doesn't work for you, don't worry – you can develop your own technique.

Keep an eye on the clock

Aim to attempt all requirements, but be ready to be ruthless and move on if your answer is not going as planned. The challenge for many is sticking to planned timings. Be aware this is difficult to achieve in the early stages of your studies and be ready to let this skill develop over time.

Question practice

Question practice is a core part of learning new topic areas. When you practice questions, you should focus on improving the Exam success skills – personal to your needs – by obtaining feedback or through a process of self-assessment.

Tackling multiple choice questions (MCQs)

MCQs are part of all Foundations in Accountancy exams.

The MCQs in your exam contain four possible answers. You have to **choose the option that best answers the question**. The incorrect options are called distracters. There is a skill in answering MCQs quickly and correctly. By practising MCQs you can develop this skill, giving you a better chance of passing the exam.

You may wish to follow the approach outlined below, or you may prefer to adapt it.

Step 1 Skim read all the MCQs and identify what appear to be the easier questions.

Step 2 Attempt each question – **starting with the easier questions** identified in Step 1. Read the question **thoroughly**. You may prefer to work out the answer before looking at the options, or you may prefer to look at the options at the beginning. Adopt the method that works best for you.

Step 3 Read the options and see if one matches your own answer. Be careful with numerical questions as the distracters are designed to match answers that incorporate common errors. Check that your calculation is correct. Have you followed the requirement exactly? Have you included every stage of the calculation?

Step 4 You may find that none of the options match your answer.

- Re-read the question to ensure that you understand it and are answering the requirement.
- Eliminate any obviously wrong answers.
- Consider which of the remaining answers is the most likely to be correct and select the option.

Step 5 If you are still unsure make a note and continue to the next question.

Step 6 Revisit unanswered questions. When you come back to a question after a break you often find you are able to answer it correctly straight away. If you are still unsure have a guess. You are not penalised for incorrect answers, so **never leave a question unanswered**!

A note of caution

After extensive practice and revision of MCQs, you may find that you recognise a question when you sit the exam. Be aware that the detail and/or requirement may be different. If the question seems familiar read the requirement and options carefully – **do not** assume that it is identical.

Using your BPP products

This Practice & Revision Kit gives you the question practice and guidance you need in the exam. Our other products can also help you pass:

- **Workbook** introduces and explains the knowledge required for your exam

You can purchase this product by visiting.www.bpp.com/learning-media.

Questions

Part A: The context and purpose of financial reporting

1 The context and purpose of financial reporting (41 mins)

1.1 Who issues IFRS® Standards?

- O The IFRS Advisory Committee
- O The stock exchange
- O The International Accounting Standards Board (the Board)
- O The government

(2 marks)

1.2 Which groups of people are most likely to be interested in the financial statements of a sole trader?

(1) Shareholders of the entity

(2) The business's bank manager

(3) The tax authorities

(4) Financial analysts

- O 1 and 2 only
- O 2 and 3 only
- O 3 and 4 only
- O 1, 2 and 3 only

(2 marks)

1.3 Identify, by indicating the relevant box in the table below, whether each of the following statements is true or false.

A supplier of goods on credit is interested only in the statement of financial position, ie an indication of the current state of affairs.	**TRUE**	**FALSE**
The objective of financial statements is to provide financial information about the reporting entity's assets, liabilities, equity, income and expenses that is useful to users of the financial statements in assessing the prospects for future net cash flows to the reporting entity and in accessing management's stewardship of the entity's economic resources.	**TRUE**	**FALSE**

(2 marks)

1.4 Which of the following are advantages of trading as a limited liability company?

(1) Operating as a limited liability company makes raising finance easier because additional shares can be issued to raise additional cash.

(2) Operating as a limited liability company is more risky than operating as a sole trader because the shareholders of a business are liable for all the debts of the business whereas the sole trader is only liable for the debts up to the amount he has invested.

- O 1 only
- O 2 only
- O Both 1 and 2
- O Neither 1 or 2

(2 marks)

1.5 Which of the following best describes corporate governance?

- O Corporate governance is the system of rules and regulations surrounding financial reporting.
- O Corporate governance is the system by which companies and other entities are directed and controlled.
- O Corporate governance is carried out by the finance department in preparing the financial statements.
- O Corporate governance is the system by which an entity monitors its impact on the natural environment.

(2 marks)

1.6 Identify which of the following statements are true.

(1) The directors of a company are ultimately responsible for the preparation of financial statements, even if the majority of the work on them is performed by the finance department.

(2) If financial statements are audited, then the responsibility for those financial statements instead falls on the auditors instead of the directors.

(3) There are generally no laws surrounding the duties of directors in managing the affairs of a company.

- O 1 only
- O 2 only
- O 2 and 3 only
- O 1 and 3 only

(2 marks)

1.7 Which of the following statements correctly describes the contents of the statement of financial position?

- O A list of ledger balances shown in debit and credit columns
- O A list of all the assets owned and all the liabilities owed by a business
- O A record of income generated and expenditure incurred over a given period
- O A record of the amount of cash generated and used by a company in a given period

(2 marks)

1.8 Which of the following statements correctly describes the contents of the statement of profit or loss?

- O A list of ledger balances shown in debit and credit columns
- O A list of all the assets owned and all the liabilities owed by a business
- O A record of income generated and expenditure incurred over a given period
- O A record of the amount of cash generated and used by a company in a given period

(2 marks)

1.9 Which of the following are true of partnerships?

(1) The partners' individual exposure to debt is limited.

(2) Financial statements for the partnership by law must be produced and made public.

(3) A partnership is not a separate legal entity from the partners themselves.

- 1 and 2 only
- 2 only
- 3 only
- 1 and 3 only

(2 marks)

1.10 Which of the following statements is/are true?

(1) Directors of companies have a duty of care to show reasonable competence in their management of the affairs of a company.

(2) Directors of companies must act honestly in what they consider to be the best interest of the company.

(3) A director's main aim should be to create wealth for the shareholders of the company.

- 1 and 2 only
- 2 only
- 1, 2 and 3
- 1 and 3 only

(2 marks)

1.11 Which of the following statements is/are true?

(1) The IFRS Interpretations Committee is a forum for the International Accounting Standards Board (the Board) to consult with the outside world.

(2) The IFRS Foundation produces IFRS Standards. The IFRS Foundation is overseen by the Board.

(3) One of the objectives of the IFRS Foundation is to bring about convergence of national accounting standards and IFRS Standards.

- 1 and 3 only
- 2 only
- 2 and 3 only
- 3 only

(2 marks)

1.12 What is the role of the International Accounting Standards Board (the Board)?

- Oversee the standard setting and regulatory process
- Formulate IFRS Standards
- Review defective accounts
- Control the accountancy profession

(2 marks)

1.13 Which of the following is **NOT** an objective of the IFRS Foundation?

- O Through the International Accounting Standards Board (the Board), develop a single set of globally accepted IFRS Standards
- O Promote the use and rigorous application of IFRS Standards
- O Ensure IFRS Standards focus primarily on the needs of global, multi-national organisations
- O Bring about the convergence of national accounting standards and IFRS Standards

(2 marks)

1.14 Which of the following statements correctly describes how IFRS Standards should be used?

- O To provide examples of best financial reporting practice for national bodies who develop their own requirements
- O To ensure high ethical standards are maintained by financial reporting professionals internationally
- O To facilitate the enforcement of a single set of global financial reporting standards
- O To prevent national bodies from developing their own financial reporting standards

(2 marks)

1.15 Which of the following is a benefit of running a business as a sole trader?

- O In the event that the business generates a loss, this is shared by the partners instead of being borne by a sole trader only.
- O Any debts of the business that cannot be met from the business assets are met from the owners' private resources.
- O In the event that the business generates a profit, this is due to the sole trader only.
- O The sole trader is not liable for the debts of the business. **(2 marks)**

1.16 Which of the following is a benefit of incorporation?

- O The company's shareholders are not personally liable for the debts of the business.
- O The company directors must ensure the accounts are filed at Companies House by a specified date.
- O Companies must comply with the provisions of the Companies Act whereas unincorporated businesses do not.
- O The company's tax charge must be shown in the statement of profit or loss. **(2 marks)**

1.17 Identify, by indicating the relevant box in the table below, whether each of the following statements is true or false.

Sole traders and partnerships are unincorporated businesses. This means there is a legal distinction between the business and their owners.	**TRUE**	**FALSE**
When a sole trader takes money from the business for personal use, this is known as drawings.	**TRUE**	**FALSE**

(2 marks)

(Total = 34 marks)

Part B: The qualitative characteristics of financial information

2 The qualitative characteristics of financial information (60 mins)

2.1 Which accounting concept should be considered if the owner of a business takes goods from inventory for their own personal use?

- O The materiality concept
- O The accruals basis
- O The going concern concept
- O The business entity concept **(2 marks)**

2.2 Sales revenue should be recognised when goods and services have been supplied to the customer; costs are incurred when goods and services have been received.

Which accounting concept governs the above?

- O The business entity concept
- O The materiality concept
- O The accruals basis
- O The duality concept **(2 marks)**

2.3 Which accounting concept states that omitting or misstating this information could influence users of the financial statements?

- O The consistency concept
- O The accruals basis
- O The materiality concept
- O The going concern concept **(2 marks)**

2.4 According to the IASB's *Conceptual Framework for Financial Reporting*, which **TWO** of the following are part of faithful representation?

(1) Neutrality

(2) Relevance

(3) Fair presentation

(4) Free from material error

- O 1 and 2
- O 2 and 3
- O 1 and 4
- O 3 and 4 **(2 marks)**

2.5 Which of the following accounting concepts means that similar items should receive a similar accounting treatment?

- O Conformity
- O Accruals
- O Matching
- O Consistency

(2 marks)

2.6 Listed below are some characteristics of financial information.

(1) Relevance

(2) Consistency

(3) Faithful representation

(4) Accuracy

Which one of these are qualitative characteristics of financial information according to the IASB's *Conceptual Framework*?

- O 1 and 2
- O 2 and 4
- O 3 and 4
- O 1 and 3

(2 marks)

2.7 Which of the following statements describes the qualitative characteristic of faithful representation?

- O Revenue earned must be matched against the expenditure incurred in earning it.
- O Having information available to decision makers in time to be capable of influencing their decisions.
- O The presentation and classification of items in the financial statements should stay the same from one period to the next.
- O Financial information should be complete, neutral and free from error.

(2 marks)

2.8 Listed below are some comments on accounting concepts.

(1) Financial statements always treat the business as a separate entity.

(2) Materiality means that only items having a physical existence may be recognised as assets.

(3) Provisions are estimates and therefore can be altered to make the financial results of a business more attractive to investors.

Which, if any, of these comments is correct, according to the IASB's *Conceptual Framework*?

- O 1 only
- O 2 only
- O 3 only
- O None of them

(2 marks)

2.9 Which of the following statements about accounting concepts and the characteristics of financial information are correct?

(1) The concept of accruals requires transactions to be reflected in the financial statements once the money or its equivalent is received or paid.

(2) Information is material if its omission or misstatement could influence the economic decisions of users taken on the basis of the financial statements.

(3) Based on faithful representation, it may sometimes be necessary to exclude material information from financial statements due to difficulties establishing an accurate figure.

- O 1 only
- O 1 and 2 only
- O 2 only
- O 2 and 3 only **(2 marks)**

2.10 The IASB's *Conceptual Framework* gives six qualitative characteristics of financial information. What are these six characteristics?

- O Relevance, Faithful representation, Comparability, Verifiability, Timeliness and Understandability
- O Accuracy, Faithful representation, Comparability, Verifiability, Timeliness and Understandability
- O Relevance, Faithful representation, Consistency, Verifiability, Timeliness and Understandability
- O Relevance, Comparability, Consistency, Verifiability, Timeliness and Understandability

(2 marks)

2.11 Which one of the following is **NOT** a qualitative characteristic of financial information according to the IASB's *Conceptual Framework*?

- O Faithful representation
- O Relevance
- O Timeliness
- O Accruals **(2 marks)**

2.12 According to the IASB's *Conceptual Framework* which of the following is **NOT** an objective of financial statements?

- O Providing information regarding the financial position of a business
- O Providing information regarding the performance of a business
- O Enabling users to assess the performance of management to aid decision making
- O Providing reliable investment advice **(2 marks)**

2.13 Identify, by indicating the relevant box in the table below, whether each of the following statements is correct or incorrect.

Companies should never change the presentation or classification of items in their financial statements, even if there is a significant change in the nature of operations.	**CORRECT**	**INCORRECT**
Companies should create provisions in times of company growth to be utilised in more difficult times, to smooth profits.	**CORRECT**	**INCORRECT**

(2 marks)

2.14 Which of the following statements about prudence is correct?

- O Prudence requires assets to be carried at their lowest possible valuation.
- O When prudence is applied, income is not recognised until the money has been received.
- O A prudent decision will mean lower expenditure.
- O Prudence does not allow for overstatement of liabilities.

(2 marks)

2.15 Complete the following sentence.

[ ] means having information available to decision makers in time to be capable of influencing their decisions. **(2 marks)**

2.16 Which of the following statements about understandability is correct?

- O Classifying, characterising and presenting information clearly and concisely makes it understandable.
- O Providing users of the financial statements with details of all transactions the entity has entered into during the year makes the information understandable.
- O Providing users of the financial statements with the information on a timely basis promotes understandability.
- O Financial information is more understandable if it faithfully represents the substance of the phenomena it purposes to represent. **(2 marks)**

2.17 According to the *Conceptual Framework for Financial Reporting*, which of the following describe relevance?

- O Complete and neutral
- O Predictive value, confirmatory value or both and free from error
- O Capable of making a difference to decisions made by users and complete
- O Capable of making a difference to decisions made by users and having a predictive value, confirmatory value or both **(2 marks)**

2.18 The *Conceptual Framework for Financial Reporting* provides a choice of measurement basis.

Complete the following sentence.

[ ] for an asset is the cost that was incurred when the asset was acquired or created and, for a liability, is the value of the consideration received when the liability was incurred. **(2 marks)**

2.19 Under an accounting concept, the commercial reality of transactions is reflected in the financial statements and this takes precedent over the legal form of arrangement.

Complete the following sentence.

The accounting concept described above is known as [▼].

Pull down list

- Accruals basis
- Materiality
- Offsetting
- Substance over form

(2 marks)

2.20 Complete the following statement.

Information can be compared:

- For the same entity over different periods
- Between different entities

This describes the enhancing characteristic of [ ]. **(2 marks)**

2.21 Complete the following statement.

'The financial statements are normally prepared on the assumption that an entity is a [ ] and will continue in operation for the foreseeable future.' **(2 marks)**

2.22 Current value accounting attempts to address some of the problems of historical cost accounting by using information updated to reflect conditions at the measurement date.

Which of the following are current value measurement basis?

(1) Fair value

(2) Value in use

(3) Current cost

O 1 only

O 1 and 2 only

O 2 and 3 only

O 1, 2 and 3 **(2 marks)**

2.23 Information that can be independently verified is generally more useful for decision making than information that cannot.

Which qualitative characteristic is being described here?

The qualitative characteristic being described here is [▼].

Pull down list

- Going concern
- Prudence
- Relevance
- Verifiability

(2 marks)

2.24 Complete the following statement.

In the general ledger, for every debit entry there is a corresponding credit entry. This is relevant to the [ ] concept of accounting. **(2 marks)**

2.25 A company has two bank accounts with different banks.

When preparing the financial statements, the bank account with a debit balance in the bank general ledger account is listed under currents assets in the statement of financial position. The bank account with a credit balance in the bank general ledger account is listed under current liabilities in the statement of financial position.

Which accounting concept requires the bank accounts described above to be presented in the statement of financial position under current assets and current liabilities?

The accounting concept is [▼].

Pull down list

- Fair presentation
- Going concern
- Offsetting
- Relevance

(2 marks)

(Total = 50 marks)

Part C: The use of double entry and accounting systems

3 Double entry bookkeeping I (46 mins)

3.1 Which one of the following can the accounting equation can be rewritten as?

- ○ Assets + profit – drawings – liabilities = closing capital
- ○ Assets – liabilities – drawings = opening capital + profit
- ○ Assets – liabilities – opening capital + drawings = profit
- ○ Assets – profit – drawings = closing capital – liabilities

(2 marks)

3.2 A trader's profit for the year may be computed by using which of the following formulae?

- ○ Opening capital + drawings – capital introduced – closing capital
- ○ Closing capital – opening capital + drawings – capital introduced
- ○ Opening capital – drawings + capital introduced – closing capital
- ○ Opening capital – drawings – capital introduced – closing capital

(2 marks)

3.3 The profit earned by a business in 20X7 was $72,500. The proprietor injected new capital of $8,000 during the year and withdrew goods for their private use which had cost $2,200.

If net assets at the beginning of 20X7 were $101,700, what were the closing net assets?

- ○ $35,000
- ○ $39,400
- ○ $168,400
- ○ $180,000

(2 marks)

3.4 The profit made by a business in 20X7 was $35,400. The proprietor injected new capital of $10,200 during the year and withdrew a monthly salary of $500.

If net assets at the end of 20X7 were $95,100, what was the proprietor's capital at the beginning of the year?

$ [ ]

(2 marks)

3.5 A sole trader took some goods costing $800 from inventory for their own use. The normal selling price of the goods is $1,600.

Which of the following journal entries would correctly record this?

		Debit ($)	Credit ($)
O	Inventory account	800	
	Purchases account		800
O	Drawings account	800	
	Purchases account		800
O	Sales account	1,600	
	Drawings account		1,600
O	Drawings account	800	
	Sales account		800

(2 marks)

3.6 A business can make a profit and yet have a reduction in its bank balance. Which of the following might cause this to happen?

- O The sale of non-current assets at a loss
- O The charging of depreciation in the statement of profit or loss
- O The lengthening of the period of credit given to customers
- O The lengthening of the period of credit taken from suppliers **(2 marks)**

3.7 The net assets of Altese, a trader, at 1 January 20X2 amounted to $128,000. During the year to 31 December 20X2 Altese introduced a further $50,000 of capital and made drawings of $48,000. At 31 December 20X2 Altese's net assets totalled $184,000.

What is Altese's total profit or loss for the year ended 31 December 20X2?

- O $54,000 profit
- O $54,000 loss
- O $42,000 loss
- O $58,000 profit **(2 marks)**

3.8 Jones Co has the following transactions:

(1) Payment of $400 to J Bloggs for a cash purchase

(2) Payment of $250 to J Doe in respect of an invoice for goods purchased last month

What are the correct ledger entries to record these transactions?

		Debit ($)	Credit ($)
O	Debit bank	650	
	Credit purchases		650
O	Debit purchases	650	
	Credit bank		650
O	Debit purchases	400	
	Debit trade payables	250	
	Credit bank		650
O	Debit bank	650	
	Credit trade payables		250
	Credit purchases		400

(2 marks)

3.9 T Tallon had the following transactions:

(1) Sale of goods on credit for $150 to F Rogit

(2) Return of goods from B Blendigg originally sold for $300 in cash to B Blendigg

What are the correct ledger entries to record these transactions?

		Debit ($)	Credit ($)
O	Debit receivables	150	
	Debit sales returns	300	
	Credit sales		150
	Credit bank		300
O	Debit sales	150	
	Debit bank	300	
	Credit receivables		150
	Credit sales returns		300
O	Debit receivables	450	
	Credit sales		150
	Credit sales returns		300
O	Debit sales returns	300	
	Debit sales	150	
	Credit bank		450

(2 marks)

3.10 Which of the following documents should accompany a return of goods to a supplier?

- O Debit note
- O Remittance advice
- O Purchase invoice
- O Credit note

(2 marks)

3.11 Giant Co's motor vehicles at cost account at 30 June 20X6 is as follows:

MOTOR VEHICLES – COST

	$		$
Balance b/d	150,500	Disposal	85,000
Additions	120,950	Balance c/d	186,450
	271,450		271,450

What opening balance should be included in the following period's trial balance for motor vehicles – cost at 1 July 20X6?

- O $271,450 DEBIT
- O $271,450 CREDIT
- O $186,450 CREDIT
- O $186,450 DEBIT

(2 marks)

3.12 Billing Co's trade payables account at 30 September 20X1 is as follows:

TRADE PAYABLES

Bank	21,600	Balance b/d	14,000
Balance c/d	11,900	Purchases	19,500
	33,500		33,500

What was the balance for trade payables in the trial balance at 1 October 20X0?

- O $14,000 DEBIT
- O $14,000 CREDIT
- O $11,900 DEBIT
- O $11,900 CREDIT

(2 marks)

3.13 Information from which of the following documents can be found in the receivables ledger?

- O Quotation
- O Sales invoices
- O Credit notes received
- O Trade discounts

(2 marks)

3.14 Identify, by indicating the relevant box in the table below, whether each of the following statements is true or false.

A debit records an increase in liabilities	**TRUE**	**FALSE**
A debit records a decrease in assets	**TRUE**	**FALSE**
A credit records an increase in liabilities	**TRUE**	**FALSE**
A credit records a decrease in capital	**TRUE**	**FALSE**

(2 marks)

3.15 What is the double entry to record credit purchases in the general ledger?

- O Debit purchases, Credit bank
- O Debit trade payables, Credit purchases
- O Debit bank, Credit purchases
- O Debit purchases, Credit trade payables **(2 marks)**

3.16 Which one of the following statements about an imprest system of petty cash is correct?

- O An imprest system for petty cash controls small cash expenditures because a fixed amount is paid into petty cash at the beginning of each period.
- O The imprest system provides a control over petty cash spending because the amount of cash held in petty cash at any time must be equal to the value of the petty cash vouchers for the period.
- O An imprest system for petty cash can operate without the need for petty cash vouchers or receipts for spending.
- O An imprest system for petty cash helps with management of small cash expenditures and reduces the risk of fraud. **(2 marks)**

3.17 Which one of the following provides evidence that an item of expenditure on petty cash has been approved or authorised?

- O Petty cash voucher
- O Record of the petty cash transaction
- O Receipt for the expense
- O Transfer of cash from the bank account into petty cash **(2 marks)**

3.18 When businesses trade, there are many different documents used to record the different stages of each transaction. Certain documents are key sources of information in an accounting system.

A new accounts assistant is being trained on the payables ledger.

From the perspective of the supplier, identify the names of the business documents described below.

Description	Business document
A document sent by a business to a credit customer requesting payment for goods or services provided.	▼
A request for payment sent by the supplier to the credit customer.	▼
A document sent by a supplier to a customer in respect of goods returned or overpayments made by the customer.	▼

Pull down list

- Credit note
- Sales invoice
- Supplier (purchase) invoice

(2 marks)

3.19 Which of the following details are provided on a supplier (purchase) invoice?

(1) Customer and supplier names and addresses

(2) Amount due, showing the net amount, income tax and gross amount due (where income tax is charged)

(3) Amount currently outstanding in respect of previous purchases

(4) Date by which the invoice must be settled

[▼]

Pull down list

- 1 and 2 only
- 1, 2 and 4 only
- 1, 2, 3 and 4
- 2 and 3 only

(2 marks)

3.20 Complete the following sentence.

A [ ] provides confirmation that goods have been received from a supplier.

It is prepared by the [ ].

(2 marks)

3.21 From time to time, customers return goods to suppliers. They may then send a formal request for the supplier to issue a credit note.

Which business document is used by customers to send a formal request for a credit note?

- O Credit note
- O Debit note
- O Remittance advice
- O Quotation

(2 marks)

(Total = 42 marks)

4 Double entry bookkeeping II **(77 mins)**

The following transactions took place at Marshall's during the week ended 6 May.

May 1 Sold $160 of goods to P Dixon on credit.

May 1 Withdrew $50 of cash from the bank account for business use.

May 2 Purchased goods priced at $380 from A Clarke, on credit, less 15% trade discount.

May 2 Repaid a debt of $120 owed to R Hill, taking advantage of a 10% settlement discount. The payment was by bank transfer.

May 3 Sold $45 of goods for cash.

May 4 Sold $80 of goods to M Maguire on credit, offering a 12.5% discount if payment made within 7 days. Marshall expects Maguire to take up this discount.

May 4 Purchased $400 of goods on credit from D Daley.

May 5 Sold $304 of goods to M Donald on credit.

May 6 Received a cheque from D Randle for $482.

May 6 Purchased $100 of goods on credit from G Perkins.

4.1 What is the total of the transactions recorded in the receivables ledger?

£ [ ] **(2 marks)**

4.2 What is the total of the transactions recorded in the payables ledger?

£ [ ] **(2 marks)**

4.3 Smith Co has the following transactions:

(1) Purchase of goods on credit from T Rader: $450

(2) Return of goods purchased on credit last month to T Rouble: $700

What are the correct ledger entries to record these transactions?

		Debit ($)	Credit ($)
O	Debit purchases	450	
	Debit purchase returns	700	
	Credit bank		450
	Credit trade payables		700
O	Debit purchases	450	
	Debit trade payables	700	
	Credit purchase returns		1,150
O	Debit purchases	450	
	Debit trade payables	250	
	Credit purchase returns		700
O	Debit purchase returns	700	
	Debit purchases	450	
	Credit trade payables		1,150

(2 marks)

4.4 Mew Ling has the following transactions:

(1) Receipt of money into the bank account from R Singh in respect of an invoice for goods sold three weeks ago

(2) Receipt of money into the bank account from S Kalu for cash sales

What are the ledger entries required to record the above transactions?

O Debit bank
Credit sales

O Debit bank
Credit sales
Credit trade receivables

O Debit sales
Credit bank

O Debit trade receivables
Debit sales
Credit bank

(2 marks)

4.5 How are credit sales recorded in the general ledger?

	Debit	Credit
O	Receivables ledger	Trade receivables
O	Trade receivables	Receivables ledger
O	Sales	Trade receivables
O	Trade receivables	Sales

(2 marks)

4.6 Identify, by indicating the relevant box in the table below, whether each of the statements is true or false.

A debit entry in the bank general ledger account will increase an overdraft in the accounts	**TRUE**	**FALSE**
A debit entry in the bank general ledger account will increase a bank balance in the accounts	**TRUE**	**FALSE**

(2 marks)

4.7 An accountant has inserted all the relevant figures into the trade payables account but has not yet balanced off the account.

TRADE PAYABLES

	$		$
Bank	100,750	Balance b/d	250,225
		Purchases	325,010

Assuming there are no other entries to be made, other than to balance off the account, what is the closing balance on the trade payables account?

O $474,485 DEBIT

O $575,235 DEBIT

O $474,485 CREDIT

O $575,235 CREDIT

(2 marks)

4.8 You are given the following information:

Trade receivables at 1 January 20X3	$10,000
Trade receivables at 31 December 20X3	$9,000
Total receipts during 20X3 (including cash sales of $5,000)	$85,000

What are sales on credit during 20X3?

- O $81,000
- O $86,000
- O $79,000
- O $84,000

(2 marks)

4.9 A business sells $100 worth of goods to a customer. The customer pays $50 immediately and will pay the remaining $50 in 30 days' time.

What is the double entry to record the purchase in the customer's accounting records?

- O DEBIT bank $50, CREDIT payables $50, CREDIT purchases $50
- O DEBIT payables $50, DEBIT bank $50, CREDIT purchases $100
- O DEBIT purchases $100, CREDIT payables $50, CREDIT bank $50
- O DEBIT purchases $100, CREDIT bank $100

(2 marks)

4.10 Tin Co purchases $250 worth of metal from Steel Co. Tin Co agrees to pay Steel Co in 60 days' time.

State how this transaction should be recorded in Steel Co's general ledger by completing the sentence below.

To record this transaction, [ ] receivables $250 and [ ] sales $250.

(2 marks)

4.11 The following totals appear in the trial balance of a business for March 20X8.

	$
Sales	40,000
Purchases	20,000
Returns inwards	2,000
Returns outward	4,000

Opening and closing inventories are both $3,000. What is the gross profit for March 20X8?

- O $22,000
- O $24,000
- O $20,000
- O $18,000

(2 marks)

4.12 William's trial balance at 30 September 20X5 includes the following balances:

Trade receivables $75,943

Receivables allowance $4,751

How should these balances be reported in William's statement of financial position as at 30 September 20X5?

- O An asset of $71,192
- O An asset of $75,943 and a liability of $4,751
- O A liability of $71,192
- O A liability of $75,943 and an asset of $4,751 **(2 marks)**

4.13 A trial balance is made up of a list of debit balances and credit balances.

Which of the following statements is correct?

- O Every debit balance represents an expense.
- O Assets are represented by debit balances.
- O Liabilities are represented by debit balances.
- O Income is included in the list of debit balances. **(2 marks)**

4.14 At 30 November 20X5 Jenny had a bank loan of $8,500 and an asset balance of $678 in her bank account.

How should these amounts be recorded on Jenny's opening trial balance at 1 December 20X5?

- O DEBIT $7,822
- O CREDIT $7,822
- O CREDIT $8,500 and DEBIT $678
- O DEBIT $8,500 and CREDIT $678 **(2 marks)**

4.15 Bert has extracted the following list of balances from his general ledger at 31 October 20X5:

	$
Sales	258,542
Opening inventory	9,649
Purchases	142,958
Expenses	34,835
Non-current assets (carrying amount)	63,960
Receivables	31,746
Payables	13,864
Bank (asset)	1,783
Capital	12,525

What is the total of the debit balances in Bert's trial balance at 31 October 20X5?

- O $267,049
- O $275,282
- O $283,148
- O $284,931 **(2 marks)**

4.16 At 31 October 20X6 Roger's trial balance included the following balances:

	$
Machinery at cost	12,890
Accumulated depreciation	8,950
Inventory	5,754
Trade receivables	11,745
Trade payables	7,830
Bank overdraft	1,675
Bank (asset)	150

What is the carrying amount of Roger's current assets at 31 October 20X6?

- O $17,649
- O $17,499
- O $15,974
- O $13,734 **(2 marks)**

4.17 Which of the following statements does **NOT** describe a way in which an effective accounting system facilitates the provision of useful accounting information?

- O By requiring authorisation in line with organisational policies
- O By processing and recording transactions in accordance with accounting rules
- O By preventing transactions from being processed inaccurately
- O By enabling transactions to be recorded as necessary to permit the preparation of financial statements **(2 marks)**

4.18 Which of the following helps to ensure that financial information is input and processed accurately in a computerised accounting system and that the data can be used to provide meaningful information to users?

- O General ledger
- O Controls
- O Sales invoices
- O Bank statements

(2 marks)

4.19 Complete the following sentences.

Businesses make [ ] to their customers. When credit customers settle the amount due to the business, they will be provided with a document confirming that the payment has been received. This document is known as a [ ].

Businesses also make [ ] from their suppliers. When businesses make a payment to settle the amount due to their suppliers, they will receive a [ ] confirmation.

(2 marks)

4.20 Financial transactions are recorded in the general ledger.

Identify the nature and function of the general ledger account described below.

This general ledger account is used to record receipts into the bank account and payments out of it. A debit balance brought down on this account in the general ledger indicates an asset account; a credit balance brought down on this account in the general ledger indicates a liability account.

[▼]

Pull down list

- Bank general ledger account
- Electricity expense account
- Trade payables account
- Trade receivables account

(2 marks)

4.21 Financial transactions are recorded in the general ledger.

Identify the nature and function of the general ledger account described below.

This general ledger account is used to record credit notes issued to credit customers in respect of items returned to the business. This represents a reduction in the income of the business.

[▼]

Pull down list

- Capital
- Carriage outwards
- Non-current assets
- Sales returns

(2 marks)

4.22 This general ledger account is used to record income earned from transactions with customers in respect of the businesses core operations.

Identify the nature and function of the general ledger account being described in the scenario.

○ Drawings (a reduction in owner's capital)

○ Sales (an income account)

○ Rent expense account (an expense account)

○ Trade receivables account (an asset account) **(2 marks)**

4.23 Select **THREE** statements which show the benefits of an accounting system to an organisation.

☐ The accounting system can be used to provide financial reports which show whether individual departments are controlling their expenditure effectively.

☐ The accounting system can be used to provide information on an organisation's competitors.

☐ The accounting system can be used to provide financial reports which show sales volumes for individual product lines.

☐ The accounting system can be used to provide information on the amount owed to each individual credit customer at any point in time. **(2 marks)**

4.24 Identify whether each of the statements is true or false.

In a computerised accounting system, sales invoices are manually input into the accounting system by the accounts assistant	**TRUE**	**FALSE**
In a computerised accounting system, sales credit notes are manually input in the accounting system by the accounts assistant	**TRUE**	**FALSE**

(2 marks)

4.25 Complete the following sentence.

Purchase invoices and purchase credit notes received from a supplier are [▼]

entered into the computerised accounting system by the accounts assistant.

Pull down list

- Automatically
- Manually

(2 marks)

4.26 Complete the following sentence.

[ ] entries are used to record business transactions in the accounting records. A [ ] entry must have a [ ] entry and a corresponding [ ] entry. **(2 marks)**

4.27 Identify which of the following are features of journal entries.

Date	**YES**	**NO**
Amount	**YES**	**NO**
General ledger account names and codes	**YES**	**NO**
Trial balance	**YES**	**NO**

(2 marks)

4.28 In respect of purchase invoices, which **TWO** of the following correctly describe how journal entries are posted into general ledger accounts?

☐ The accounts assistant enters details of the amount per the purchase invoice and the invoice date into the computerised accounting system

☐ Purchase invoices are created within the accounting system

☐ The invoice must be coded both to the relevant payables ledger account and the purchases expense account

☐ Income tax can be ignored when purchase invoices are input into the payables ledger

(2 marks)

4.29 Identify, by selecting the relevant box in the table below, whether each of the statements is true or false.

In a computerised accounting system, the total of the receivables ledger balances and the trade receivables balance must be reconciled on a regular basis	**TRUE**	**FALSE**
The trade receivables general ledger account is used to establish the amount due from each individual credit customer	**TRUE**	**FALSE**

(2 marks)

4.30 Businesses need accounting software packages which meet the needs of their organisation. There are two main types of accounting software packages they can acquire.

Match the terms to the descriptions provided.

Description	Term
A computer software package tailor made for the accounting requirements of a particular client	▼
A computer software package that can be used by multiple organisations	▼

Pull down list

- Bespoke accounting software package
- Off the shelf accounting software package

(2 marks)

4.31 There are various ways in which computerised accounting software can be stored, accessed and updated.

Complete the following sentences.

The data and software can be held remotely on the computer servers of the service provider hosting the service. This is known as [ ] .

Alternatively, the data and software can be installed locally on the computers of its accounting staff. In this situation the accounting staff will access the accounting software and data through the organisation's [ ] . **(2 marks)**

4.32 There is certain information that will be input into the computerised accounting system that will not change frequently. For example, in respect of customers, the name and address of the customers, the sales tax details, the credit limit, and any specific arrangements that have been agreed with particular customers.

What term is given to this type of information?

This type of information is known as [ ] . **(2 marks)**

(Total = 64 marks)

Part D: Recording transactions and events

5 Sales tax (19 mins)

5.1 W is registered for sales tax. The managing director has asked four staff in the accounts department why the output tax for the last quarter does not equal 20% of sales (20% is the rate of tax). Which one of the following four replies she received was **NOT** correct?

- O The company had some exports that were not liable to sales tax.
- O The company made some sales of zero-rated products.
- O The company made some sales of exempt products.
- O The company sold some products to businesses not registered for sales tax. **(2 marks)**

5.2 The following information relates to Eva Co's sales tax for the month of March 20X3:

	$
Sales (including sales tax)	109,250
Purchases (net of sales tax)	64,000

Sales tax is charged at a flat rate of 15%. Eva Co's sales tax account showed an opening credit balance of $4,540 at the beginning of the month and a closing debit balance of $2,720 at the end of the month.

What was the total sales tax paid to regulatory authorities during the month of March 20X3?

$ [ ] **(2 marks)**

5.3 Alana is not registered for sales tax purposes. She has recently received an invoice for goods for resale which cost $500 before sales tax, which is levied at 15%. The total value was therefore $575.

What is the correct entry to be made in Alana's general ledger in respect of the invoice?

- O DEBIT Purchases $500, DEBIT Sales tax $75, CREDIT Payables $575
- O DEBIT Purchases $575, CREDIT Sales tax $75, CREDIT Payables $500
- O DEBIT Purchases $500, CREDIT Payables $500
- O DEBIT Purchases $575, CREDIT Payables $575 **(2 marks)**

5.4 Information relating to Lauren Co's transactions for the month of May 20X4 is shown below:

	$
Sales (including sales tax)	140,000*
Purchases (net of sales tax)	65,000

Note. * Lauren Co's sales for the month of $140,000 included $20,000 of sales exempt from sales tax.

Sales tax is charged at a flat rate of 20%. Lauren Co's sales tax account had a zero balance at the beginning of the month and at the end of the month.

What was the total sales tax paid to regulatory authorities at the end of May 20X4 (to the nearest $)?

- O $7,000
- O $20,000
- O $23,333
- O $13,000

(2 marks)

5.5 A business commenced with capital in cash of $1,000. Inventory costing $800 plus sales tax is purchased on credit, and half is sold for $1,000 plus sales tax, the customer paying in cash at once. The sales tax rate is 20%.

What would the accounting equation after these transactions show?

- O Assets $1,800 less Liabilities $200 equals Capital $1,600
- O Assets $2,200 less Liabilities $1,000 equals Capital $1,200
- O Assets $2,600 less Liabilities $800 equals Capital $1,800
- O Assets $2,600 less Liabilities $1,000 equals Capital $1,600

(2 marks)

5.6 Trade receivables and payables in the financial statements of a sales tax registered trader will appear as described by which of the following?

- O Inclusive of sales tax in the statement of financial position
- O Exclusive of sales tax in the statement of financial position
- O The sales tax is deducted and added to the sales tax account in the statement of financial position
- O Sales tax does not appear in the statement of financial position because the business simply acts as a collector on behalf of the tax authorities

(2 marks)

5.7 Which of the following correctly describe the entry in the sales account for a sale for a sales tax registered trader?

- O Credited with the total of sales made, including sales tax
- O Credited with the total of sales made, excluding sales tax
- O Debited with the total of sales made, including sales tax
- O Debited with the total of sales made, excluding sales tax

(2 marks)

5.8 Sales (including sales tax) amounted to $27,612.50, and purchases (excluding sales tax) amounted to $18,000. What is the balance on the sales tax account, assuming all items are subject to sales tax at 17.5%?

- O $962.50 DEBIT
- O $962.50 CREDIT
- O $1,682.10 CREDIT
- O $1,682.10 CREDIT

(2 marks)

(Total = 16 marks)

6 Inventory **(55 mins)**

6.1 The inventory value for the financial statements of Global Co for the year ended 30 June 20X3 was based on an inventory count on 7 July 20X3, which gave a total inventory value of $950,000.

Between 30 June and 7 July 20X3, the following transactions took place.

	$
Purchase of goods	11,750
Sale of goods (mark up on cost at 15%)	14,950
Goods returned by Global Co to supplier	1,500

What figure should be included in the financial statements for inventories at 30 June 20X3?

$ [ ] **(2 marks)**

6.2 Which of the following costs may be included when arriving at the cost of finished goods inventory for inclusion in the financial statements of a manufacturing company?

(1) Carriage inwards

(2) Carriage outwards

(3) Depreciation of factory plant

(4) Finished goods storage costs

(5) Factory supervisors' wages

- O 1 and 5 only
- O 2, 4 and 5 only
- O 1, 3 and 5 only
- O 1, 2, 3 and 4 only **(2 marks)**

6.3 The closing inventory at cost of Darcy Co at 31 January 20X3 amounted to $284,700.

The following items were included at cost in the total:

(1) 400 coats, which had cost $80 each and normally sold for $150 each. Owing to a defect in manufacture, they were all sold after the reporting date at 50% of their normal price. Selling expenses amounted to 5% of the proceeds.

(2) 800 skirts, which had cost $20 each. These too were found to be defective. Remedial work in February 20X3 cost $5 per skirt, and selling expenses for the batch totalled $800. They were sold for $28 each.

What should the inventory value be according to IAS 2 *Inventories* after considering the above items?

- O $276,400
- O $281,200
- O $282,800
- O $329,200 **(2 marks)**

6.4 Jennings Co values its inventory using the first in, first out (FIFO) method. At 1 May 20X2 Jennings Co had 700 engines in inventory, valued at $190 each.

During the year ended 30 April 20X3 the following transactions took place:

20X2	
1 July	Purchased 500 engines at $220 each
1 November	Sold 400 engines for $160,000
20X3	
1 February	Purchased 300 engines at $230 each
15 April	Sold 250 engines for $125,000

What is the value of Jenning Co's closing inventory of engines at 30 April 20X3?

- O $188,500
- O $195,500
- O $166,000
- O None of these figures

(2 marks)

6.5 Identify, by indicating the relevant box in the table below, whether each of the following statements about the valuation of inventory are correct or incorrect, according to IAS 2 *Inventories*.

Inventory items are normally to be valued at the higher of cost and net realisable value.	**CORRECT**	**INCORRECT**
The cost of goods manufactured by an entity will include materials and labour only. Overhead costs cannot be included.	**CORRECT**	**INCORRECT**
LIFO (last in, first out) cannot be used to value inventory.	**CORRECT**	**INCORRECT**
First in first out (FIFO) and Average cost (AVCO) are acceptable methods that can be used to value inventory.	**CORRECT**	**INCORRECT**

(2 marks)

6.6 Wilson Co has an accounting date of 31 October and carried out a physical check of inventory on 4 November 20X3, leading to an inventory value at cost at this date of $483,700.

Between 1 November 20X3 and 4 November 20X3 the following transactions took place:

(1) Goods costing $38,400 were received from suppliers.

(2) Goods that had cost $14,800 were sold for $20,000.

(3) A customer returned, in good condition, some goods which had been sold to him in October for $600 and which had cost $400.

(4) The company returned goods that had cost $1,800 in October to the supplier, and received a credit note for them.

What figure should appear in the company's financial statements at 31 October 20X3 for closing inventory, based on this information?

- O $458,700
- O $505,900
- O $508,700
- O $461,500

(2 marks)

6.7 In preparing its financial statements for the current year, Jackson Co's closing inventory was understated by $300,000.

What will be the effect of this error if it remains uncorrected?

- O The current year's profit will be overstated and next year's profit will be understated.
- O The current year's profit will be understated but there will be no effect on next year's profit.
- O The current year's profit will be understated and next year's profit will be overstated.
- O The current year's profit will be overstated but there will be no effect on next year's profit.

(2 marks)

6.8 The financial year of Mitex Co ended on 31 December 20X1. An inventory count on 4 January 20X2 gave a total inventory value of $527,300.

The following transactions occurred between January 1 and January 4.

	$
Purchases of goods	7,900
Sales of goods (gross profit margin 40% on sales)	15,000
Goods returned to a supplier	800

What inventory value should be included in Mitex Co's financial statements at 31 December 20X1?

- O $525,400
- O $527,600
- O $529,200
- O $535,200

(2 marks)

6.9 Which of the following statements about IAS 2 *Inventories* is correct?

- O Production overheads should be included in cost on the basis of a company's normal level of activity in the period.
- O In determining the cost of inventories, trade discounts received must be deducted and selling costs must be added.
- O In arriving at the cost of inventories, FIFO, LIFO and weighted average cost formulas are acceptable.
- O It is permitted to value finished goods inventories at materials plus labour cost only, without adding production overheads.

(2 marks)

6.10 You are preparing the financial statements for a business. The cost of the items in closing inventory is $41,875. This includes some items which cost $1,960 and which were damaged in transit. You have estimated that it will cost $360 to repair the items, and they can then be sold for $1,200.

What is the correct inventory valuation for inclusion in the financial statements?

- O $39,915
- O $40,755
- O $41,515
- O $42,995

(2 marks)

6.11 S sells three products – Basic, Super and Luxury. The following information was available at the year end.

	Basic	*Super*	*Luxury*
	$ per unit	*$ per unit*	*$ per unit*
Original cost	6	9	18
Estimated selling price	9	12	15
Selling and distribution costs	1	4	5
	units	units	units
Units of inventory	200	250	150

What is the value of inventory at the year end?

- O $4,200
- O $4,700
- O $5,700
- O $6,150

(2 marks)

6.12 An inventory record card shows the following details.

February	1	50 units in stock at a cost of $40 per unit
	7	100 units purchased at a cost of $45 per unit
	14	80 units sold
	21	50 units purchased at a cost of $50 per unit
	28	60 units sold

What is the value of inventory at 28 February using the FIFO method?

- O $2,450
- O $2,700
- O $2,950
- O $3,000

(2 marks)

6.13 IAS 2 *Inventories* defines the items that may be included in computing the cost of an inventory of finished goods manufactured by a business.

Which one of the following lists consists only of items which may be included in the cost of inventories, according to IAS 2?

- O Supervisor's wages, carriage inwards, carriage outwards, raw materials
- O Raw materials, carriage inwards, costs of storage of finished goods, plant depreciation
- O Plant depreciation, carriage inwards, raw materials, supervisor's wages
- O Carriage outwards, raw materials, supervisor's wages, plant depreciation **(2 marks)**

6.14 The closing inventory of X amounted to $116,400 **excluding** the following two inventory lines:

(1) 400 items which had cost $4 each. All were sold after the reporting period for $3 each, with selling expenses of $200 for the batch.

(2) 200 different items which had cost $30 each. These items were found to be defective at the end of the reporting period. Rectification work after the statement of financial position amounted to $1,200, after which they were sold for $35 each, with selling expenses totalling $300.

Which of the following total figures should appear in the statement of financial position of X for inventory?

- O $122,300
- O $121,900
- O $122,900
- O $123,300 **(2 marks)**

6.15 The inventory value for the financial statements of Q for the year ended 31 December 20X4 was based on an inventory count on 4 January 20X5, which gave a total inventory value of $836,200.

Between 31 December and 4 January 20X5, the following transactions took place:

	$
Purchases of goods	8,600
Sales of goods (profit margin 30% on sales)	14,000
Goods returned by Q to supplier	700

What adjusted figure should be included in the financial statements for inventories at 31 December 20X4?

- O $838,100
- O $853,900
- O $818,500
- O $834,300 **(2 marks)**

6.16 Changer Co has decided to switch from using the FIFO method of inventory valuation to using the average cost method (AVCO).

In the first accounting period where the change is made, opening inventory valued by the FIFO method was $53,200. Closing inventory valued by the AVCO method was $59,800.

Total purchases and during the period were $136,500. Using the continuous AVCO method, opening inventory would have been valued at $56,200.

What is the cost of materials that should be included in the statement of profit or loss for the period?

- O $129,900
- O $132,900
- O $135,900
- O $140,100

(2 marks)

6.17 Which one of the following statements about the use of a continuous inventory system is **INCORRECT**?

- O In a retail organisation, a continuous inventory system can be used to keep track of the quantity of each stock item available in its distribution centres.
- O Under continuous inventory, the cost of each receipt of inventory and the cost of each issue from inventory is recorded individually.
- O A continuous inventory system removes the need for periodic physical inventory counts.
- O Both the FIFO and average cost (AVCO) methods of pricing inventory may be used within a continuous inventory system.

(2 marks)

6.18 The information below relates to inventory item Z.

March	1	50 units held in opening inventory at a cost of $40 per unit
	17	50 units purchased at a cost of $50 per unit
	31	60 units sold at a selling price of $100 per unit

Under AVCO, what is the value of inventory held for item Z at the end of March 31?

- O $4,000
- O $1,800
- O $2,000
- O $2,500

(2 marks)

6.19 A firm has the following transactions with its product R.

1 January 20X1	Opening inventory: nil
1 February 20X1	Buys 10 units at $300 per unit
11 February 20X1	Buys 12 units at $250 per unit
1 April 20X1	Sells 8 units at $400 per unit
1 August 20X1	Buys 6 units at $200 per unit
1 December 20X1	Sells 12 units at $400 per unit

The firm uses continuous weighted average cost (AVCO) to value its inventory.

What is the inventory value at the end of the year? (Give your answer to 2 decimal places)

$ [ ]

(2 marks)

6.20 A firm has the following transactions with its product Q.

1 December 20X1	Opening inventory: Nil
2 December 20X1	Buys 10 units at $300 per unit
9 December 20X1	Buys 12 units at $250 per unit
10 December 20X1	Sells 8 units at $400 per unit
11 December 20X1	Buys 6 units at $200 per unit
21 December 20X1	Sells 12 units at $400 per unit

The firm uses periodic weighted average cost (AVCO) to value its inventory.

What is the inventory value at the end of the year? (Give your answer to 2 decimal places)

$ ______ **(2 marks)**

6.21 Inventory is generally accounted for as a year-end adjustment in the adjusted trial balance via a journal entry.

Indicate whether the following statements are true or false in respect of explaining why inventory is generally accounted for as a year-end adjustment via a journal entry.

Opening inventory is automatically shown in the initial trial balance, however, this figure needs to be updated for goods which have been purchased and sold during the year, to calculate closing inventory.	**TRUE**	**FALSE**
Inventory is often a small balance in the financial statements, therefore a late journal entry is appropriate.	**TRUE**	**FALSE**
Posting closing inventory as a journal entry ensures that it is correctly accounted for both as a reduction in cost of sales (statement of profit or loss) and as an asset (statement of financial position).	**TRUE**	**FALSE**
The quantity of each line of inventory is often counted during a year end inventory count; once this information is known, inventory can be valued and a closing inventory figure posted to the adjusted trial balance as a journal entry.	**TRUE**	**FALSE**

(2 marks)

6.22 Inventory can be counted on a continuous basis throughout the year or at a physical inventory count at the year end (or more frequently if required).

Complete the following sentence.

An advantage of the ______ is that at any point in time an organisation will know the quantity of each line of inventory held in the warehouse. **(2 marks)**

6.23 A company has the following information regarding sales and cost of sales for the year ended 31 December 20XX.

	$	$
Sales		184,000
Cost of sales		
Opening inventory	35,500	
Purchases	70,200	

Closing inventory has been valued at $33,600 using the FIFO method and $32,800 using the AVCO method.

Complete the following sentences to show the gross profit for the year using both the FIFO and AVCO methods. Then state which method gives the higher gross profit figure for the year.

Gross profit for the year using the FIFO method is $ [ ]

Gross profit for the year using the AVCO method is $ [ ]

Which method give a higher gross profit for the year (FIFO or AVCO? [ ]

(2 marks)

(Total = 46 marks)

7 Tangible non-current assets I (46 mins)

7.1 What is the purpose of charging depreciation in financial statements?

- O To allocate the cost of a non-current asset over the accounting periods expected to benefit from its use
- O To ensure that funds are available for the eventual replacement of the asset
- O To reduce the cost of the asset in the statement of financial position to its estimated market value
- O To account for the 'wearing-out' of the asset over its life **(2 marks)**

7.2 Which of the statements below correctly states the purpose of the asset register?

- O An internal control to ensure details of all assets are readily available in the event of loss or theft
- O To ensure the organisation is aware of the age of plant and machinery
- O An internal control to ensure information relating to non-current assets in the general ledger and the financial statements is correct
- O To enable the organisation to comply with IAS 16 *Property, Plant and Equipment*

(2 marks)

7.3 An asset register showed a carrying amount of $67,460. A non-current asset costing $15,000 had been sold for $4,000, making a loss on disposal of $1,250. No entries had been made in the asset register for this disposal.

What is the correct balance on the asset register, once the disposal has been accounted for?

$ [ ] **(2 marks)**

7.4 An organisation's asset register shows a carrying amount of $145,600. The non-current asset account in the general ledger shows a carrying amount of $135,600. The difference could be due to an asset that was disposed of not having been deducted from the asset register.

Which one of the following could represent that asset?

- O Asset with disposal proceeds of $15,000 and a profit on disposal of $5,000
- O Asset with disposal proceeds of $15,000 and a carrying amount of $5,000
- O Asset with disposal proceeds of $15,000 and a loss on disposal of $5,000
- O Asset with disposal proceeds of $5,000 and a carrying amount of $5,000 **(2 marks)**

7.5 Which one of the following would occur if the purchase of computer stationery was debited to the computer equipment at cost account?

- O An overstatement of profit and an overstatement of non-current assets
- O An understatement of profit and an overstatement of non-current assets
- O An overstatement of profit and an understatement of non-current assets
- O An understatement of profit and an understatement of non-current assets

(2 marks)

7.6 Which one of the following statements correctly describes non-current assets?

- O Assets that form part of the working capital of the business
- O Assets which are intended to be used by the business on a continuing basis, including both tangible and intangible assets that do not meet the IAS 1 *Presentation of Financial Statements* definition of a current asset
- O Non-monetary assets without physical substance that are controlled by the entity and from which future benefits are expected to flow
- O Assets in the form of materials or supplies to be consumed in the production process

(2 marks)

7.7 Happy Co bought a property four years ago on 1 January for $170,000. Since then property prices have risen substantially and the property has been revalued at $210,000.

The property was estimated as having a useful life of 20 years when it was purchased. What is the balance on the revaluation surplus reported in the statement of financial position?

- O $210,000
- O $136,000
- O $74,000
- O $34,000 **(2 marks)**

7.8 A business purchased a motor car on 1 July 20X3 for $20,000. It is to be depreciated at 20% per year on the straight line basis, assuming a residual value at the end of five years of $4,000, with a proportionate depreciation charge in the years of purchase and disposal.

The $20,000 cost was correctly entered in the bank general ledger account but posted to the debit of the motor vehicles repairs account.

How will the business profit for the year ended 31 December 20X3 be affected by the error?

- O Understated by $18,400
- O Understated by $16,800
- O Overstated by $18,400
- O Overstated by $16,800 **(2 marks)**

7.9 Right Co's policy is to charge depreciation on plant and machinery at 20% per year on cost, with proportional depreciation for items purchased or sold during a year.

Right Co's plant and machinery at cost account for the year ended 30 September 20X3 is shown below.

PLANT AND MACHINERY – COST

		$			$
20X2			*20X3*		
1 Oct	Balance b/d	200,000	30 Jun	Transfer disposal account	40,000
			30 Sep	Balance c/d	210,000
20X3					
1 Apr	Cash-purchase of plant	50,000			
		250,000			250,000

What should be the depreciation charge for plant and machinery (excluding any profit or loss on the disposal) for the year ended 30 September 20X3?

- O $43,000
- O $51,000
- O $42,000
- O $45,000 **(2 marks)**

7.10 The plant and machinery at cost account of Tolly Co for the year ended 30 June 20X4 was as follows:

PLANT AND MACHINERY – COST

		$			$
20X3			*20X3*		
1 Jul	Balance	240,000	30 Sep	Transfer disposal account	60,000
20X4			*20X4*		
1 Jan	Cash – purchase of plant	160,000	30 Jun	Balance	340,000
		400,000			400,000

Tolly Co's policy is to charge depreciation at 20% per year on the straight line basis, with proportionate depreciation in the years of purchase and disposal.

What should be the depreciation charge for the year ended 30 June 20X4?

- O $68,000
- O $64,000
- O $61,000
- O $55,000

(2 marks)

7.11 A manufacturing company receives an invoice on 29 February 20X2 for work done on one of its machines. $25,500 of the cost is actually for a machine upgrade, which will improve efficiency. The accounts department do not notice and charge the whole amount to maintenance costs. Machinery is depreciated at 25% per year on a straight line basis, with a proportional charge in the years of acquisition and disposal.

By what amount will the profit for the year to 30 June 20X2 be understated?

- O $19,125
- O $25,500
- O $23,375
- O $21,250

(2 marks)

7.12 W bought a new printing machine. The machine was purchased for $80,000. The installation costs were $5,000 and the employees received training on how to use the machine, at a cost of $2,000. Before using the machine to print customers' orders, a test was undertaken and the paper and ink cost $1,000.

What should be the cost of the machine in the company's statement of financial position?

$ [ ]

(2 marks)

7.13 What are the correct ledger entries to record an acquisition of a non-current asset on credit?

	Debit	Credit
O	Non-current assets – cost	Receivables
O	Payables	Non-current assets – cost
O	Non-current assets – cost	Payables
O	Non-current assets – cost	Revaluation surplus

(2 marks)

7.14 Alpha sells machine B for $50,000 cash on 30 April 20X4. Machine B cost $100,000 when it was purchased and has a carrying amount of $65,000 at the date of disposal. What are the journal entries to record the disposal of machine B?

O	DEBIT Accumulated depreciation	$35,000	
	DEBIT Loss on disposal (SPL)	$15,000	
	DEBIT Bank	$50,000	
	CREDIT Non-current assets – cost		$100,000
O	DEBIT Accumulated depreciation	$65,000	
	DEBIT Loss on disposal (SPL)	$35,000	
	CREDIT Non-current assets – cost		$100,000
O	DEBIT Accumulated depreciation	$35,000	
	DEBIT Bank	$50,000	
	CREDIT Non-current assets		$65,000
	CREDIT Profit on disposal (SPL)		$20,000
O	DEBIT Non-current assets	$65,000	
	DEBIT Accumulated depreciation	$35,000	
	CREDIT Bank		$50,000
	CREDIT Profit on disposal (SPL)		$50,000

(2 marks)

QUESTIONS

7.15 Identify, by selecting the relevant box in the table below, whether each of the following statements is true or false.

IAS 16 Property, Plant and Equipment requires entities to disclose the purchase date of each asset.	**TRUE**	**FALSE**
The carrying amount of a non-current asset is the cost or valuation of that asset less accumulated depreciation.	**TRUE**	**FALSE**
IAS 16 Property, Plant and Equipment permits entities to make a transfer from the revaluation surplus to retained earnings for excess depreciation on revalued assets.	**TRUE**	**FALSE**
Once decided, the useful life of a non-current asset should not be changed.	**TRUE**	**FALSE**

(2 marks)

7.16 The following information relates to questions 7.16 and 7.17.

Gusna Co purchased a building on 31 December 20X1 for $750,000. At the date of acquisition, the useful life of the building was estimated to be 25 years and depreciation is calculated using the straight line method. At 31 December 20X6, an independent valuer valued the building at $1,000,000 and the revaluation was recognised in the financial statements. Gusna's accounting policies state that excess depreciation arising on revaluation of non-current assets can be transferred from the revaluation surplus to retained earnings.

What is the depreciation charge on the building for the year ended 31 December 20X7?

- O $40,000
- O $50,000
- O $30,000
- O $42,500

(2 marks)

7.17 Identify the correct debit/credit entries to record the transfer of excess depreciation.

Retained earnings $20,000 – [▼]

Revaluation surplus $20,000 – [▼]

Revaluation surplus $12,500 – [▼]

Retained earnings $12,500 – [▼]

Pull down list

- Both
- Credit entry
- Debit entry
- Neither

(2 marks)

7.18 Which of the following should be disclosed for tangible non-current assets according to IAS 16 *Property, Plant and Equipment*?

(1) Depreciation methods used and the total depreciation allocated for the period

(2) A reconciliation of the carrying amount of non-current assets at the beginning and end of the period

(3) For revalued assets, whether an independent valuer was involved in the valuation

(4) For revalued assets, the effective date of the revaluation

- O 2 and 4 only
- O 1 and 2 only
- O 1, 2, 3 and 4
- O 3 and 4 only

(2 marks)

7.19 On 1 October 20X1, X Co purchased a property for $400,000. The property had a useful life of 40 years and was depreciated on a straight line basis. On 1 October 20X5, the property was revalued to $432,000. The remaining useful life at that date was 36 years. The company wishes to make the allowed transfer of excess depreciation between the revaluation surplus and retained earnings accounts.

Which of the following correctly records the transfer at 30 September 20X6?

	Debit	Credit
O	Retained earnings $2,000	Revaluation surplus $2,000
O	Revaluation surplus $2,000	Retained earnings $2,000
O	Retained earnings $12,000	Revaluation surplus $12,000
O	Revaluation surplus $12,000	Retained earnings $12,000

(2 marks)

(Total = 38 marks)

8 Tangible non-current assets II **(53 mins)**

8.1 A car was purchased by a newsagent business in May 20X0 for:

	$
Cost	10,000
Road tax	150
Total	10,150

The business adopts a date of 31 December as its year end.

The car was traded in for a replacement vehicle in August 20X3 at an agreed value of $5,000.

It has been depreciated at 25% per year on the diminishing balance method, charging a full year's depreciation in the year of purchase and none in the year of sale.

What was the profit or loss on disposal of the vehicle during the year ended December 20X3?

$ [ ] profit **(2 marks)**

8.2 The carrying amount of a Billing's non-current assets was $200,000 at 1 August 20X0. During the year ended 31 July 20X1, the company sold non-current assets for $25,000 on which it made a loss of $5,000. The depreciation charge for the year was $20,000.

What was the carrying amount of non-current assets at 31 July 20X1?

- O $150,000
- O $155,000
- O $160,000
- O $180,000

(2 marks)

8.3 Y purchased some plant on 1 January 20X0 for $38,000. The payment for the plant was correctly entered in the bank general ledger account but was entered on the debit side of the plant repairs account.

Y charges depreciation on the straight line basis at 20% per year, with a proportionate charge in the years of acquisition and disposal, and assuming no scrap value at the end of the life of the asset.

How will Y's profit for the year ended 31 March 20X0 be affected by the error?

- O Understated by $30,400
- O Understated by $36,100
- O Understated by $38,000
- O Overstated by $1,900

(2 marks)

8.4 B acquired a lorry on 1 May 20X0 at a cost of $30,000. The lorry has an estimated useful life of four years, and an estimated resale value at the end of that time of $6,000. B charges depreciation on the straight line basis, with a proportionate charge in the period of acquisition.

What will the depreciation charge for the lorry be in B's accounting period to 30 September 20X0?

- O $3,000
- O $2,500
- O $2,000
- O $5,000

(2 marks)

8.5 At 31 December 20X3 Q, a limited liability company, owned a building that had cost $800,000 ten years ago.

It was being depreciated at 2% per year.

On 31 December 20X3 a revaluation to $1,000,000 was recognised. At this date the building had a remaining useful life of 40 years.

What is the balance on the revaluation surplus at 31 December 20X3 and the depreciation charge in the statement of profit or loss for the year ended 31 December 20X4?

	Depreciation charge for year ended 31 December 20X4 (statement of profit or loss)	Revaluation surplus as at 31 December 20X3 (statement of financial position)
	$	$
O	25,000	200,000
O	25,000	360,000
O	20,000	200,000
O	20,000	360,000

(2 marks)

8.6 Which of the following best explains what is meant by 'asset expenditure'?

- O Expenditure on non-current assets, including repairs and maintenance
- O Expenditure on expensive assets
- O Expenditure relating to the issue of share capital
- O Expenditure relating to the acquisition or improvement of non-current assets **(2 marks)**

8.7 Which of the following costs would be classified as asset expenditure for a restaurant business?

- O A replacement for a broken window
- O Repainting the restaurant
- O An illuminated sign advertising the business name
- O Cleaning of the kitchen floors **(2 marks)**

8.8 Which one of the following costs on the invoice for a new company car would be shown as an expense in the statement of profit or loss?

- O Road tax
- O Number plates
- O Fitted stereo
- O Delivery costs **(2 marks)**

8.9 Lance is entering an invoice for a new item of equipment in the accounts. The invoice shows the following costs:

Water treatment equipment	$39,800
Delivery	$1,100
Maintenance charge	$3,980
Sales tax	$7,854
Invoice total	$52,734

Lance is registered for sales tax. What is the total value of asset expenditure on the invoice?

- O \$39,800
- O \$40,900
- O \$44,880
- O \$52,734 **(2 marks)**

8.10 Which one of the following assets may be classified as a non-current asset in the financial statements of a business?

- O A tax refund due next year
- O A motor vehicle held for resale
- O A computer used in the office
- O Cleaning products used to clean the office floors **(2 marks)**

8.11 Which of the following items should be included in current assets?

(1) Assets which are not intended to be converted into cash

(2) Assets which will be converted into cash in the long term

(3) Assets which will be converted into cash in the near future

- O 1 only
- O 2 only
- O 3 only
- O 2 and 3 **(2 marks)**

8.12 Which of the following statements describes current assets?

- O Assets which are currently located on the business premises
- O Assets which are used to conduct the organisation's current business
- O Assets which are expected to be converted into cash in the short-term
- O Assets which are not expected to be converted into cash in the short-term

(2 marks)

8.13 Gamma purchases a motor vehicle on 30 September 20X1 for $15,000 on credit. Gamma has a policy of depreciating motor vehicles using the diminishing balance method at 15% per year, pro rata in the years of purchase and sale.

What are the correct ledger entries to record the purchase of the vehicle at 30 September 20X1 and what is the depreciation charge for the year ended 30 November 20X1?

	Purchase of motor vehicle on 30.9.X1			Depreciation charge for year ended 30.11.X1
O	DEBIT Non-current assets – cost CREDIT Payables	$15,000	$15,000	$2,250
O	DEBIT Payables CREDIT Non-current assets – cost	$15,000	$15,000	$2,250
O	DEBIT Non-current assets –cost CREDIT Payables	$15,000	$15,000	$375
O	DEBIT Payables CREDIT Non-current assets – cost	$15,000	$15,000	$375

(2 marks)

8.14 Banjo Co purchased a building on 30 June 20X8 for $1,250,000. At acquisition, the useful life of the building was 50 years. Depreciation is calculated on the straight line basis. Ten years later, on 30 June 20Y8 when the carrying amount of the building was $1,000,000, the building was revalued to $1,600,000. Banjo Co has a policy of transferring the excess depreciation on revaluation from the revaluation surplus to retained earnings.

Assuming no further revaluations take place, what is the balance on the revaluation surplus at 30 June 20Y9?

- O $335,000
- O $310,000
- O $560,000
- O $585,000

(2 marks)

8.15 A non-current asset (cost $15,000, depreciation $10,000) is given in part exchange for a new asset costing $20,500. The agreed trade-in value was $5,500. Which of the following will be included in the statement of profit or loss?

- O A profit on disposal $5,500
- O A loss on disposal $4,500
- O A loss on purchase of a new asset $5,500
- O A profit on disposal $500

(2 marks)

8.16 Baxter Co purchased an asset for $100,000 on 1.1.X1. It had an estimated useful life of five years and it was depreciated using the straight line method. On 1.1.X3 Baxter Co revised the remaining estimated useful life to eight years.

What is the carrying amount of the asset at 31.12.X3?

- O $40,000
- O $52,500
- O $40,000
- O $62,500

(2 marks)

8.17 Senakuta Co purchased a machine with an estimated useful life of five years for $34,000 on 30 September 20X5. Senakuta Co planned to scrap the machine at the end of its useful life and estimated that the scrap value at the purchase date was $4,000. On 1 October 20X8, Senakuta revised the scrap value to $2,000 due to the decreased value of scrap metal.

What is the depreciation charge for the year ended 30 September 20X9?

- O $7,000
- O $6,800
- O $2,800
- O $6,400

(2 marks)

8.18 Evans Co purchased a machine with an estimated useful life of ten years for $76,000 on 30 September 20X5. The machine had a residual value of $16,000.

What are the ledger entries to record the depreciation charge for the machine in the year ended 30 September 20X8?

O	DEBIT Depreciation charge	$6,000	
	CREDIT Accumulated depreciation		$6,000
O	DEBIT Depreciation charge	$6,000	
	DEBIT Non-current assets	$12,000	
	CREDIT Accumulated depreciation		$18,000
O	DEBIT Accumulated depreciation	$6,000	
	CREDIT Depreciation charge		$6,000
O	DEBIT Accumulated depreciation	$18,000	
	CREDIT Non-current assets		$18,000

(2 marks)

8.19 Banter Co purchased an office building on 1 January 20X1. The building cost was $1,600,000 and this was depreciated by the straight line method at 2% per year, assuming a 50-year life and nil residual value. The building was revalued to $2,250,000 on 1 January 20X6. The useful life was not revised. The excess depreciation charge will be transferred from the revaluation surplus to retained earnings each year. The company's financial year ends on 31 December.

What is the balance on the revaluation surplus at 31 December 20X6?

$ [ ]

(2 marks)

8.20 Digger Co purchased an asset on 1 January 20X3 at a cost of $1,000,000. It is depreciated over 50 years by the straight line method (nil residual value), with a proportionate charge for depreciation in the year of acquisition and the year of disposal. At 31 December 20X4 the asset was re-valued to $1,200,000. There was no change in the expected useful life of the asset.

The asset was sold on 30 June 20X5 for $1,195,000.

What profit or loss on disposal of the asset will be reported in the statement of profit or loss of Digger Co for the year ended 31 December 20X5?

- O Profit of $7,500
- O Profit of $235,000
- O Profit of $247,500
- O Loss of $5,000

(2 marks)

8.21 On 1 January 20X7 a building with a carrying amount of $700,000 was revalued to $750,000. The remaining useful life at that date was 25 years.

On 1 January 20X9 the building was sold for $800,000.

What profit on disposal of the building will be reported in the statement of profit or loss for the year ended 31 December 20X7?

- O $110,000
- O $50,000
- O $160,000
- O $156,000

(2 marks)

8.22 Company J's head office building had a carrying amount of $400,000 at 1 January 20X4 and 30 years useful life remaining. It was revalued on that date to $600,000 with no change to the useful life.

On 1 January 20X6, following a property slump, it was sold for $450,000.

What amount (if any) should be charged against profit or loss as loss on disposal?

- O $150,000
- O $110,000
- O $50,000
- O $Nil

(2 marks)

(Total = 44 marks)

9 Intangible non-current assets **(34 mins)**

9.1 Identify, by clicking on the relevant box in the table below, whether each of the following statements about research and development expenditure are true or false, according to IAS 38 *Intangible Assets*.

Research expenditure, other than asset expenditure on research facilities, should be recognised as an expense as incurred.	**TRUE**	**FALSE**
In deciding whether development expenditure qualifies to be recognised as an asset, it is necessary to consider whether there will be adequate finance available to complete the project.	**TRUE**	**FALSE**
Development expenditure recognised as an asset must be amortised over a period not exceeding five years.	**TRUE**	**FALSE**

(2 marks)

9.2 According to IAS 38 *Intangible Assets*, which of the following statements about research and development expenditure are correct?

(1) If certain conditions are met, an entity may decide to capitalise development expenditure.

(2) Research expenditure, other than asset expenditure on research facilities, must be written off as incurred.

(3) Capitalised development expenditure must be amortised over a period not exceeding five years.

(4) Capitalised development expenditure must be disclosed in the statement of financial position under intangible non-current assets.

- O 1, 2 and 4 only
- O 1 and 3 only
- O 2 and 4 only
- O 3 and 4 only

(2 marks)

9.3 According to IAS 38 *Intangible Assets*, which of the following statements concerning the accounting treatment of research and development expenditure are true?

(1) Development costs recognised as an asset must be amortised over a period not exceeding five years.

(2) Research expenditure, other than asset expenditure on research facilities, should be recognised as an expense as incurred.

(3) In deciding whether development expenditure qualifies to be recognised as an asset, it is necessary to consider whether there will be adequate finance available to complete the project.

(4) Development projects must be reviewed at each reporting date, and expenditure on any project no longer qualifying for capitalisation must be amortised through the statement of profit or loss and other comprehensive income over a period not exceeding five years.

O 1 and 4

O 2 and 4

O 2 and 3

O 1 and 3 **(2 marks)**

9.4 Which of the following **CANNOT** be recognised as an intangible non-current asset in GHK's statement of financial position at 30 September 20X1?

O GHK spent $12,000 researching a new type of product. The research is expected to lead to a new product line in three years' time.

O GHK purchased another entity, BN on 1 October 20X0. Goodwill arising on the acquisition was $15,000.

O GHK purchased a brand name from a competitor on 1 November 20X0, for $65,000.

O GHK spent $21,000 during the year on the development of a new product. The product is being launched on the market on 1 December 20X1 and is expected to be profitable. **(2 marks)**

9.5 According to IAS 38 *Intangible Assets*, which of the following are intangible non-current assets in the financial statements of Iota Co?

(1) A patent for a new glue purchased for $20,000 by Iota Co

(2) Development costs capitalised in accordance with IAS 38

(3) A licence to broadcast a television series, purchased by Iota Co for $150,000

(4) A state of the art factory purchased by Iota Co for $1.5 million

O 1 and 3 only

O 1, 2 and 3 only

O 2 and 4 only

O 2, 3 and 4 only **(2 marks)**

9.6 In its first year of trading to 31 July 20X6, Camp Co incurred the following expenditure on research and development, none of which related to the cost of non-current assets: $12,000 on successfully devising processes for converting seaweed into chemicals X, Y and Z and $60,000 on developing a headache pill based on chemical Z. No commercial uses have yet been discovered for chemicals X and Y. Commercial production and sales of the headache pill commenced on 1 April 20X6 and are expected to produce steady profitable income during a five-year period before being replaced. Adequate resources exist to achieve this.

What is the maximum amount of development costs that must be carried forward at 31 July 20X6 under IAS 38 *Intangible Assets*?

- O $48,000
- O $56,000
- O $60,000
- O $72,000

(2 marks)

9.7 A manufacturer incurs the following costs: $38,000 developing new techniques that will be put in place shortly to cut production costs; $27,000 researching a new process to improve the quality of the standard product and $8,000 on market research into the commercial viability of a new type of product. It is company policy to capitalise costs whenever permitted by IAS 38 *Intangible Assets*.

How much should be charged as research and development expenditure in profit or loss? (ignore amortisation)

- O $73,000
- O $35,000
- O $27,000
- O $38,000

(2 marks)

9.8 Which **TWO** of the following conditions would preclude any part of the development expenditure to which it relates from being capitalised?

(1) The development is incomplete.

(2) The benefits flowing from the completed development are expected to be less than its cost.

(3) Funds are unlikely to be available to complete the development.

(4) The development is expected to give rise to more than one product.

- O 1 and 2
- O 2 and 3
- O 3 and 4
- O 1 and 4

(2 marks)

9.9 Theta Co purchased a patent on 31 December 20X3 for $250,000. Theta Co expects to use the patent for ten years, after which it will be valueless.

According to IAS 38 *Intangible Assets*, what amount will be amortised in Theta Co's statement of profit or loss and other comprehensive income for the year ended 31 December 20X4?

$ [ ]

(2 marks)

9.10 PF purchased a quota for carbon dioxide emissions for $15,000 on 30 April 20X6 and capitalised it as an intangible asset in its statement of financial position. PF estimates that the quota will have a useful life of three years. What is the journal entry required to record the amortisation of the quota in the accounts for the year ended 30 April 20X9?

O	DEBIT Expenses	$15,000	
	CREDIT Accumulated amortisation		$15,000
O	DEBIT Expenses	$5,000	
	CREDIT Accumulated amortisation		$5,000
O	DEBIT Intangible assets	$5,000	
	CREDIT Accumulated amortisation		$5,000
O	DEBIT Accumulated amortisation	$15,000	
	CREDIT Intangible assets		$15,000

(2 marks)

9.11 What is the purpose of amortisation?

- O To allocate the cost of an intangible non-current asset over its useful life
- O To ensure that funds are available for the eventual purchase of a replacement non-current asset
- O To reduce the cost of an intangible non-current asset in the statement of financial position to its estimated market value
- O To account for the risk associated with intangible assets **(2 marks)**

9.12 Which of the following items (that all generate future economic benefits, and whose costs can be measured reliably), is an intangible non-current asset?

(1) Computer hardware owned by a business

(2) Operating software that operates the computer hardware in (1)

(3) A patent bought by a business

(4) An extension to an office building owned by a business

- O All four items
- O 1, 2 and 4 only
- O 1 and 2 only
- O 3 only **(2 marks)**

9.13 What is the purpose of charging amortisation on intangible non-current assets in the financial statements?

- O To reflect the fact that greater benefit is derived from intangible non-current assets in the early years of their useful life
- O To ensure that any fall in value of the intangible non-current assets is reflected in the financial statements annually
- O To provide a market value of intangible non-current asset in the financial statements at the year end
- O To allocate the cost of the intangible non-current asset over the accounting periods expected to benefit from its use **(2 marks)**

9.14 Identify whether the following statements are true or false.

Development expenditure must be recognised as an intangible asset in the statement of financial position, if the relevant criteria in IAS 38 Intangible Assets have been met.	**TRUE**	**FALSE**
When a company engages in research, it may be searching for new products or looking to design possible new or improved processes.	**TRUE**	**FALSE**
Research expenditure is recognised as an intangible asset in the statement of financial position.	**TRUE**	**FALSE**
The IAS 38 Intangible Assets definition of research includes the intention of the entity to complete the intangible asset and use or sell it, and also the ability to use or sell the intangible asset.	**TRUE**	**FALSE**

(2 marks)

(Total = 28 marks)

10 Accruals and prepayments (46 mins)

10.1 Mega Co receives rent for subletting part of its office block.

Rent, receivable quarterly in advance, is received as follows:

Date of receipt	Period covered		$
1 October 20X1	3 months to	31 December 20X1	7,500
30 December 20X1	3 months to	31 March 20X2	7,500
4 April 20X2	3 months to	30 June 20X2	9,000
1 July 20X2	3 months to	30 September 20X2	9,000
1 October 20X2	3 months to	31 December 20X2	9,000

Based on these receipts, what entries should appear in Mega Co's financial statements for the year ended 30 November 20X2?

	Statement of profit or loss	*Statement of financial position*
O	$34,000 DEBIT	Rent in arrears (DEBIT) $3,000
O	$34,500 CREDIT	Rent received in advance (CREDIT) $6,000
O	$34,000 CREDIT	Rent received in advance (CREDIT) $3,000
O	$34,000 CREDIT	Rent in arrears (DEBIT) $3,000

(2 marks)

10.2 Active Co pays rent quarterly in arrears on 1 January, 1 April, 1 July and 1 October each year. The rent was increased from $90,000 per year to $120,000 per year as from 1 October 20X2.

What rent expense and accrual should be included in Active Co's financial statements for the year ended 31 January 20X3?

	Rent expense	*Accrual*
	$	$
O	100,000	20,000
O	100,000	10,000
O	97,500	10,000
O	97,500	20,000

(2 marks)

10.3 At 31 March 20X2 Fire Co had oil in hand to be used for heating costing $8,200 and an unpaid heating oil bill for $3,600.

At 31 March 20X3 the heating oil in hand was $9,300 and there was an outstanding heating oil bill of $3,200.

Payments made for heating oil during the year ended 31 March 20X3 totalled $34,600.

Based on these figures, what expense should appear in Fire Co's statement of profit or loss for heating oil for the year?

$ [ ] **(2 marks)**

10.4 Jelly Co has sublet part of its offices and in the year ended 30 November 20X3 the rent receivable was:

Until 30 June 20X3	$8,400 per year
From 1 July 20X3	$12,000 per year

Rent was paid quarterly in advance on 1 January, April, July, and October each year.

What entries should appear in Jelly Co's financial statements for the year ended 30 November 20X3?

	Rent receivable	*Statement of financial position*
O	$9,900	$2,000 in sundry payables
O	$9,900	$1,000 in sundry payables
O	$10,200	$1,000 in sundry payables
O	$9,900	$2,000 in sundry receivables

(2 marks)

10.5 A business compiling its financial statements for the year to 31 July each year pays rent quarterly in advance on 1 January, 1 April, 1 July and 1 October each year. The annual rent was increased from $60,000 per year to $72,000 per year as from 1 October 20X3.

What amount should appear for rent expense in the business's statement of profit or loss for the year ended 31 July 20X4?

- O $69,000
- O $62,000
- O $70,000
- O $63,000

(2 marks)

10.6 One of the products a garage sells to motorists is diesel fuel. Diesel fuel in inventory at 1 November 20X7 was $12,500, and there were invoices awaited for $1,700. During the year to 31 October 20X8, diesel fuel invoices of $85,400 were paid, and a delivery worth $1,300 had yet to be invoiced. (This was the only outstanding balance on the diesel fuel payable account at the year end). At 31 October 20X8, the inventory of diesel fuel was valued at $9,800.

What is the value of diesel fuel to be charged to the garage's statement of profit or loss for the year to 31 October 20X8?

- O $87,700
- O $89,400
- O $88,500
- O $91,100

(2 marks)

10.7 The electricity account for the year ended 30 June 20X1 was as follows.

	$
Opening balance for electricity accrued at 1 July 20X0	300
Payments made during the year	
1 August 20X0 for three months to 31 July 20X0	600
1 November 20X0 for three months to 31 October 20X0	720
1 February 20X1 for three months to 31 January 20X1	900
30 June 20X1 for three months to 30 April 20X1	840
1 August 20X1 for three months to 31 July 20X1	840

Which of the following is the appropriate entry for electricity?

	Accrued expense at 30 June 20X1	**Charge to SPL year ended 30 June 20X1**
O	$Nil	$3,060
O	$460	$3,320
O	$560	$3,320
O	$560	$3,420

(2 marks)

10.8 The year end of M Co is 30 November 20X0. The company pays for its gas by a standing order of $600 per month. On 1 December 20W9, the statement from the gas supplier showed that M Co had overpaid by $200. M Co received gas bills for the four quarters commencing on 1 December 20W9 and ending on 30 November 20X0 for $1,300, $1,400, $2,100 and $2,000 respectively.

Which of the following is the correct charge for gas in M Inc's statement of profit or loss for the year ended 30 November 20X0?

O $6,800
O $7,000
O $7,200
O $7,400 **(2 marks)**

10.9 A business compiling its financial statements for the year to 31 January pays rent quarterly in advance on 1 January, 1 April, 1 July and 1 October each year. After remaining unchanged for some years, the rent was increased from $24,000 per year to $30,000 per year as from 1 July 20X0.

Which of the following figures is the rent expense which should appear in the statement of profit or loss for year ended 31 January 20X1?

O $27,500
O $29,500
O $28,000
O $29,000 **(2 marks)**

10.10 Blint, a limited liability company, receives rent for subletting part of its office premises to a number of tenants.

In the year ended 31 December 20X4 Blint received cash of $318,600 from its tenants.

Details of rent in advance and in arrears at the beginning and end of 20X4 are as follows:

	31 December 20X4	*31 December 20X3*
	$	*$*
Rent received in advance	28,400	24,600
Rent owing by tenants	18,300	16,900

All rent owing was subsequently received.

What is the figure for rental income that Blint should include in its statement of profit or loss for 20X4?

$ [ ] **(2 marks)**

10.11 During 20X4, Hild Co paid a total of $60,000 for rent, covering the period from 1 October 20X3 to 31 March 20X5.

What balances should appear in Hild Co's financial statements for the year ended 31 December 20X4?

	Statement of profit or loss	***Statement of financial position***
	$	**$**
O	40,000	10,000 prepayment
O	40,000	15,000 prepayment
O	50,000	10,000 accrual
O	50,000	15,000 accrual

(2 marks)

10.12 The trainee accountant at Judd Co has forgotten to make an accrual for rent for December in the financial statements for the year ended 31 December 20X2. Rent is charged in arrears at the end of February, May, August and November each year. The bill payable in February is expected to be $30,000. Judd Co's draft statement of profit or loss shows a profit of $25,000 and draft statement of financial position shows net assets of $275,000.

What is the profit for the year and what is the net asset position after the accrual has been included in the financial statements?

	Profit for the year	***Net asset position***
O	$15,000	$265,000
O	$15,000	$285,000
O	$35,000	$265,000
O	$35,000	$285,000

(2 marks)

10.13 Buster's draft financial statements for the year to 31 October 20X5 report a loss of $1,486. When he prepared the financial statements, Buster did not include an accrued expense of $1,625 and a prepaid expense of $834.

What is Buster's profit or loss for the year to 31 October 20X5 following the inclusion of the accrued expense and prepaid expense?

- O A loss of $695
- O A loss of $2,277
- O A loss of $3,945
- O A profit of $1,807

(2 marks)

10.14 Bookz Co pays royalties to writers annually in February, the payment covering the previous calendar year.

As at the end of December 20X2, Bookz Co had accrued $100,000 in royalties due to writers. However, a check of the royalty calculation performed in January 20X3 established that the actual figure due to be paid by Bookz Co to writers was $150,000.

Before this under-accrual was discovered, Bookz Co's draft statement of profit or loss for the accounting year ended 31 December 20X2 showed a profit of $125,000 and their draft statement of financial position showed net assets of $375,000.

What will Bookz Co's profit and net asset position be after an entry to correct the under-accrual has been corrected?

	Profit for the year	Net asset position
O	$175,000	$425,000
O	$125,000	$375,000
O	$75,000	$325,000
O	$25,000	$225,000

(2 marks)

10.15 Danya owns a small shop and the following information concerns the heat and light account for the year to 31 March 20X7:

	Gas	*Electricity*
At 31 March 20X6	1,000 prepaid expenses	500 accrued expenses
At 31 March 20X7	2,000 accrued expenses	1,200 prepaid expenses

During the year, Danya made payments of $5,000 for gas and $7,800 for electricity.

What is the total heat and light expense for the year ended 31 March 20X7?

- O $14,100
- O $13,100
- O $12,500
- O $11,500

(2 marks)

10.16 NB Ltd has a year end of 31 December 20X2.

On 14 December 20X2, NB Ltd receives $2,000 income in advance in respect of marketing services it will provide to a client in the next financial period.

What is the journal to record this income in the financial statements for the year end 31 December 20X2?

- O Debit Deferred income $2,000, Credit Sales (marketing income) $2,000
- O Debit Sales (marketing income) $2,000, Credit Deferred income $2,000
- O Debit Accrued income $2,000, Credit Sales (marketing income) $2,000
- O Debit Sales (marketing income) $2,000, Credit Accrued income $2,000 **(2 marks)**

10.17 VR Ltd has a year end of 30 September 20X3.

On 1 August 20X3 VR Ltd pay their annual buildings insurance premium of $6,600 in full.

What is the journal required to record the adjustment required in respect of this accrual/prepayment in the financial statements for 30 September 20X3?

- O Debit Prepaid expenses $1,100, Credit Insurance expense $1,100
- O Debit Insurance expense $1,100, Credit Prepaid expenses $1,100
- O Debit Prepaid expenses $5,500, Credit Insurance expense $5,500
- O Debit Insurance expense $5,500, Credit Prepaid expenses $5,500 **(2 marks)**

10.18 In the accounting records YN Ltd has accrued rent expenses brought forward from the previous year ended 31 March 20X4 of $3,490. When preparing the financial statements for the year ended 31 March 20X5 this accrued expense must be reversed.

State the journal entry required to reverse the accrued expenses brought forward from the previous year so that the financial statements for the year ended 31 March 20X5 can be prepared.

Debit [ ]

Credit [ ] **(2 marks)**

10.19 BB Ltd has earned rental income of $9,500 as at 30 April 20X6. BB Ltd have not received this income or raised an invoice for this amount.

State the journal required to record this income in the financial statements at 30 April 20X6.

Debit [ ]

Credit [ ] [ ] **(2 marks)**

(Total = 38 marks)

11 Receivables and payables (53 mins)

11.1 Identify, by indicating the relevant box in the table below, whether each of the following statements is true or false.

Payables represent money the business owes.	TRUE	FALSE
Payables are an asset.	TRUE	FALSE
Receivables represent money owed to the business	TRUE	FALSE

(2 marks)

11.2 At 31 December 20X2 Bunting Co's receivables totalled $400,000 and an allowance for receivables of $50,000 had been brought forward from the year ended 31 December 20X1.

It was decided to write off irrecoverable debts totalling $38,000. The allowance for receivables was to be adjusted to the equivalent of 10% of the receivables.

What charge for receivables expense should appear in Bunting Co's statement of profit or loss for the year ended 31 December 20X2?

- O $74,200
- O $51,800
- O $28,000
- O $24,200

(2 marks)

11.3 At 1 July 20X2 the receivables allowance of Q was $18,000.

During the year ended 30 June 20X3 irrecoverable debts totalling $14,600 were written off. The receivables allowance required was to be $16,000 as at 30 June 20X3.

What amount should appear in Q's statement of profit or loss for receivables expense for the year ended 30 June 20X3?

- O $12,600
- O $16,600
- O $48,600
- O $30,600

(2 marks)

11.4 At 30 September 20X2 Tester Co's allowance for receivables amounted to $38,000, which was equivalent to 5% of the receivables at that date.

At 30 September 20X3 receivables totalled $868,500. It was decided to write off $28,500 of debts as irrecoverable. The allowance for receivables required was to be the equivalent of 5% of receivables.

What should be the charge in the statement of profit or loss for the year ended 30 September 20X3 for receivables expense?

$ ____________

(2 marks)

11.5 At 1 July 20X3 a limited liability Sugar Co had an allowance for receivables of $83,000.

During the year ended 30 June 20X4 irrecoverable debts totalling $146,000 were written off. At 30 June 20X4 a receivables allowance of $218,000 was required.

What amount should appear in the company's statement of profit or loss for the year ended 30 June 20X4 for the receivables expense?

- O $155,000
- O $364,000
- O $281,000
- O $11,000

(2 marks)

11.6 Pepper Co has received a bank receipt for a debt that was previously written off as irrecoverable. Which of the following is the correct double entry to record the bank receipt?

	Debit	***Credit***
O	Irrecoverable debts expense	Trade receivables
O	Bank	Irrecoverable debts expense
O	Allowance for receivables	Trade receivables
O	Bank	Allowance for receivables

(2 marks)

11.7 At 31 December 20X4 Whistle Co's trade receivables totalled $864,000 and the allowance for receivables was $48,000.

It was decided that irrecoverable debts totalling $13,000 were to be written off. The allowance for receivables was to be adjusted to the equivalent of 5% of the receivables.

What amounts should appear in the statement of financial position for trade receivables (after deducting the allowance) and in the statement of profit or loss for receivables expense?

	Statement of profit or loss	***Statement of financial position***
	$	**$**
O	8,200	807,800
O	7,550	808,450
O	18,450	808,450
O	55,550	808,450

(2 marks)

11.8 Which of the following would a decrease in the allowance for receivables result in?

- O An increase in liabilities
- O A decrease in working capital
- O A decrease in profit for the year
- O An increase in profit for the year

(2 marks)

11.9 Jupiter Co has been notified that a customer has been declared bankrupt. The company had previously included this customers' balance within the allowance for receivables in a previous period.

Which of the following is the correct double entry to account for this new information?

	Debit	Credit
O	Irrecoverable debts	Receivables
O	Receivables	Irrecoverable debts
O	Allowance for receivables	Receivables
O	Receivables	Allowance for receivables

(2 marks)

11.10 An increase in an allowance for receivables of $8,000 has been treated as a reduction in the allowance in the financial statements. Which of the following explains the resulting effects?

- O Profit for the year is overstated by $16,000, receivables overstated by $8,000
- O Profit for the year is understated by $16,000, receivables understated by $16,000
- O Profit for the year is overstated by $16,000, receivables overstated by $16,000
- O Gross profit is overstated by $16,000, receivables overstated by $16,000 **(2 marks)**

11.11 At 1 January 20X1, there was an allowance for receivables of $3,000. During the year, $1,000 of debts were written off as irrecoverable, and $800 of debts previously written off were recovered. At 31 December 20X1, it was decided to adjust the allowance for receivables to 5% of receivables which are $20,000.

What amount should be included in the statement of profit or loss as the receivables expense for the year?

$ [ ]

Please enter whether it is CREDIT or DEBIT: [ ] **(2 marks)**

11.12 Top Co has total receivables outstanding of $280,000. The accountant believes that approximately 1% of these balances will not be collected, so wishes to make an allowance of $28,000. No previous allowance has been made for receivables.

Which of the following is the correct double entry to create this allowance?

	Debit	*Credit*
O	Irrecoverable debts	Allowance for receivables
O	Allowance for receivables	Receivables
O	Irrecoverable debts	Receivables
O	Receivables	Allowance for receivables

(2 marks)

11.13 At the beginning of the year, the allowance for receivables was $850. At the year end, the allowance required was $1,000. During the year $500 of irrecoverable debts were written off, which includes $100 previously included in the allowance for receivables.

What is the charge to statement of profit or loss for receivables expense for the year?

- O $1,500
- O $1,000
- O $650
- O $550

(2 marks)

11.14 Which **TWO** of the following statements are correct?

- ☐ An aged receivables analysis shows how long invoices for each customer have been outstanding
- ☐ A credit limit is a tool applied by the credit control department to make suppliers provide goods on time
- ☐ Receivables are included in the statement of financial position net of the receivables allowance
- ☐ Credit limits are applied to customers who purchase goods using cash only

(2 marks)

11.15 At 31 May 20X7 Roberta's trial balance included the following items.

	$
Inventory at 1 June 20X6	23,856
Trade receivables	55,742
Trade payables	32,165
Bank overdraft	5,855
Loan due for repayment in 20X9	15,000

What is the carrying amount of Roberta's current liabilities at 31 May 20X7?

- O $38,020
- O $53,020
- O $61,597
- O $76,597

(2 marks)

11.16 Which one of the following statements is **NOT** a benefit of offering credit facilities to customers?

- O Improved convenience for the customer
- O The separation of product and service delivery from payment
- O Provides time for appropriate payment approval procedures
- O Fewer irrecoverable debts

(2 marks)

11.17 What is the correct double entry for discounts received?

	Debit	Credit
O	Trade payables	Expenses
O	Expenses	Trade payables
O	Discounts received (income)	Trade payables
O	Trade payables	Discounts received (income)

(2 marks)

11.18 Which of the following is/are examples of payables of a business?

(1) Interest owed from the bank

(2) Loans and advances to employees

(3) Money owed from customers

(4) Tax owed to the tax authority

O 1 and 3 only

O 2 and 3 only

O 2 and 4 only

O 4 only **(2 marks)**

11.19 Which of the following is/are examples of payables of a business?

(1) An estimation of tax owed to the tax authority for the year just ended

(2) $500 owed to a supplier for invoiced goods

(3) An estimation of probable repair costs under warranty claims

O 1 and 2 only

O 1 and 3 only

O 2 only

O 1, 2 and 3 **(2 marks)**

11.20 A business commenced trading on 1 January 20X1. The following transactions with Supplier A have been recorded in the purchase ledger.

	1 January 20X1	Opening balance	$nil
(1)	1 January 20X1	Purchase of goods	$50
(2)	1 February 20X1	Purchase of goods	$435
(3)	30 March 20X1	Payment	$385
	31 March 20X1	Closing balance	$100

On 31 March 20X1, the business receives the following statement from the supplier.

	Opening balance		$nil
(4)	1 January 20X1	Invoice #365	$50
(5)	1 February 20X1	Invoice #490	$435
(6)	31 March 20X1	Invoice #533	$35
	Closing balance		$520

Which transactions should be noted as reconciling items on the supplier statement reconciliation at 31 March 20X1?

- O 3 only
- O 6 only
- O 3 and 6 only
- O 1 to 6

(2 marks)

11.21 Indicate whether the following statements are true or false.

An aged receivables analysis often analyses customers by the age of their invoices.	**TRUE**	**FALSE**
In an aged receivables analysis, customer invoices are often analysed in terms of the balances being due for 30+ days, 60+ days and 90+ days.	**TRUE**	**FALSE**
An aged receivables analysis is a useful tool when a business reviews the credit limits that should be offered to existing customers.	**TRUE**	**FALSE**
A year-end aged receivables analysis is included in the financial statements.	**TRUE**	**FALSE**

(2 marks)

11.22 Which **TWO** of the following are costs of offering credit facilities to customers?

- ☐ Offering credit facilities to customers is an administrative expense as a receivables function is required to monitor and chase overdue debts.
- ☐ Trade discounts are offered to credit customers to encourage them to purchase goods and services from the business.
- ☐ Offering credit facilities to customers encourages them to purchase goods and services from a business.
- ☐ Where credit customers are given a period of time to settle their debts, the business offering the credit is providing finance to them and during this time, is unable to use this money elsewhere in the business. **(2 marks)**

(Total = 44 marks)

12 Provisions and contingencies (31 mins)

12.1 Identify, by indicating the relevant box in the table below, whether each of the following statements about provisions and contingencies is true or false.

A company should disclose details of the change in carrying amount of a provision from the beginning to the end of the year.	**TRUE**	**FALSE**
Contingent assets must be recognised in the financial statements in accordance with the prudence concept.	**TRUE**	**FALSE**
Contingent liabilities must be treated as actual liabilities and provided for if it is probable that they will arise.	**TRUE**	**FALSE**

(2 marks)

12.2 Which of the following statements about contingent assets and contingent liabilities are correct?

(1) A contingent asset should be disclosed by note if an inflow of economic benefits is probable.

(2) A contingent liability should be disclosed by note if it is probable that a transfer of economic benefits to settle it will be required, with no provision being made.

(3) No disclosure is required for a contingent liability if it is not probable that a transfer of economic benefits to settle it will be required.

(4) No disclosure is required for either a contingent liability or a contingent asset if the likelihood of a payment or receipt is remote.

- O 1 and 4 only
- O 2 and 3 only
- O 2, 3 and 4
- O 1, 2 and 4

(2 marks)

12.3 A former director of Biss Co has commenced an action against the company claiming substantial damages for wrongful dismissal. The company's solicitors have advised that the former director is unlikely to succeed with his claim, although the chance of Biss Co paying any monies to the ex-director is not remote. The solicitors' estimates of Biss Co's potential liabilities are:

	$
Legal costs (to be incurred whether the claim is successful or not)	50,000
Settlement of claim if successful	500,000
	550,000

According to IAS 37 *Provisions, Contingent Liabilities and Contingent Assets*, how should this claim be treated in Bliss Co's financial statements?

- O Provision of $550,000
- O Disclose a contingent liability of $550,000
- O Disclose a provision of $50,000 and a contingent liability of $500,000
- O Provision for $500,000 and a contingent liability of $50,000

(2 marks)

12.4 Identify, by indicating the relevant box in the table below, the correct action to be taken in the financial statements in respect of each item.

The company gives warranties on its products at no extra cost to the customer. The company's statistics show that about 5% of sales give rise to a warranty claim.	**CREATE A PROVISION**	**DISCLOSURE NOTE ONLY**	**NO ACTION**
The company has guaranteed the overdraft of another company. The likelihood of a liability arising under the guarantee is assessed as possible.	**CREATE A PROVISION**	**DISCLOSURE NOTE ONLY**	**NO ACTION**

(2 marks)

12.5 Which of the following statements about the requirements of IAS 37 *Provisions, Contingent Liabilities and Contingent Assets* are correct?

(1) A contingent asset should be disclosed by note if an inflow of economic benefits is probable.

(2) No disclosure of a contingent liability is required if the possibility of a transfer of economic benefits arising is remote.

(3) Contingent assets must not be recognised in financial statements unless an inflow of economic benefits is virtually certain to arise.

○ All three statements are correct

○ 1 and 2 only

○ 1 and 3 only

○ 2 and 3 only **(2 marks)**

12.6 Wanda Co allows customers to return faulty goods within 14 days of purchase. At 30 November 20X5 a provision of $6,548 was made for a refund liability (sales returns). At 30 November 20X6, the provision was re-calculated and should now be $7,634.

What should be reported in Wanda Co's statement of profit or loss for the year to 31 October 20X6 in respect of the provision?

○ A charge of $7,634

○ A credit of $7,634

○ A charge of $1,086

○ A credit of $1,086 **(2 marks)**

12.7 Doggard Co is a business that sells second hand cars. If a car develops a fault within 30 days of the sale, Doggard Co will repair it free of charge

At 30 April 20X4 Doggard Co had made a provision for repairs of $2,500. At 30 April 20X5 Doggard Co calculated that the provision should be $2,000.

What entry should be made for the provision in Doggard Co's statement of profit or loss for the year to 30 April 20X5?

- O A charge of $500
- O A credit of $500
- O A charge of $2,000
- O A credit of $2,000 **(2 marks)**

12.8 Which of the following best describes a provision according to IAS 37 *Provisions, Contingent Liabilities and Contingent Assets*?

- O A provision is a liability of uncertain timing or amount
- O A provision is a possible obligation of uncertain timing or amount
- O A provision is a credit balance set up to offset a contingent asset so that the effect on the statement of financial position is nil
- O A provision is a possible asset that arises from past events **(2 marks)**

12.9 Which of the following items does the statement below describe?

According to IAS 37 *Provisions, Contingent Liabilities and Contingent Assets*, 'A possible obligation that arises from past events and whose existence will be confirmed only by the occurrence or non-occurrence of one or more uncertain future events not wholly within the entity's control'.

- O A provision
- O A current liability
- O A contingent liability
- O A contingent asset **(2 marks)**

12.10 Montague's paint shop has suffered some bad publicity as a result of a customer claiming to be suffering from skin rashes as a result of using a new brand of paint sold by Montague's shop. The customer launched a court action against Montague in November 20X3, claiming damages of $5,000. Montague's lawyer has advised him that the most probable outcome is that he will have to pay the customer $3,000.

What amount should Montague include as a provision in his financial statements for the year ended 31 December 20X3?

$ [ ] **(2 marks)**

12.11 Mobiles Co sells goods with a one year free warranty under which customers are covered for any defect that becomes apparent within a year of purchase. In calendar year 20X4, Mobiles Co sold 100,000 units.

The company expects warranty claims for 5% of units sold. Half of these claims will be for a major defect, with an average claim value of $50. The other half of these claims will be for a minor defect, with an average claim value of $10.

What amount should Mobiles Co include as a provision in the statement of financial position for the year ended 31 December 20X4?

- O $125,000
- O $25,000
- O $300,000
- O $150,000

(2 marks)

12.12 When a provision is needed that involves a number of outcomes, the provision is calculated using the expected value of expenditure. The expected value of expenditure is the total expenditure of:

- O Each possible outcome
- O Each possible outcome weighted according to the probability of each outcome happening
- O Each possible outcome divided by the number of outcomes
- O Each possible outcome multiplied by the number of outcomes

(2 marks)

12.13 X Co sells goods with a free one year warranty and had a provision for warranty claims of $64,000 at 31 December 20X0. During the year ended 31 December 20X1, $25,000 in claims were paid to customers. On 31 December 20X1, X Co estimated that the following claims will be paid in the following year:

Scenario	*Probability*	*Anticipated cost*
Worst case	5%	$150,000
Best case	20%	$25,000
Most likely	75%	$60,000

What amount should X Co record in the statement of profit or loss for the year ended 31 December 20X1 in respect of the provision?

- O $57,500
- O $6,500
- O $18,500
- O $39,000

(2 marks)

(Total = 26 marks)

13 Capital structure and finance costs (34 mins)

13.1 The issued share capital of Alpha, a limited liability company, is as follows:

	$
Ordinary shares of 10c each	1,000,000
8% Redeemable preference shares of 50c each	500,000

In the year ended 31 October 20X2, the company has paid the preference dividend for the year and an interim dividend of 2c per share on the ordinary shares. A final ordinary dividend of 3c per share was proposed, after the reporting date.

What amount will be shown as dividends in the statement of changes in equity at 31 October 20X2?

$ [ ] **(2 marks)**

13.2 When a company makes a rights issue of equity shares which of the following effects will the issue have?

(1) Assets are increased

(2) Retained earnings are reduced

(3) Share premium account is reduced

(4) Investments are increased

- O 1 only
- O 1 and 2
- O 3 only
- O 1 and 4

(2 marks)

13.3 A company made an issue for cash of 1,000,000 50c shares at a premium of 30c per share.

Which one of the following journal entries correctly records the issue?

		Debit	Credit
		$	**$**
O	Share capital	500,000	
	Share premium	300,000	
	Bank		800,000
O	Bank	800,000	
	Share capital		500,000
	Share premium		300,000
O	Bank	1,300,000	
	Share capital		1,000,000
	Share premium		300,000
O	Share capital	1,000,000	
	Share premium		300,000
	Bank		1,300,000

(2 marks)

13.4 At 31 December 20X1 the capital structure of Venus Co was as follows:

	$
100,000 ordinary shares of 50c each	50,000
Share premium account	180,000

During 20X2 Venus Co made a bonus issue of one ordinary share for every two held, using the share premium account for the purpose, and later issued for cash another 60,000 ordinary shares of 50c each at a price of 80c per share.

What is Venus Co's capital structure at 31 December 20X2?

	Ordinary share capital	*Share premium account*
	$	**$**
O	130,000	173,000
O	105,000	173,000
O	130,000	137,000
O	105,000	137,000

(2 marks)

13.5 An organisation's year end is 30 September. On 1 January 20X6 the organisation took out a loan of $100,000 with annual interest of 12%. The interest is payable in equal instalments on the first day of April, July, October and January in arrears.

How much should be charged to the statement of profit or loss (SPL) for the year ended 30 September 20X6, and how much should be accrued on the statement of financial position (SOFP)?

	SPL	**SOFP**
O	$12,000	$3,000
O	$9,000	$3,000
O	$9,000	NIL
O	$6,000	$3,000

(2 marks)

13.6 Identify, by identifying the relevant box in the table below, whether each of the following statements about company financial statements is true or false, according to IFRS Standards.

Dividends paid on ordinary shares should be included in the statement of profit or loss and other comprehensive income.	**TRUE**	**FALSE**
Dividends paid on redeemable preference shares are treated in the same way as dividends paid on ordinary shares.	**TRUE**	**FALSE**
The statement of profit or loss and other comprehensive income shows the gain on revaluation of non-current assets for the period.	**TRUE**	**FALSE**

(2 marks)

13.7 At 30 June 20X2 Walker Co's capital structure was as follows:

	$
500,000 ordinary shares of 25c each	125,000
Share premium account	100,000

In the year ended 30 June 20X3 the company made a rights issue of one share for every two held at $1 per ordinary share and this was taken up in full. Later in the year the company made a bonus issue of one ordinary share for every five held, using the share premium account for the purpose.

What was Walker Co's capital structure at 30 June 20X3?

	Ordinary share capital	***Share premium account***
	$	**$**
O	450,000	25,000
O	225,000	325,000
O	225,000	250,000
O	212,500	262,500

(2 marks)

13.8 At 30 June 20X2 a Runner Co had $1 million 8% loan notes in issue, interest being paid half-yearly on 30 June and 31 December.

On 30 September 20X2 Runner Co redeemed $250,000 of these loan notes at par, paying interest due to that date.

On 1 April 20X3 Runner Co issued $500,000 7% loan notes, interest payable half-yearly on 31 March and 30 September.

What figure should appear in Runner Co's statement of profit or loss for interest payable in the year ended 30 June 20X3?

$ [ ]

(2 marks)

13.9 A limited liability company issued 50,000 ordinary shares of 25c each at a premium of 50c per share. The cash received was correctly recorded but the full amount was credited to the ordinary share capital account.

Which one of the following journal entries is needed to correct this error?

		Debit	Credit
		$	$
O	Share premium account	25,000	
	Share capital account		25,000
O	Share capital account	25,000	
	Share premium account		25,000
O	Share capital amount	37,500	
	Share premium account		37,500
O	Share capital account	25,000	
	Bank		25,000

(2 marks)

13.10 Which one of the following journal entries could correctly record a bonus issue of shares?

		Debit	Credit
		$	$
O	Bank	100,000	
	Ordinary share capital		100,000
O	Ordinary share capital	100,000	
	Share premium		100,000
O	Share premium	100,000	
	Ordinary share capital		100,000
O	Investments	100,000	
	Bank		100,000

(2 marks)

13.11 Which of these statements about limited liability companies is/are correct?

(1) A company might make a bonus issue of shares to raise funds for expansion.

(2) No cash is received when a company makes a rights issue of shares, instead other reserves (usually share premium) are capitalised and reclassified as share capital.

(3) A rights issue of shares dilutes the shareholding of existing shareholders if they do not take up their rights.

- O 1 and 3
- O 2 and 3
- O 1 and 2
- O 3 only

(2 marks)

13.12 At 1 January 20X0 the capital structure of Q, a limited liability company, was as follows:

	$
Issued share capital 1,000,000 ordinary shares of 50c each	500,000
Share premium account	300,000

On 1 April 20X0 the company made an issue of 200,000 50c ordinary shares at $1.30 each, and on 1 July the company made a bonus (capitalisation) issue of one share for every four in issue at the time, using the share premium account for the purpose.

Which of the following correctly states the company's ordinary share capital and share premium account at 31 December 20X0?

	Ordinary ***share capital***	***Share premium account***
O	$750,000	$230,000
O	$875,000	$285,000
O	$750,000	$310,000
O	$750,000	$610,000

(2 marks)

13.13 According to the illustrative financial structure in IAS 1 *Presentation of Financial Statements*, where should dividends paid during the year be presented?

O Statement of profit or loss and other comprehensive income

O Statement of changes in equity

O Statement of financial position

O None of these **(2 marks)**

13.14 On 31 March 2016, Yellow, a limited liability company, issued share capital of $50,000 (25c ordinary shares). The company also has an investment of 50,000 50c ordinary shares in Blue, a limited liability company.

The following is an extract from Yellow's ledger accounts:

DIVIDEND

	$		$
		30 September 2016 Bank	5,000

Which of the following statements is correct?

O Yellow has paid an interim dividend of 5c per share

O Yellow has received a 20% interim dividend

O Yellow has received a 10% interim dividend

O Yellow has paid a 10% interim dividend **(2 marks)**

(Total = 28 marks)

Part E: Preparing a trial balance

14 Trial balance (15 mark question) (18 mins)

Mr Yousef

The following balances have been extracted from the ledger of Mr Yousef, a sole trader at 31 May 20X6.

Task 1

Indicate whether each of these balances are debit or credit balances (Mr Yousef is not overdrawn at the bank).

	Debit	Credit
Sales – $138,078	○	○
Purchases – $82,350	○	○
Carriage – $5,144	○	○
Drawings – $7,800	○	○
Rent and insurance – $6,622	○	○
Postage and stationery – $3,001	○	○
Advertising – $1,330	○	○
Salaries and wages – $26,420	○	○
Irrecoverable debts – $877	○	○
Allowance for receivables – $130	○	○
Receivables – $12,120	○	○
Payables – $6,471	○	○
Cash on hand – $177	○	○
Bank – $1,002	○	○
Inventory as at 1 June 20X5 – $11,927	○	○
Equipment at cost – $58,000	○	○
Accumulated depreciation – $19,000	○	○
Capital at 1 June 20X5 – $53,091	○	○

Task 2

The following additional information as at 31 May 20X6 is available.

1	Rent of $210 is to be accrued.
2	Insurance has been prepaid by $880.
3	$2,211 of carriage represents carriage inwards on purchases (the remainder being carriage outwards).
4	Equipment is to be depreciated at 15% per year using the straight line method.
5	The allowance for receivables is to be increased by $40.
6	Inventory at the close of business has been valued at $13,551.

Calculate cost of sales at 31 May 20X6.

$ [ ]

Task 3

Complete this sentence:

Profit for the year will be [▼] by the rent accrual and [▼] by the insurance prepayment.

Pull down list

- Decreased
- Increased

Task 4

If profit for the year ended 31 May 20X6 is $5,888, what will be the capital balance at 31 May 20X6?

$ [ ]

Task 5

Calculate the carrying amount of equipment at 31 May 20X6.

$ [ ]

(Total = 15 marks)

15 Trade receivables and trade payables (53 mins)

15.1 You are given the following information:

Receivables at 1 January 20X3	$10,000
Receivables at 31 December 20X3	$9,000
Total receipts during 20X3 (including cash sales of $5,000)	$85,000

What is the figure for sales on credit during 20X3?

$ [ ] **(2 marks)**

15.2 A supplier sends you a statement showing a balance outstanding of $14,350. Your own records show a balance outstanding of $14,500.

Which one of the following could be the reason for this difference?

- O The supplier sent an invoice for $150 which you have not yet received
- O The supplier has allowed you $150 cash discount which you had omitted to enter in your ledgers
- O You have paid the supplier $150 which he has not yet accounted for
- O You have returned goods worth $150 which the supplier has not yet accounted for

(2 marks)

15.3 Your trade payables account has a balance at 1 October 20X8 of $34,500 credit. During October, credit purchases were $78,400, cash purchases were $2,400 and payments made to suppliers, excluding cash purchases, and after deducting settlement discounts of $1,200, were $68,900. Purchase returns were $4,700.

What was the closing balance?

- O $38,100
- O $40,500
- O $47,500
- O $49,900 **(2 marks)**

15.4 A trade receivables account had a closing balance of $8,500. It contained a contra to the trade payables account of $400, but this had been entered on the wrong side of the trade receivables account.

What is the correct balance on the trade receivables account?

- O $7,700 DEBIT
- O $8,100 DEBIT
- O $8,400 DEBIT
- O $8,900 DEBIT **(2 marks)**

15.5 Which of the following items could appear on the credit side of a trade receivables account?

(1) Bank receipts from customers

(2) Irrecoverable debts written off

(3) Increase in allowance for receivables

(4) Sales

(5) Credits for goods returned by customers

(6) Refunds to customers

- O 1, 2, and 5
- O 1, 2, 3 and 6
- O 3, 4 and 5
- O 4 and 6 **(2 marks)**

15.6 An inexperienced bookkeeper has drawn up the following trade receivables account:

TRADE RECEIVABLES

	$		$
Opening balance	180,000	Credit sales	190,000
Bank receipts from credit customers	232,200	Irrecoverable debts written off	1,500
Sales returns	8,000	Contras against payables	2,400
Refunds to credit customers	3,300	Closing balance (balancing figure)	229,600
	423,500		423,500

What should the closing balance be after correcting the errors made in preparing the account?

- O $130,600
- O $129,200
- O $142,400
- O $214,600

(2 marks)

15.7 The trade payables account below contains a number of errors:

TRADE PAYABLES

	$		$
Opening balance (amounts owed to suppliers)	318,600	Purchases	1,268,600
Bank payments to suppliers	1,364,300	Contras against debit balances in receivables ledger	48,000
Purchases returns	41,200	Discounts received	8,200
Refunds received from suppliers	2,700	Closing balance	402,000
	1,726,800		1,726,800

All items relate to credit purchases.

What should the closing balance be when all the errors are corrected?

- O $128,200
- O $509,000
- O $224,200
- O $144,600

(2 marks)

15.8 The following trade receivables account has been prepared by a trainee accountant:

TRADE RECEIVABLES

	$		$
Opening balance	308,600	Bank receipts from credit customers	148,600
Credit sales	154,200	Interest charged on overdue accounts	2,400
Cash sales	88,100	Irrecoverable debts written off	4,900
Contras against credit balances in payables ledger	4,600	Allowance for receivables	2,800
		Closing balance	396,800
	555,500		555,500

What should the closing balance be once all errors are corrected?

$ [ ] **(2 marks)**

15.9 The following trade receivables account prepared by a trainee accountant contains a number of errors:

TRADE RECEIVABLES

	$		$
20X4		*20X4*	
1 Jan Balance b/d	614,000	31 Dec Credit sales	301,000
31 Jan Bank receipts from credit customers	311,000	31 Dec Irrecoverable debts written off	35,400
Contras against amounts due to suppliers in the payables ledger	8,650	31 Dec Interest charged on overdue accounts	1,600
		31 Dec Balance c/d	595,650
	933,650		933,650

What should the closing balance on the trade receivables account be after the errors in it have been corrected?

- O $561,550
- O $578,850
- O $581,550
- O $568,350 **(2 marks)**

15.10 Your organisation sold goods to PQ Co for $800 less trade discount of 20% and settlement discount of 5% for payment within 14 days. At the time of the sale, you expect PQ to take up the settlement discount. The invoice was settled by bank transfer five days later.

Which one of the following gives the entries required to record **BOTH** of these transactions?

		Debit	Credit
		$	$
○	Trade receivables		608
	Sales		608
	Bank	608	
	Trade receivables	608	
○	Trade receivables		640
	Sales		640
	Bank	640	
	Trade receivables	640	
○	Trade receivables		608
	Sales		608
	Bank	640	
	Trade receivables	608	
	Sales		32
○	Trade receivables		640
	Sales		640
	Bank	608	
	Sales	32	
	Trade receivables	640	

(2 marks)

15.11 On 15 June 20X2, the accounts assistant at Bees Co receives a supplier statement from Nicholas Co. The balance per Nicholas Co's supplier statement shows that Bees Co has an outstanding balance of $35,040. However, in Bees Co's accounting records, the balance per Nicholas Co's payables ledger is $32,980.

Which of the following statements could explain the difference?

- ☐ A payment was made by Bees Co to Nicholas Co but has not yet been received by Nicholas Co.
- ☐ Goods have been despatched by Nicholas Co to Bees Co but have not yet been received into Bees Co's warehouse
- ☐ A transposition error was made when recording an invoice received on 10 June; the invoice was for $1,200 but was accidently recorded as $2,100.
- ☐ Bees Co has not recorded a settlement discount given by Nicholas Co in the payables ledger **(2 marks)**

15.12 Which of the following lists is composed only of items which would appear on the credit side of the trade receivables account?

- O Bank receipts from customers, sales returns, irrecoverable debts written off, contras against amounts due to suppliers in the payable ledger
- O Sales, refunds to customers, irrecoverable debts written off
- O Bank receipts from customers, interest charged on overdue accounts, irrecoverable debts written off
- O Sales, refunds to customers, interest charged on overdue accounts, contras against amounts due to suppliers in the payable ledger **(2 marks)**

15.13 The following trade receivables account has been prepared by a trainee accountant for the month of January 20X5:

TRADE RECEIVABLES

	$		$
20X5		*20X5*	
Balance b/d	318,650	Bank receipts from credit customers	181,140
Credit sales	163,010	Interest charged on overdue accounts	280
Cash sales	84,260	Irrecoverable debts written off	1,390
		Sales returns from credit customers	3,990
		Balance c/d	379,120
	565,920		565,920

What should the balance c/d at 31 January 20X5 be after correcting the errors in the account?

- O $294,860
- O $298,200
- O $295,420
- O $379,680 **(2 marks)**

15.14 At 1 April 20X9, the trade payables account showed a balance of $142,320.

At the end of April the general ledger showed the following balances:

	$
Purchases	183,800
Returns outwards	27,490
Returns inwards	13,240
Payments to payables, after deducting $1,430 cash discount	196,360

It is also discovered that:

(1) The purchases figure is net of sales tax at 17.5%; the other figures all include sales tax.

(2) A customer's balance of $2,420 has been offset against their balance of $3,650 in the payables ledger.

What is the corrected balance on the trade payables account?

- O $130,585
- O $144,835
- O $98,429
- O $128,985

(2 marks)

15.15 The balance on Jude Co's trade payables account is $31,554. The accountant at Jude Co has discovered that she has not recorded:

- A settlement discount of $53 received from a supplier; and
- A supplier's invoice for $622.What amount should be reported for payables on Jude Co's statement of financial position?

- O $30,879
- O $30,985
- O $32,123
- O $32,229

(2 marks)

15.16 On 31 March 20X7, the accountant at Borris Co is reconciling the balance on the Lima Co's payables ledger account with the supplier statement received from Lima Co on the same date.

The balance per the payables ledger of Lima's account is $20,254 and the balance per the supplier statement received from Lima Co dated 31 March 20X7 is $18,700.

Which of the following statements could explain the difference?

- O Contra entry being accidentally omitted from the supplier statement
- O Invoice received from Lima being recorded on the debit side of the payables ledger
- O An invoice received from a different supplier being allocated against Lima's account in the payables ledger
- O A bank payment being duplicated in the payables ledger

(2 marks)

15.17 How should the balance on the trade payables account be presented in the final financial statements?

- O As an expense account
- O As a non-current liability
- O As a current asset
- O As a current liability

(2 marks)

15.18 Y Ltd keeps a trade receivables account as part of its accounting system.

The following transactions take place in March:

(1) Invoices totalling $5,000 are raised to Customer X in March. These invoices offer the customer a 5% discount if they pay within 14 days. Of these invoices, Y Ltd expects invoices amounting to $2,000 to be paid with the discount taken.

(2) Customer Z pays cash of $2,850 for invoices with face values of $3,000. They took advantage of discounts totalling $150 for early payment, however Y Ltd had not expected Customer Z to take up the discounts.

Which of the following entries correctly record these transactions?

- O DEBIT trade receivables $5,000, CREDIT sales $5,000, DEBIT bank $2,850, CREDIT trade receivables $2,850
- O DEBIT trade receivables $4,900, CREDIT sales $4,900, DEBIT bank $2,850, DEBIT sales $150, CREDIT trade receivables $3,000
- O DEBIT trade receivables $5,000, CREDIT sales $5,000, DEBIT bank $2,850, DEBIT sales $150, CREDIT trade receivables $3,000
- O DEBIT trade receivables $4,900, CREDIT sales $4,900, DEBIT bank $2,850, CREDIT trade receivables $2,850 **(2 marks)**

15.19 You are an accounts assistant at Cuppa Supplies, a company that sells cups and mugs. The following is an extract from a sales invoice raised by the bookkeeper in your company to a customer, Oasis Café.

Invoice No:	**3242**			
Date:	**31 October 20X6**			
Description	**Qty**	**Unit Price** **$**		**Net amount** **$**
Coffee cups	200	5.00		1,000.00
			Sales Value	1,000.00
			Sales Tax	0.00
			Amount Payable	1,000.00
A discount of 5% of the full price applies if payment is made within seven days.				
If you pay within seven days, the discounted price is:				950.00

Senior management at your company do not expect Oasis Café to take advantage of the discount. However, you receive a payment from Oasis Café on 3 November 20X6.

Which one of the following gives the entries required to record **BOTH** of these transactions?

		Debit	Credit
		$	**$**
O	Trade receivables	950	
	Sales		950
	Bank	950	
	Trade receivables		950
O	Trade receivables	1,000	
	Sales		1,000
	Bank	950	
	Trade receivables		950
O	Trade receivables	1,000	
	Sales		1,000
	Bank	950	
	Sales	50	
	Trade receivables		1,000
O	Trade receivables	950	
	Sales		950
	Bank	950	
	Sales	50	
	Trade receivables		1,000

(2 marks)

15.20 D Co's year-end total of the list of receivables ledger balances is $560,000. The following errors have been identified:

(1) An irrecoverable receivable balance of $30,000 has not been written off in the relevant customer's account in the receivables ledger.

(2) Early settlement discounts of $12,500, which were not expected to be taken at the time the invoice was raised, have been omitted from the receivables ledger balances.

What is the total of the list of receivables ledger balances **AFTER** the errors were corrected?

- O $547,000
- O $530,000
- O $542,500
- O $517,500

(2 marks)

15.21 Complete the following sentence.

The trade payables account shows the total of the amount owed to all [ ] .

The trade payables account forms part of the [ ] and therefore is part of the [ ] system.

(2 marks)

15.22 Indicate which **TWO** of the following are reasons for reconciling the balances on individual supplier accounts to external documents.

☐ It is important that transactions with suppliers are recorded completely and accurately in the accounting records.

☐ Some suppliers will not send supplier statements to the businesses they trade with.

☐ It is inevitable that there will be items in transit (for example, goods that have been despatched but not received), therefore there will usually be difference between the balance per the individual supplier account and the balance per the supplier statement.

☐ The reconciliation enables the accounts assistant to verify to an independent source that the balances on the individual supplier accounts are accurate. **(2 marks)**

(Total = 44 marks)

16 Bank reconciliations **(36 mins)**

16.1 Your bank general ledger account at 31 December 20X3 shows a balance of $565 overdrawn. On comparing this with your bank statement at the same date, you discover the following.

(1) A cheque for $57 drawn by you on 29 December 20X3 has not yet been presented for payment.

(2) A cheque for $92 from a customer, which was paid into the bank on 24 December 20X3, has been dishonoured on 31 December 20X3.

What is the correct bank balance to be shown in the statement of financial position at 31 December 20X3?

○ $714 overdrawn

○ $657 overdrawn

○ $473 overdrawn

○ $53 overdrawn **(2 marks)**

16.2 The bank general ledger account shows a bank balance of $5,675 overdrawn at 31 August 20X5. It is subsequently discovered that a standing order for $125 has been entered twice, and that a dishonoured cheque for $450 has been debited in the bank general ledger account instead of credited.

What is the correct bank balance?

$ [ ] overdrawn **(2 marks)**

16.3 A business had a balance at the bank of $2,500 at the start of the month. During the following month, it paid for materials invoiced at $1,000 less trade discount of 20% and settlement discount of 10%. It received a cheque from a customer in respect of an invoice for $200, subject to settlement discount of 5%.

What was the balance at the bank at the end of the month?

○ $1,970

○ $1,980

○ $1,990

○ $2,000 **(2 marks)**

16.4 The bank statement on 31 October 20X7 showed an overdraft of $800. On reconciling the bank statement, it was discovered that a cheque drawn by your company for $80 had not been presented for payment, and that a cheque for $130 from a customer had been dishonoured on 30 October 20X7, but that this had not yet been notified to you by the bank.

What is the correct bank balance to be shown in the statement of financial position at 31 October 20X7?

- O $1,010 overdrawn
- O $880 overdrawn
- O $750 overdrawn
- O $720 overdrawn

(2 marks)

16.5 The following information relates to a bank reconciliation.

(1) The bank balance in the bank general ledger account before taking the items below into account was $8,970 overdrawn.

(2) Bank charges of $550 on the bank statement have not been entered in the bank general ledger account.

(3) The bank has credited the account in error with $425 which belongs to another customer.

(4) Cheque payments totalling $3,275 have been entered in the bank general ledger account but have not been presented for payment.

(5) Cheques totalling $5,380 have been correctly entered on the debit side of the bank general ledger account but have not been paid in at the bank.

What was the balance as shown by the bank statement **BEFORE** taking the above items into account?

- O $9,520 overdrawn
- O $11,200 overdrawn
- O $9,520 in credit
- O $11,200 in credit

(2 marks)

16.6 The following bank reconciliation statement has been prepared by a trainee accountant:

Bank reconciliation 30 September 20X2

	$
Balance per bank statement (overdrawn)	36,840
Add: lodgements credited after date	51,240
	88,080
Less: unpresented cheques	43,620
Balance per bank general ledger account (credit)	44,460

Assuming the amounts stated for items other than the bank general ledger account balance are correct, what should the bank general ledger account balance be?

- O $44,460 CREDIT as stated
- O $60,020 CREDIT
- O $29,220 DEBIT
- O $29,220 CREDIT

(2 marks)

16.7 Listed below are some possible causes of difference between the bank general ledger account balance and the bank statement balance when preparing a bank reconciliation.

Which **TWO** of these items require an entry in the bank general ledger account?

☐ Cheque paid in, subsequently dishonoured

☐ Bank charges

☐ Lodgements credited after date

☐ Cheques not yet presented **(2 marks)**

16.8 In preparing a company's bank reconciliation statement at March 20X3, the following items are causing the difference between the bank general ledger account balance and the bank statement balance:

(1) Bank charges $380

(2) Lodgements not credited $4,580

(3) Unpresented cheques $1,475

(4) Direct debit $350

(5) Cheque paid in by the company and dishonoured $400

Which of these items will require an entry in the bank general ledger account?

○ 2, 3 and 4

○ 1,4 and 5

○ 3 and 4

○ 1 and 5 **(2 marks)**

16.9 The following bank reconciliation statement has been prepared by a trainee accountant:

	$
Overdraft per bank statement	3,860
Less: unpresented cheques	9,160
	5,300
Add: deposits credited after date	16,690
Bank general ledger account as calculated above	21,990

What should be the correct balance per the bank general ledger account?

○ $21,990 balance at bank as stated

○ $3,670 balance at bank

○ $11,390 balance at bank

○ $3,670 overdrawn **(2 marks)**

16.10 Which of the following statements about bank reconciliations are correct?

(1) A difference between the bank general ledger account and the bank statement must be corrected by means of a journal entry.

(2) In preparing a bank reconciliation, lodgements recorded before date in the bank general ledger account but credited by the bank after date should reduce an overdrawn balance in the bank statement.

(3) Bank charges not yet entered in the bank general ledger account should be dealt with by an adjustment in the bank reconciliation statement.

(4) If a cheque received from a customer is dishonoured after date, a credit entry in the bank general ledger account is required.

- O 2 and 4
- O 1 and 4
- O 2 and 3
- O 1 and 3

(2 marks)

16.11 The following information relates to a bank reconciliation.

(1) The bank balance in the bank general ledger account before taking the items below into account was $8,970 overdrawn.

(2) Bank charges of $550 on the bank statement have not been entered in the bank general ledger account.

(3) The bank has credited the account in error with $425 which belongs to another customer.

(4) Cheque payments totalling $3,275 have been entered in the bank general ledger account but have not been presented for payment.

(5) Cheques totalling $5,380 have been correctly entered on the debit side of the bank general ledger account but have not been paid in at the bank.

What was the balance as shown by the bank statement **before** taking the items above into account?

$ [ ] overdrawn

(2 marks)

16.12 The following attempt at a bank reconciliation statement has been prepared by Q Co:

	$
Overdraft per bank statement	38,600
Add: deposits not credited	41,200
	79,800
Less: unpresented cheques	3,300
Overdraft per bank general ledger account	76,500

Assuming the bank statement balance of $38,600 to be correct, what **should** the bank general ledger account balance be?

- O $76,500 overdrawn, as stated
- O $5,900 overdrawn
- O $700 overdrawn
- O $5,900 bank general ledger account **(2 marks)**

16.13 After checking a business bank general ledger account against the bank statement, which of the following items could require an entry in the bank general ledger account?

(1) Bank charges

(2) A cheque from a customer which was dishonoured

(3) Cheque not presented

(4) Deposits not credited

(5) Credit transfer entered in bank statement

(6) Standing order entered in bank statement.

- O 1, 2, 5 and 6
- O 3 and 4
- O 1, 3, 4 and 6
- O 3, 4, 5 and 6 **(2 marks)**

16.14 The following bank reconciliation statement has been prepared for a Red Co:

	$
Overdraft per bank statement	39,800
Add: Deposits credited after date	64,100
	103,900
Less: Unpresented cheques presented after date	44,200
Overdraft per bank general ledger account	59,700

Assuming the amount of the overdraft per the bank statement of $39,800 is correct, what should be the balance in the bank general ledger account?

- O $158,100 overdrawn
- O $19,900 overdrawn
- O $68,500 overdrawn
- O $59,700 overdrawn **(2 marks)**

16.15 Listed below are four potential causes of difference between a company's bank general ledger account balance and its bank statement balance as at 30 November 20X3:

(1) Cheques recorded and sent to suppliers before 30 November 20X3 but not yet presented for payment

(2) Bank charges

(3) Cheques paid in before 30 November 20X3 but not credited by the bank until 3 December 20X3

(4) A cheque recorded and paid in before 30 November 20X3 but dishonoured by the bank

Which one of the following alternatives correctly analyses these items into those requiring an entry in the bank general ledger account and those that would feature in the bank reconciliation?

	Bank general ledger account entry	**Bank reconciliation**
O	1, 3	2, 4
O	2, 4	1, 3
O	2, 3	1, 4
O	2, 4	1, 4

(2 marks)

(Total = 30 marks)

17 Correction of errors (44 mins)

17.1 The debit side of a trial balance totals $800 more than the credit side.

Which one of the following errors would fully account for the difference?

- O $400 paid for plant maintenance has been correctly entered in the bank general ledger account and credited to the plant asset account.
- O Credit note issued to a customer of $400 has been debited to trade receivables.
- O A receipt of $800 for commission receivable has been omitted from the records.
- O The petty cash balance of $800 has been omitted from the trial balance. **(2 marks)**

17.2 The bookkeeper of Peri made the following mistakes:

A credit entry for sales returns of $384 was recorded in the purchases returns account

A debit entry for purchases returns of $296 was recorded in the sales returns account.

Which one of the following journal entries will correct the errors?

		Debit	Credit
		$	$
O	Sales returns	768	
	Purchases returns		592
	Suspense accounts		176
O	Sales returns	88	
	Purchases returns	88	
	Suspense accounts		176
O	Sales returns	680	
	Purchases returns		680
O	Suspense account	176	
	Sales returns		88
	Purchases returns		88

(2 marks)

17.3 White Co's trial balance failed to agree, the totals being:

DEBIT	$815,602
CREDIT	$808,420

Which one of the following errors could fully account for the difference?

- O The omission from the trial balance of the balance on the insurance expense account $7,182 debit.
- O Settlement discounts received from suppliers of $3,591 were credited in error to the purchases account.
- O No entries made in the records for cash sales totalling $7,182.
- O The purchases returns total of $3,591 was included in the trial balance as a debit balance. **(2 marks)**

17.4 The debit side of a trial balance totals $50 more than the credit side. Which one of the following could this be due to?

- O A purchase of goods for $50 being omitted from the trade payables account.
- O A sale of goods for $50 being omitted from the trade receivables account.
- O An invoice of $25 for electricity being credited to the electricity account.
- O A receipt for $50 from a customer being omitted from the bank general ledger account.

(2 marks)

17.5 Which one of the following is an error of principle?

- O Plant and machinery purchased was credited to a non-current assets account.
- O Plant and machinery purchased was debited to the purchases account.
- O Plant and machinery purchased was debited to the equipment account.
- O Plant and machinery purchased was credited to the equipment account. **(2 marks)**

17.6 What is an error of commission?

- O An error where a transaction has not been recorded.
- O An error where one side of a transaction has been recorded in the wrong account, and that account is of a different class to the correct account.
- O An error where one side of a transaction has been recorded in the wrong account, and that account is of the same class as the correct account.
- O An error where the numbers in the posting have been transposed. **(2 marks)**

17.7 Where a transaction is entered into the correct ledger accounts, but the wrong amount is used, what is the error known as?

- O An error of omission
- O An error of original entry
- O An error of commission
- O An error of principle **(2 marks)**

17.8 Daily Co's statement of profit or loss and other comprehensive income for the year ended 31 December 20X4 showed a profit for the year of $83,600. It was later found that $18,000 paid for the purchase of a motor van had been debited to motor expenses account. It is the company's policy to depreciate motor vans at 25% per year, with a full year's charge in the year of acquisition.

What is Daily Co's profit for the year after adjusting for this error?

$ [ ] **(2 marks)**

17.9 An organisation restores its petty cash balance to $250 at the end of each month. During October, the total expenditure column in the petty cash records was calculated as being $210, and the imprest was restored by this amount. The analysis columns posted to the general ledger totalled only $200.

Which one of the following would this error cause?

- O The trial balance being $10 higher on the debit side
- O The trial balance being $10 higher on the credit side
- O No imbalance in the trial balance
- O The petty cash balance being $10 lower than it should be

(2 marks)

17.10 Profit for the year was calculated as being $10,200. It was later discovered that asset expenditure of $3,000 had been treated as expenditure in the statement of profit or loss, and revenue receipts of $1,400 had been treated as asset receipts.

What is the profit for the year after correcting this error?

- O $5,800
- O $8,600
- O $11,800
- O $14,600

(2 marks)

17.11 The accountant at Investotech discovered the following errors after calculating the company's profit for 20X3:

(1) A non-current asset costing $50,000 has been included in the purchases account.

(2) Stationery costing $10,000 has been included as closing inventory of raw materials, instead of stationery expenses.

What is the effect of these errors on gross profit and profit for the year?

- O Understatement of gross profit by $40,000 and understatement of profit for the year by $30,000
- O Understatement of both gross profit and profit for the year by $40,000
- O Understatement of gross profit by $60,000 and understatement of profit for the year by $50,000
- O Overstatement of both gross profit and profit for the year by $60,000

(2 marks)

17.12 A purchase return of $48 has been wrongly posted to the debit of the sales returns account, but has been correctly entered in the supplier's account.

Which of the following statements about the trial balance would be correct?

- O The credit side to be $48 more than the debit side
- O The debit side to be $48 more than the credit side
- O The credit side to be $96 more than the debit side
- O The debit side to be $96 more than the credit side

(2 marks)

17.13 Two types of common errors in bookkeeping are errors of **principle** and errors of **transposition**.

Which of the following correctly states whether or not these errors will be revealed by extracting a trial balance?

	Errors of principle	Errors of transposition
O	Will be revealed	Will not be revealed
O	Will be revealed	Will be revealed
O	Will not be revealed	Will not be revealed
O	Will not be revealed	Will be revealed

(2 marks)

17.14 The following are balances on the accounts of Luigi, a sole trader, as at the end of the current financial year and after all entries have been processed and the profit for the year has been calculated.

	$
Non-current assets	85,000
Receivables	7,000
Trade payables	3,000
Bank loan	15,000
Allowance for depreciation, non-current assets	15,000
Inventory	4,000
Accruals	1,000
Prepayments	2,000
Bank overdraft	2,000

What is the balance on Luigi's capital account?

O $59,000

O $66,000

O $62,000

O $64,000 **(2 marks)**

17.15 The following balances have been extracted from the general ledger accounts of Tanya, but the figure for the bank loan is unknown. There are no other accounts in the main ledger.

	$
Payables	27,000
Capital	66,000
Purchases	160,000
Sales	300,000
Other expenses	110,000
Receivables	33,000
Purchase returns	2,000
Non-current assets	120,000
Bank (asset)	18,000
Bank loan	[Unknown]

What is the credit balance on the bank loan account?

$ [ ] **(2 marks)**

17.16 Beta Co has total assets of $650,000 and profit for the year of $150,000 recorded in the financial statements for the year ended 31 December 20X3. Inventory costing $50,000, with a resale value of $75,000, was received into the warehouse on 2 January 20X4 and included in the inventory value that was recorded in the financial statements at 31 December 20X3.

What would the total assets figure in the statement of financial position, and the adjusted profit for the year figure be, after adjusting for this error?

	Total assets (SOFP)	*Profit for the year*
O	$700,000	$200,000
O	$600,000	$100,000
O	$725,000	$225,000
O	$600,000	$75,000

(2 marks)

17.17 The electricity account for Jingles Co for the year ended 30 June 20X1 was as follows.

	$
Opening balance for electricity accrued at 1 July 20X0	300
Payments made during the year	
1 August 20X0 for three months to 31 July 20X0	600
1 November 20X0 for three months to 31 October 20X0	720
1 February 20X1 for three months to 31 January 20X1	900
30 June 20X1 for three months to 30 April 20X1	840

Jingles Co expects the next bill due in September to be for the same amount as the bill received in June.

What are the appropriate amounts for electricity to be included in the financial statements of Jingles Co for the year ended 30 June 20X1?

	Statement of financial position	Statement of profit or loss
O	$560	$3,320
O	$560	$3,060
O	$860	$3,320
O	$860	$3,060

(2 marks)

17.18 Paula Co is reviewing its receivables ledger and has discovered the following items:

(1) An invoice for $110 had been recorded in the receivables ledger as $1,100.

(2) A credit note sent to a customer in respect of sales returns has been debited to the receivables ledger.

Indicate whether a debit or credit entry should be made in the receivables ledger in respect of each of the items.

	Item 1	*Item 2*
O	Debit	Debit
O	Credit	Credit
O	Debit	Credit
O	Credit	Debit

(2 marks)

(Total = 36 marks)

18 Suspense accounts (31 mins)

18.1 When Q's trial balance failed to agree, a suspense account was opened for the difference. The trial balance totals were:

DEBIT	$864,390
CREDIT	$860,930

The following errors were found in the general ledger:

(1) In recording an issue of shares at par, bank receipts of $333,000 was credited to the ordinary share capital account as $330,000.

(2) Cash $2,800 paid for plant repairs was correctly accounted for in the bank general ledger account but was credited to the plant asset account.

(3) The petty cash balance of $500 had been omitted from the trial balance.

(4) A cheque for $78,400 paid for the purchase of a motor car was debited to the motor vehicles account as $87,400.

Which of these errors will require an entry to the suspense account to correct them?

- O 2 and 4 only
- O 3 and 4 only
- O 1, 2 and 3 only
- O 1, 2, 3 and 4 **(2 marks)**

18.2 What will the balance on the suspense account be after making the necessary entries to correct the errors affecting the suspense account?

- O $2,440 DEBIT
- O $15,560 CREDIT
- O $13,640 DEBIT
- O $3,440 DEBIT **(2 marks)**

18.3 Cat Co's trial balance totals were:

Debit	$387,642	
Credit		$379,511

A suspense account was opened for the difference.

Which one of the following errors would have the effect of reducing the difference when corrected?

- O The petty cash balance of $500 has been omitted from the trial balance.
- O $4,000 received for rent of part of the office has been correctly recorded in the bank general ledger account and debited to the rent account.
- O $3,000 paid for repairs to plant has been debited to the plant asset account.
- O An invoice for Mr A Smith for $400 has been posted to the account of Mrs B Smith in error. **(2 marks)**

18.4 A trial balance extracted from a sole trader's records failed to agree, and a suspense account was opened for the difference.

Which of the following errors would require an entry in the suspense account in correcting them?

(1) Sales returns were mistakenly debited to the purchases returns account.

(2) Cash received from the sale of a non-current asset was correctly entered in the bank general ledger account but was debited to the disposal account.

(3) The balance on the rent account was omitted from the trial balance.

(4) Goods taken from inventory by the proprietor had been recorded by crediting drawings account and debiting purchases account.

- O All four items
- O 2 and 3 only
- O 2 and 4 only
- O 1 and 3 only **(2 marks)**

18.5 A suspense account was opened when a trial balance fai ed to agree. The following errors were later discovered.

- A gas bill of $420 had been recorded in the gas accou nt as $240.
- A sales invoice to a customer for $50 had been credited to trade receivables.
- Interest received of $70 had been entered in the bank general ledger account only.

What was the original balance on the suspense account?

- O DEBIT $210
- O CREDIT $210
- O DEBIT $160
- O CREDIT $160

(2 marks)

18.6 Dog Co's trial balance failed to agree, the difference of $25,000 being posted to a suspense account.

Subsequent investigation revealed the difference was due to one side of an entry to record the purchase of machinery for $25,000, by cheque, failing to post to the plant and machinery account.

Which of the following journal entries would correct the error?

		Debit	Credit
		$	**$**
O	Plant and machinery	25,000	
	Bank general ledger account		25,000
O	Suspense account	25,000	
	Plant and machinery		25,000
O	Plant and machinery	25,000	
	Suspense account		25,000
O	Bank general ledger account	25,000	
	Suspense account		25,000

(2 marks)

18.7 The trial balance of Z failed to agree, the totals being:

Debit	$836,200	
Credit		$819,700

A suspense account was opened for the amount of the difference and the following errors were found and corrected:

(1) A discount received balance of $5,100 had not been posted to the discount received account.

(2) A cheque for $19,000 received from a customer was correctly entered in the bank general ledger account but was posted to the trade receivables account as $9,100.

What will the remaining balance be on the suspense account **after** the correction of these errors?

$ [ ] credit **(2 marks)**

18.8 The trial balance of C, a limited liability company, did not agree, and a suspense account was opened for the difference. Checking in the bookkeeping system revealed a number of errors.

Which **TWO** of the following errors would require an entry to the suspense account as part of the process of correcting them?

- ☐ $4,600 paid for motor van repairs was correctly treated in the bank general ledger account but was credited to motor vehicles asset account.
- ☐ $360 received from B, a customer, was credited in error to the account of BB.
- ☐ $9,500 paid for rent was debited to the rent account as $5,900.
- ☐ Sales returns had been debited in error to the purchases returns account.
- ☐ No entries have been made to record a cash sale of $100. **(2 marks)**

18.9 The suspense account shows a debit balance of $100. What could this balance be due to?

- O Recording the receipt of $100 from the owner of the business correctly in the bank general ledger account but omitting the entry in the capital account
- O Omitting the bank overdraft balance of $100 from the trial balance
- O Undercasting the sales account by $100
- O Undercasting the purchases account by $100 **(2 marks)**

18.10 A suspense account shows a credit balance of $130. Which of the following options could this be due to?

- O Recording a credit sale as $2,440 instead of $2,310 in both the sales account and the receivables account
- O Recording a purchase of $130 twice in the purchases account
- O Failing to write off an irrecoverable debt of $130
- O Recording an electricity bill paid of $65 by debiting the bank account and crediting the electricity account **(2 marks)**

18.11 Chocolate Co has a suspense account balance in its trial balance of $560 credit.

It was discovered that discounts allowed of $700 have been debited to, instead of credited to, the trade receivables account.

What is the remaining balance on the suspense account after this error has been adjusted for?

- O $140 DEBIT
- O $840 DEBIT
- O $1,260 CREDIT
- O $1,960 CREDIT **(2 marks)**

18.12 M Co's trial balance does not agree and therefore a suspense account with a debit balance of $3,000 has been opened.

Which of the following errors could explain this difference?

- O A receipt of $3,000 from a credit customer has been credited to the trade payables account instead of the trade receivables account.
- O The interest received account of $1,500 has been omitted from the trial balance.
- O Equipment repairs of $3,000 have been incorrectly capitalised as part of plant and equipment.
- O A $1,500 bank balance has been shown in the trial balance as an overdraft of $1,500.

(2 marks)

18.13 On 1 October 20X6, N Co had 400,000 25c ordinary shares in issue. On 1 January 20X7 there was a rights issue of one for five at $1.50. The entry in the share premium account was omitted in error and as a result the trial balance at 30 September 20X7 did not agree.

What balance would have been entered in the suspense account when it was opened?

- O $400,000 DEBIT
- O $400,000 CREDIT
- O $100,000 DEBIT
- O $100,000 CREDIT

(2 marks)

(Total = 26 marks)

19 Shuswap **(18 mins)**

The draft statement of financial position shown below has been prepared for Shuswap, a limited liability company, as at 31 December 20X4:

	Cost	Accumulated depreciation	Carrying amount
	$'000	$'000	$'000
Assets			
Non-current assets			
Land and buildings	9,000	1,000	8,000
Plant and equipment	21,000	9,000	12,000
	30,000	10,000	20,000
Current assets			
Inventories			3,000
Receivables			2,600
Cash at bank			1,900
Total assets			27,500
Equity and liabilities			
Equity			
Issued share capital (ordinary shares of 50c each)			6,000
Retained earnings			12,400
Non-current liabilities			
Loan notes (redeemable 20Y0)			2,000
Current liabilities			
Trade payables			2,100
			22,500
Suspense account			5,000
			27,500

19.1 Some inventory items included in the draft statement of financial position at cost $500,000 were sold after the reporting date for $400,000, with selling expenses of $40,000.

Which of the following statements is correct?

- O Inventory should be debited with $140,000 at 31.12.20X4.
- O Inventory should be credited with $140,000 at 31.12.20X4.
- O Bank should be credited with $140,000 at 31.12.20X4.
- O No adjustment should be made because the inventory was sold after the year end.

(2 marks)

19.2 The suspense account is made up of two items:

(1) The proceeds of the issue of 4,000,000 50c shares at $1.10 per share, credited to the suspense account from the bank general ledger account.

(2) The balance of the account is the proceeds of sale of some plant on 1 January 20X4 with a carrying amount at the date of sale of $700,000 and which had originally cost $1,400,000. No other accounting entries have yet been made for the disposal apart from the bank general ledger account entry for the receipt of the proceeds. Depreciation on plant has been charged at 25% (straight line basis) in preparing the draft statement of financial position without allowing for the sale. The depreciation for the year relating to the plant sold should be adjusted for in full.

Task 1

What is the profit or loss on disposal of the plant?

$ [ ] [ ] /Profit **(1.5 marks)**

Task 2

What is the amount of the depreciation adjustment that should be made for the year to 31.12.20X4?

$ [ ] **(1.5 marks)**

(Total = 3 marks)

19.3 A year end journal to clear the suspense account is given below.

Task 1

Prepare the double entry by selecting the correct option for each row. (Use the information given under Task 2 to help you.)

	Credit	Debit	Neither DEBIT nor CREDIT
Issued share capital	○	○	○
Share premium	○	○	○
Bank	○	○	○
Plant and equipment – cost	○	○	○
Plant and equipment – disposal account	○	○	○
Suspense account	○	○	○

(4 marks)

Task 2

After the suspense account has been cleared, what will be the balances on these accounts?

Share capital $ [ ]

Share premium $ [ ] **(3 marks)**

(Total = 7 marks)

19.4 Irrecoverable debts of $200,000 are to be written off at 31.12.20X4.

Will the following adjustments be debited or credited to retained earnings?

	Debit	Credit	Neither DEBIT nor CREDIT
Irrecoverable debts	○	○	○
Depreciation adjustment (Task 2)	○	○	○
Inventory adjustment (Task 1)	○	○	○

(3 marks)

(Total = 15 marks)

20 Malright (18 mins)

You are presented with the following trial balance of Malright, a limited liability company, at 31 October 20X7.

	DEBIT	*CREDIT*
	$'000	$'000
Buildings at cost	740	
Buildings, accumulated depreciation, 1 November 20X6		60
Plant at cost	220	
Plant, accumulated depreciation, 1 November 20X6		110
Bank balance		70
Revenue		1,800
Purchases	1,140	
Inventory at 1 November 20X6	160	
Cash	20	
Trade payables		250
Trade receivables	320	
Administrative expenses	325	
Allowance for receivables, at 1 November 20X6		10
Retained earnings at 1 November 20X6		130
$1 ordinary shares		415
Share premium account		80
	2,925	2,925

20.1 Do each of the above items belong on the statement of financial position (SOFP) as at 31 October 20X7?

	On SOFP	Not on SOFP
Buildings at cost	O	O
Buildings, accumulated depreciation, 1 November 20X6	O	O
Plant at oost	O	O
Plant, accumulated depreciation, 1 November 20X6	O	O
Bank balance	O	O
Revenue	O	O
Purchases	O	O
Inventory at 1 November 20X6	O	O
Cash	O	O
Trade payables	O	O
Trade receivables	O	O
Administrative expenses	O	O
Allowance for receivables, at 1 November 20X6	O	O
Retained earnings at 1 November 20X6	O	O
$1 ordinary shares	O	O
Share premium account	O	O

(4 marks)

20.2 The allowance for receivables is to be increased to 5% of trade receivables. The allowance for receivables is treated as an administrative expense.

Task 1

The year-end journal for allowance for receivables is given below. Prepare the double entry by selecting the correct option for each row.

	DEBIT	CREDIT	Neither DEBIT nor CREDIT
Trade receivables	O	O	O
Administrative expenses	O	O	O
Allowance for receivables	O	O	O
Revenue	O	O	O

(1.5 marks)

Task 2

Complete the following:

The amount included in the statement of profit or loss after the allowance is increased to 5% of trade receivables is $ [ ] **(1.5 marks)**

(Total = 3 marks)

20.3 Plant is depreciated at 20% per year using the diminishing balance method and buildings are depreciated at 5% per year on their original cost. Depreciation is treated as a cost of sales expense.

Task 1

The year-end journal for buildings and plant depreciation is given below. Using the information above, prepare the double entry by selecting the correct option for each row.

	DEBIT	CREDIT	Neither DEBIT nor CREDIT
Administrative expenses	○	○	○
Cost of sales	○	○	○
Buildings cost	○	○	○
Plant costs	○	○	○
Buildings accumulated depreciation	○	○	○
Plant accumulated depreciation	○	○	○

(2 marks)

Task 2

Calculate the depreciation charge for the below for the year ended 31 October 20X7. Use the information above to help you.

Buildings $ [ ]

Plant $ [ ] **(2 marks)**

(Total = 4 marks)

20.4 Closing inventory is $75,000.

Ignoring the depreciation charge calculated earlier, what is the cost of sales for the year?

$ [ ] **(1 mark)**

20.5 An invoice of $15,000 for energy costs relating to the quarter ended 30 November 20X7 was received on 2 December 20X7. Energy costs are included in administrative expenses.

Complete the following statements:

Task 1

The double entry to post the year end adjustments for energy costs is:

	Debit	**Credit**
Accrual	O	O
Administrative expenses	O	O

(1.5 marks)

Task 2

The amount to be posted within the year end adjustment double entry above is

$ [ ] **(1.5 marks)**

(Total = 3 marks)

(Total = 15 marks)

21 Tonson (18 mins)

The information below has been extracted from the accounting records of Tonson, a limited liability company, as at 31 October 20X6.

	DEBIT	*CREDIT*
	$'000	$'000
Inventory at 1 November 20X5	350	
Administrative expenses	1,106	
Share premium account		200
Retained earnings at 1 November 20X5		315
Allowance for receivables at 1 November 20X5		40
Sales revenue		5,780
Bank		79
Returns inward	95	
Trade payables		340
Loan note interest	33	
Trade receivables	900	
Purchases	3,570	
7% loan notes		470
Irrecoverable debts	150	
$1 ordinary shares		1,800
Land at cost	740	
Buildings at cost	1,500	

	DEBIT	CREDIT
	$'000	$'000
Motor vehicles at cost	240	
Furniture and equipment at cost	1,200	
Accumulated depreciation at 1 November 20X5		
Buildings		360
Motor vehicles		80
Furniture and equipment		420
	9,884	9,884

21.1 Do each of the above items belong in the statement of profit or loss (P/L) as at 31 October 20X6?

	P/L	Not P/L
Inventory at 1 November 20X5	○	○
Administrative expenses	○	○
Share premium account	○	○
Retained earnings at 1 November 20X5	○	○
Allowance for receivables at 1 November 20X5	○	○
Sales revenue	○	○
Bank	○	○
Returns inward	○	○
Trade payables	○	○
Loan note interest	○	○
Trade receivables	○	○
Purchases	○	○
7% loan notes	○	○
Irrecoverable debts	○	○
$1 ordinary shares	○	○
Land at cost	○	○
Buildings at cost	○	○
Motor vehicles at cost	○	○
Furniture and equipment at cost	○	○
Accumulated depreciation at 1 November 20X5: Buildings	○	○
Accumulated depreciation at 1 November 20X5: Motor vehicles	○	○
Accumulated depreciation at 1 November 20X5: Furniture and equipment	○	○

(5 marks)

21.2 Buildings are depreciated at 5% of cost. At 31 October 20X6 the buildings were professionally valued at $1,800,000 and the directors wish this valuation to be incorporated into the financial statements.

Depreciation is to be charged as follows:

(1) Motor vehicles at 20% of carrying amount

(2) Furniture and equipment at 20% of cost

What will be the carrying amount of the following assets in the financial statements at 31 October 20X6?

Land $ [ ]

Buildings $ [ ]

Motor vehicles $ [ ]

Furniture and equipment $ [ ]

(4 marks)

21.3 Inventory at 31 October 20X6 was valued at $275,000 based on its original cost. However, $45,000 of this inventory has been in the warehouse for over two years and the directors have agreed to sell it in November 20X6 for a cash price of $20,000.

The administrative expenses include $5,000 which relates to November 20X6.

The allowance for receivables is to be increased to the equivalent of 5% of trade receivables.

There are wages and salaries outstanding of $40,000 for the year ended 31 October 20X6.

Will the following items be debited or credited to profit for the year?

Inventory valuation adjustment	**DEBIT**	**CREDIT**
Administrative expenses relating to November 20X6	**DEBIT**	**CREDIT**
Increase in allowance for receivables	**DEBIT**	**CREDIT**
Outstanding wages and salaries	**DEBIT**	**CREDIT**

(3 marks)

21.4 During October 20X6 a bonus issue of one for ten shares was made to ordinary shareholders. This has not been entered into the accounting records. The share premium account was used for this purpose.

Task 1

Complete this sentence:

The bonus issue will [▼] Tonson's cash balance.

Pull down list

- Decrease
- Increase
- Not affect

Task 2

What will be the balances on these accounts following the bonus issue?

Share capital $ [ ]

Share premium $ [ ] **(1.5 marks)**

(Total = 6 marks)

(Total = 18 marks)

22 Emma **(18 mins)**

Set out below are the financial statements of Emma, a limited liability company.

STATEMENT OF PROFIT OR LOSS FOR THE YEAR ENDED 31 DECEMBER 20X2

	$'000
Sales revenue	2,553
Cost of sales	1,814
Gross profit	739
Distribution costs	125
Administrative expenses	204
Finance costs	60
Profit before tax	350
Income tax expense	240
Profit for the year	110

STATEMENTS OF FINANCIAL POSITION AS AT 31 DECEMBER

	20X2	*20X1*
	$'000	$'000
Non-current assets		
Tangible assets	380	305
Intangible assets	250	200
Investments		25
	630	530
Current assets		
Inventories	150	102
Receivables	390	315
Cash in hand	52	1
	592	418
	1,222	948

	20X2	20X1
	$'000	$'000
Equity and liabilities		
Share capital ($1 ordinary shares)	200	150
Share premium account	160	150
Revaluation surplus	100	91
Retained earnings	160	100
	620	491
Non-current liabilities		
Long-term loan	100	–
Current liabilities		
Trade payables	127	119
Bank overdraft	85	98
Taxation	290	240
	502	457
	1,222	948

Additional information

(1) The proceeds of the sale of non-current asset investments amounted to $30,000.

(2) Fixtures and fittings, with an original cost of $85,000 and a carrying amount of $45,000, were sold for $32,000 during the year.

(3) The following information relates to property, plant and equipment.

Some items of PPE were revalued during the year.

	31.12.20X2	*31.12.20X1*
	$'000	$'000
Cost/valuation	720	595
Accumulated depreciation	340	290
Carrying amount	380	380

(4) 50,000 $1 ordinary shares were issued during the year at a premium of 20c per share.

Required

Complete the following sections of the statement of cash flows for the year ended 31 December 20X2 for Emma.

(15 marks)

STATEMENT OF CASH FLOWS FOR THE YEAR ENDED 31 DECEMBER 20X2 (extract)

	$'000	Add/Subtract
Cash flows from operating activities		
Profit before tax/Profit after tax		
Adjustments for:		
Depreciation		
Loss on sale for non-current assets		
Profit on sale of non-current asset investments		
Movement in inventories		
Movement in receivables		
Movement in payables		
Income taxes paid		
Cash flows from investing activities		
Purchase of intangible non-current assets		
Purchase of tangible non-current assets		
Receipts from sale of non-current assets		
Cash flows from financing activities		
Proceeds from issue of share capital		
Dividends paid		
Long-term loan		

23 Sioux **(18 mins)**

The following information is available for Sioux, a limited liability company:

STATEMENTS OF FINANCIAL POSITION

				31 December
		20X4		*20X3*
	$'000	$'000	$'000	$'000
Non-current assets				
Cost or valuation		11,000		8,000
Accumulated depreciation		(5,600)		(4,800)
Carrying amount		5,400		3,200

	$'000	31 December 20X4 $'000	$'000	20X3 $'000
Current assets				
Inventories	3,400		3,300	
Receivables	3,800		2,900	
Cash at bank	400	7,600	100	6,800
		13,000		10,000
Equity and liabilities				
Capital and equity				
Ordinary share capital	1,000		1,000	
Revaluation surplus	1,500		1,000	
Retained earnings	3,100	5,600	2,200	4,200
Non-current liabilities				
10% Loan notes		3,000		2,000
Current liabilities				
Trade payables	3,700		3,200	
Income tax	700	4,400	600	3,800
		13,000		10,000

SUMMARISED STATEMENT OF PROFIT OR LOSS FOR THE YEAR ENDED 31 DECEMBER 20X4

	$'000
Profit from operations	2,650
Finance cost (loan note interest)	(300)
	2,350
Income tax expense	(700)
Profit for the year	1,650

Notes.

1 During the year non-current assets which had cost $800,000, with a carrying amount of $350,000, were sold for $500,000.

2 The revaluation surplus arose from the revaluation of some land that was not being depreciated.

3 The 20X3 income tax liability was settled at the amount provided for at 31 December 20X3.

4 The additional loan notes were issued on 1 January 20X4. Interest was paid on 30 June 20X4 and 31 December 20X4.

5 Dividends paid during the year amounted to $750,000.

Required

Complete the following statement of cash flows for the year ended 31 December 20X2 for Sioux.

(15 marks)

STATEMENT OF CASH FLOWS FOR THE YEAR ENDED 31 DECEMBER 20X4

	$'000	*Add/Subtract*
Profit before tax/Profit after tax (indicate 'Before tax' or 'After tax' in right hand column)		
Depreciation		
Profit on disposal		
Movement in inventories		
Movement in receivables		
Movement in payables		
Tax paid		
Cash flows from investing activities		
Payments to acquire non-current assets		
Proceeds from sale of non-current assets		
Cash flows from financing activities		
Proceeds from issue of loan notes		
Dividends paid		
Net increase in cash (indicate 'Increase' or 'Decrease' in right hand column)		
Cash at 1 January 20X4		
Cash at 31 December 20X4		

24 Snowdrop (18 mins)

The following information has been extracted from the draft financial statements of Snowdrop, a limited liability company.

STATEMENTS OF FINANCIAL POSITION AS AT 31 MAY

		20X5		*20X4*
	$'000	$'000	$'000	$'000
Non-current assets		4,600		2,700
Current assets				
Inventory	580		500	
Trade receivables	360		230	
Bank	0		170	
		940		900
Total assets		5,540		3,600

	$'000	20X5 $'000	$'000	20X4 $'000
Equity and liabilities				
Equity				
Ordinary share capital		3,500		2,370
Share premium		300		150
Retained earnings		1,052		470
		4,852		2,990
Non-current liabilities				
10% Loan note (redeemable 31 May 20X5)		0		100
Current liabilities				
Trade payables	450		365	
Taxation	180		145	
Bank overdraft	58		0	
		688		510
		5,540		3,600

Additional information

(1) The statement of profit or loss for the year ended 31 May 20X5 shows the following.

	$'000
Operating profit	1,042
Interest payable	(10)
Profit before taxation	1,032
Taxation	(180)
Profit for the year	852

(2) During the year dividends paid were $270,000.

(3) Profit before taxation had been arrived at after charging $700,000 for depreciation on non-current assets.

(4) During the year non-current assets with a carrying amount of $200,000 were sold for $180,000.

Required

Complete the following statement of cash flows for the year ended 31 May 20X5 for Snowdrop.

(15 marks)

SNOWDROP LIMITED STATEMENT OF CASH FLOWS FOR THE YEAR ENDED 31 MAY 20X5

	$'000	Add/Subtract
Cash flows from operating activities		
Profit before tax/Profit after tax (indicate 'Before tax' or 'After tax' in right hand column)		
Adjustments for		
Depreciation		
Loss on disposal of non-current assts		
Movement in inventories		
Movement in receivables		
Movement in payables		
Income taxes paid		
Cash flow from investing activities		
Purchase of non-current assets		
Receipts from sales of tangible non-current assets		
Cash flows from financing activities		
Issue of share capital		
Dividends paid		
Repayment of long term borrowing		
Net increase/(decrease) in cash and cash equivalents (indicate 'Increase' or 'Decrease' in right hand column)		
Cash and cash equivalents at the beginning of period		
Cash and cash equivalents at end of period		

Note. Dividends paid should be shown under financing activities.

25 Geofrost (18 mins)

Geofrost is preparing its statement of cash flows for the year ended 31 October 20X7. You have been presented with the following information.

STATEMENT OF PROFIT OR LOSS FOR THE YEAR ENDED 31 OCTOBER 20X7

	$'000
Profit before tax	15,000
Taxation	(4,350)
Profit for the year	10,650

STATEMENTS OF FINANCIAL POSITION AS AT 31 OCTOBER

		20X7		20X6
	$'000	$'000	$'000	$'000
Non-current assets		44,282		26,574
Current assets				
Inventory	3,560		9,635	
Trade receivables	6,405		4,542	
Cash	2,045		1,063	
		12,010		15,240
Total assets		56,292		41,814
Equity and liabilities				
Equity				
Ordinary share capital		19,365		17,496
Retained earnings		17,115		6,465
		36,480		23,961
Non-current liabilities				
9% loan notes		8,000		10,300
Current liabilities				
Bank overdraft	1,230		429	
Trade payables	7,562		4,364	
Taxation	3,020		2,760	
		11,812		7,553
Total equity and liabilities		56,292		41,814

Additional information

(1) Depreciation expense for the year was $4,658,000.

(2) Assets with a carrying amount of $1,974,000 were disposed of at a profit of $720,000.

Required

Complete the following statement of cash flows for the year ended 31 October 20X7 for Geofrost.

(15 marks)

	$	Add/Subtract
Cash flows from operating activities		
Profit before tax/Profit after tax (indicate 'Before tax' or 'After tax' in right hand column)		
Adjustments for		
Depreciation		
Profit on disposal of non-current assets		
Movement in inventory		
Movement in receivables		
Movement in payables		
Tax paid		
Cash flows from investing activities		
Payments to acquire tangible non-current assets		
Proceeds from sale of non-current assets		
Cash flows from financing activities		
Proceeds from issue of share capital		
Repayment of long term borrowing		
Net increase/(decrease) in cash in cash and cash equivalents (indicate 'Increase' or 'Decrease' in right hand column)		
Cash and cash equivalents at the beginning of period		
Cash and cash equivalents at end of period		

26 Incomplete records (38 mins)

26.1 A business has compiled the following information for the year ended 31 October 20X2:

	$
Opening inventory	386,200
Purchases	989,000
Closing Inventory	422,700

The gross profit as a percentage of sales is always 40%.

Based on these figures, what is the sales revenue for the year?

- O $952,500
- O $1,333,500
- O $1,587,500
- O $1,524,000

(2 marks)

26.2 Which of the following calculations could produce an acceptable figure for a trader's profit for a period if no accounting records had been kept?

- O Closing net assets plus drawings minus capital introduced minus opening net assets
- O Closing net assets minus drawings plus capital introduced minus opening net assets
- O Closing net assets minus drawings minus capital introduced minus opening net assets
- O Closing net assets plus drawings plus capital introduced minus opening net assets

(2 marks)

26.3 A sole trader fixes his prices to achieve a gross profit percentage on sales revenue of 40%. All his sales are for cash. He suspects that one of his sales assistants is stealing cash from sales revenue.

His trading account for the month of June 20X3 is as follows:

	$
Recorded sales revenue	181,600
Cost of sales	114,000
Gross profit	67,600

Assuming that the cost of sales figure is correct, how much cash could the sales assistant have taken?

- O $5,040
- O $8,400
- O $22,000
- O It is not possible to calculate a figure from this information

(2 marks)

26.4 A is a sole trader who does not keep full accounting records. The following details relate to her transactions with credit customers and suppliers for the year ended 30 November 20X3.

	$
Trade receivables, 1 December 20X2	130,000
Trade payables, 1 December 20X2	60,000
Bank receipts from customers	687,800
Bank payments to suppliers	302,800
Discounts received	2,960
Irrecoverable debts	4,160
Amount due from a customer who is also a supplier offset against an amount due for goods supplied by him	2,000
Trade receivables, 30 November 20X3	181,000
Trade payables, 30 November 20X3	84,000

Based on the above information, what should be the figure for sales revenue in A's statement of profit or loss for the year ended 30 November 20X3?

$ [ ] **(2 marks)**

26.5 Based on the above information, what figure should appear in A's statement of profit or loss for the year ended 30 November 20X3 for purchases?

- O $283,760
- O $325,840
- O $329,760
- O $331,760

(2 marks)

26.6 A sole trader fixes her prices by adding 50% to the cost of all goods purchased. On 31 October 20X3 a fire destroyed a considerable part of the inventory and all inventory records.

Her trading account for the year ended 31 October 20X3 included the following figures:

	$	$
Sales		281,250
Opening inventory at cost	183,600	
Purchases	249,200	
	432,800	
Closing inventory at cost	204,600	
		228,200
Gross profit		53,050

Using this information, what inventory loss has occurred?

- O $61,050
- O $87,575
- O $40,700
- O $110,850

(2 marks)

26.7 A fire on 30 September 20X2 destroyed some of a company's inventory and its inventory records.

The following information is available:

	$
Inventory 1 September 20X2	318,000
Sales for September 20X2	612,000
Purchases for September 20X2	412,000
Inventory in good condition at 30 September 20X2	214,000

Standard gross profit percentage on sales is 25%.

Based on this information, what is the value of inventory lost?

- O $96,000
- O $271,000
- O $26,400
- O $57,000

(2 marks)

26.8 A business's bank balance increased by $750,000 during its last financial year. During the same period, it issued shares of $1 million and repaid a loan note of $750,000. It purchased non-current assets for $200,000 and charged depreciation of $100,000. Working capital (other than the bank balance) increased by $575,000.

What was its profit for the year?

- O $1,175,000
- O $1,275,000
- O $1,325,000
- O $1,375,000

(2 marks)

26.9 A sole trader's business made a profit of $32,500 during the year ended 31 March 20X8. This figure was after deducting $100 per week wages for himself. In addition, he put his home telephone bill through the business accounting records, amounting to $400 plus sales tax at 17.5%. He is registered for sales tax and therefore has charged only the net amount to his statement of profit or loss and other comprehensive income.

His capital at 1 April 20X7 was $6,500. What was his capital at 31 March 20X8?

- O $33,730
- O $33,800
- O $38,930
- O $39,000

(2 marks)

26.10 Senji does not keep proper accounting records, and it is necessary to calculate her total purchases for the year ended 31 January 20X3 from the following information:

		$
Trade payables:	31 January 20X2	130,400
	31 January 20X3	171,250
Payment to suppliers		888,400
Cost of goods taken from inventory by Senji for her personal use		1,000
Refunds received from suppliers		2,400
Discounts received		11,200

What should be the figure for purchases, in Senji's financial statements for the year ended 31 January 20X3?

$ [ ]

(2 marks)

26.11 Aluki fixes prices to make a standard gross profit percentage on sales of 20%.

The following information for the year ended 31 January 20X3 is available to compute her sales total for the year.

		$
Inventory:	1 February 20X2	243,000
	31 January 20X3	261,700
Purchases		595,400
Purchases returns		41,200

What is the sales figure for the year ended 31 January 20X3?

- O $669,375
- O $702,600
- O $772,375
- O $741,480

(2 marks)

26.12 Alpha is a sole trader who does not keep proper accounting records.

Alpha's first year of trading was 20X4. From reviewing Alpha's bank statements and the incomplete records relating to cash maintained, the following summary has been compiled.

Bank and cash summary, Alpha, 20X4

	$
Cash received from credit customers and paid into the bank	381,600
Expenses paid out of cash received from credit customers before banking	6,800
Cash sales	112,900

Other information, Alpha, 20X4

Irrecoverable debts written off	7,200
Closing balance of trade receivables	0

Which of the following correctly represents Alpha's sales figure for 20X4?

- O $508,500
- O $112,900
- O $381,600
- O $494,100

(2 marks)

26.13 A sole trader who does not keep full accounting records wishes to calculate her sales revenue for the year.

The information available is:

(a)	Opening inventory	$17,000
(b)	Closing inventory	$24,000
(c)	Purchases	$91,000
(d)	Standard gross profit percentage on sales revenue	40%

Which of the following is the sales figure for the year calculated from these figures?

- O $117,600
- O $108,000
- O $210,000
- O $140,000

(2 marks)

26.14 On 31 December 20X0 the inventory of Vole Co was completely destroyed by fire. The following information is available:

(1) Inventory at 1 December 20X0 at cost $28,400

(2) Purchases for December 20X0 $49,600

(3) Sales for December 20X0 $64,800

(4) Standard gross profit percentage on sales revenue 30%

Based on this information, which of the following is the amount of inventory destroyed?

- O $45,360
- O $32,640
- O $40,971
- O $19,440

(2 marks)

26.15 The following information is available for the year ended 31 December 20X4 for a trader who does not keep proper accounting records:

	$
Inventories at 1 January 20X4	38,000
Inventories at 31 December 20X4	45,000
Purchases	637,000

Gross profit percentage on sales = 30%

Based on this information, what was the trader's sales figure for the year?

- O $900,000
- O $819,000
- O $920,000
- O $837,200

(2 marks)

26.16 Wanda keeps no accounting records. The following information is available about her position and transactions for the year ended 31 December 20X4:

	$
Net assets at 1 January 20X4	210,000
Drawings during 20X4	48,000
Capital introduced during 20X4	100,000
Net assets at 31 December 20X4	400,000

Based on this information, what was Wanda's profit for 20X4?

- O $42,000
- O $242,000
- O $138,000
- O $338,000

(2 marks)

(Total = 32 marks)

27 Company financial statements (24 mins)

27.1 Which of the following items may appear as current liabilities in a company's statement of financial position?

(1) Revaluation surplus

(2) Loan due for repayment within one year

(3) Taxation

(4) Preference dividend payable on redeemable preference shares

- O 1, 2 and 3
- O 1, 2 and 4
- O 1, 3 and 4
- O 2, 3 and 4

(2 marks)

27.2 Which **TWO** of the following might appear as an item in a company's statement of changes in equity?

- ☐ Profit on disposal of properties
- ☐ Surplus on revaluation of properties
- ☐ Equity dividends proposed after the reporting date
- ☐ Issue of share capital

(2 marks)

27.3 At 31 December 20X2 the following matters require inclusion in a company's financial statements:

(1) On 1 January 20X2 the company made a loan of $12,000 to an employee, repayable on 30 April 20X3, charging interest at 2% per year. On the due date she repaid the loan and paid the whole of the interest due on the loan to that date.

(2) The company has paid insurance $9,000 in 20X2, covering the year ending 31 August 20X3.

(3) In January 20X3 the company received rent from a tenant $4,000 covering the six months to 31 December 20X2.

For these items, what total figures should be included in the company's statement of financial position at 31 December 20X2?

	Receivables and prepayments	***Payables and accruals***
	$	**$**
O	22,000	240
O	22,240	NIL
O	10,240	NIL
O	16,240	6,000

(2 marks)

27.4 Which of the following items are required to be disclosed by a limited liability company, either on the face of their main financial statements or in the notes, according to IFRS Standards?

(1) Share capital

(2) Dividends proposed

(3) Depreciation and amortisation

O 1 and 2 only

O 1 and 3 only

O 2 and 3 only

O 1, 2, and 3 **(2 marks)**

27.5 Identify, by indicating the relevant box in the table below, whether each of the following statements about the financial statements of a limited company is true or false, according to IFRS Standards.

In preparing a statement of cash flows, either the direct or the indirect method may be used. Both lead to the same figure for net cash from operating activities.	**TRUE**	**FALSE**
Loan notes can be classified as current or non-current liabilities.	**TRUE**	**FALSE**
Financial statements must disclose a company's total expense for depreciation, if material.	**TRUE**	**FALSE**
A company must disclose, by note, details of all adjusting events allowed for in the financial statements.	**TRUE**	**FALSE**

(2 marks)

27.6 Which **TWO** of the following could be presented as separate items in the statement of changes in equity required by IAS 1 *Presentation of Financial Statements* as part of a company's financial statements?

☐ Dividends on equity shares paid during the period

☐ Loss on sale of investments

☐ Proceeds of an issue of ordinary shares

☐ Dividends proposed after the year end **(2 marks)**

27.7 Which one of the following items is **NOT** presented under the heading 'equity' on a company statement of financial position?

○ Share premium account

○ Retained earnings

○ Revaluation surplus

○ Loan stock **(2 marks)**

27.8 The correct ledger entries needed to record the issue of 200,000 $1 shares at a premium of 30c, and paid for in full, would be:

○	DEBIT Ordinary share capital	$200,000	
	CREDIT Share premium account		$60,000
	CREDIT Bank		$140,000
○	DEBIT Bank	$260,000	
	CREDIT Ordinary share capital		$200,000
	CREDIT Share premium account		$60,000
○	DEBIT Ordinary share capital	$200,000	
	CREDIT Share premium account		$60,000
	CREDIT Bank		$260,000
○	DEBIT Bank	$200,000	
	DEBIT Share premium account	$60,000	
	CREDIT Ordinary share capital		$260,000

(2 marks)

27.9 Which of the following statements about limited liability companies' accounting is/are correct?

(1) A revaluation surplus arises when a non-current asset is sold at a profit.

(2) The authorised share capital of a company is the maximum nominal value of shares and loan notes the company may issue.

(3) IAS 10 *Events After the Reporting Period* requires all non-adjusting events to be disclosed in the notes to the financial statements.

- O 1 and 2
- O 2 only
- O 3 only
- O None of the statements are correct **(2 marks)**

27.10 Fruitz Co has a tax liability relating to 20X1 brought forward in 20X2 of $16,000. This liability is finally agreed at $18,500, which is paid in 20X2.

Fruitz Co's accountant estimates their tax liability for profits earned in 20X2 will be $20,000.

What will be the charge for taxation in Fruitz Co's statement of profit or loss for the year ended 31 December 20X2?

$ [ ] **(2 marks)**

(Total = 20 marks)

28 Disclosure notes (22 mins)

28.1 Which of the following best describes the purpose of disclosure notes in the financial statements?

- O To provide more detail for the users of financial statements about the information in the statement of financial position and statement of profit or loss and other comprehensive income.
- O To allow companies to present their financial results in a more favourable way by only disclosing some things in the notes and not on the main financial statements.
- O To give all the detail of all the transactions that occurred during the period because the main financial statements only present a summary.
- O To explain the accounting treatment adopted where management have chosen not to apply IFRS® Standards. **(2 marks)**

28.2 For which class or classes of assets should a company disclose in the notes to the financial statements a reconciliation of the opening carrying amount to the closing carrying amount, showing the movements in the period?

(1) Cash
(2) Intangible assets
(3) Tangible non-current assets
(4) Trade receivables

- O 3 only
- O 2 and 3 only
- O 1 and 4 only
- O 1 only **(2 marks)**

28.3 Which of the following should be disclosed in the note to the financial statements for inventories?

(1) The date the inventories were purchased or manufactured and/or how long they have been held as inventories
(2) The amount of inventories carried at net realisable value
(3) The accounting policies adopted in measuring inventories
(4) The useful life of the inventories

- O 3 only
- O 2 and 3 only
- O 1 and 4 only
- O 1 only **(2 marks)**

28.4 Which of the following should be disclosed in the note to the financial statements for intangible assets?

(1) The method of amortisation used

(2) A reconciliation of the carrying amount at the beginning and end of the period

(3) The useful life of the assets

(4) The net realisable value of any deferred development costs capitalised

- O 1, 2 and 3 only
- O 2 and 3 only
- O 3 and 4 only
- O 2 only **(2 marks)**

28.5 Which of the following statements is/are correct?

(1) IAS 37 *Provisions, Contingent Liabilities and Contingent Assets* requires disclosure in the notes to the financial statements of the uncertainties affecting the outcome of a provision.

(2) IAS 10 *Events After the Reporting Period* requires disclosure of the nature and financial effect of a non-adjusting event after the reporting period in the notes to the financial statements.

- O 1 only
- O 2 only
- O Both 1 and 2
- O Neither 1 or 2 **(2 marks)**

28.6 A certain IFRS Standard requires that the following disclosure is made in a note to the financial statements:

(1) A brief description of its nature

(2) Where practicable an estimate of the financial effect

(3) An indication of the uncertainties relating to the amount or timing of any outflow

(4) The possibility of any reimbursement

Which of the following does the above disclosure apply to?

- O Provisions
- O Contingent liabilities
- O Contingent assets
- O Events after the reporting period **(2 marks)**

28.7 Which of the following should be disclosed in the note to the financial statements for tangible non-current assets?

(1) The market value of all assets classified as tangible non-current assets, whether they have been revalued or not

(2) A reconciliation of the carrying amount of non-current assets at the beginning and end of the period

(3) For revalued assets, the methods and significant assumptions applied in estimating the fair value

(4) For revalued assets, the carrying amount of each class of assets that would have been included in the financial statements had the assets been carried at cost less depreciation

- O 1, 2 and 3 only
- O 2 and 3 only
- O 2, 3 and 4 only
- O 1 and 4 only

(2 marks)

28.8 Which of the following are required as disclosures by IAS 2 *Inventories*?

(1) The amount of write-downs of inventories in the period that have been recognised as an expense

(2) The original cost of inventories that are carried at net realisable value

(3) The carrying amount of inventories classified by type (for example, raw materials, work in progress)

- O 1 and 2 only
- O 1 and 3 only
- O 2 and 3 only
- O 1, 2 and 3

(2 marks)

28.9 Which one of the following is a disclosure about non-adjusting events required by IAS 10 *Events After the Reporting Period*?

- O Dividends declared before the end of the reporting period and paid after the end of the reporting period
- O The nature of both material and non-material non-adjusting events
- O The date that the non-adjusting event occurred
- O An estimate of the financial effect of the event, unless a reasonable estimate cannot be made

(2 marks)

(Total = 18 marks)

29 Events after the reporting period (22 mins)

29.1 Which of the following material events after the reporting period and before the financial statements are approved by the directors should be adjusted for in those financial statements?

(1) A valuation of property providing evidence of impairment in value at the reporting period

(2) Sale of inventory held at the end of the reporting period for less than cost

(3) Discovery of fraud or error affecting the financial statements

(4) The insolvency of a customer with a debt owing at the end of the reporting period which is still outstanding

- O All of them
- O 1, 2 and 4 only
- O 3 and 4 only
- O 1, 2 and 3 only

(2 marks)

29.2 The draft financial statements of a limited liability company are under consideration. The accounting treatment of the following material events which occurred after the end of the reporting period needs to be determined.

According to IAS 10 *Events After the Reporting Period*, which **TWO** of the events require an adjustment to the figures in the draft financial statements?

- ☐ The bankruptcy of a major customer, with a substantial debt outstanding at the end of the reporting period
- ☐ A fire destroying some of the company's inventory (the company's going concern status is not affected)
- ☐ An issue of shares to finance expansion
- ☐ Sale for less than cost of some inventory held at the end of the reporting period

(2 marks)

29.3 In finalising the financial statements of a company for the year ended 30 June 20X4, which of the following material matters should be adjusted for?

(1) A customer who owed $180,000 at the end of the reporting period went bankrupt in July 20X4.

(2) The sale in August 20X4 for $400,000 of some inventory items valued in the statement of financial position at $500,000.

(3) A factory with a carrying amount of $3,000,000 was seriously damaged by a fire in July 20X4. The factory was back in production by August 20X4 but its value was reduced to $2,000,000.

(4) The company issued 1,000,000 ordinary shares in August 20X4.

- O All four items
- O 1 and 2 only
- O 1 and 4 only
- O 2 and 3 only

(2 marks)

29.4 IAS 10 *Events After the Reporting Period* regulates the extent to which events after the reporting period should be reflected in financial statements.

Which one of the following lists of such events consists only of items that, according to IAS 10, should normally be classified as non-adjusting?

- O Insolvency of an account receivable which was outstanding at the end of the reporting period, issue of shares or loan notes, an acquisition of another company
- O Issue of shares or loan notes, changes in foreign exchange rates, major purchases of non-current assets
- O An acquisition of another company, destruction of a major non-current asset by fire, discovery of fraud or error which shows that the financial statements were incorrect
- O Sale of inventory which gives evidence about its value at the end of the reporting period, issue of shares or loan notes, destruction of a major non-current asset by fire

(2 marks)

29.5 Which of the following events occurring after the reporting period are classified as adjusting, if material?

(1) The sale of inventories valued at cost at the end of the reporting period for a figure in excess of cost

(2) A valuation of land and buildings providing evidence of an impairment in value at the year end

(3) The issue of shares and loan notes

(4) The insolvency of a customer with a balance outstanding at the year end

- O 1 and 3
- O 2 and 4
- O 2 and 3
- O 1 and 4

(2 marks)

29.6 The financial statements of Overexposure Co for the year ended 31 December 20X1 are to be approved on 31 March 20X2. Before they are approved, the following events take place.

(1) On 14 February 20X2 the directors took the strategic decision to sell their investment in Quebec Co despite the fact that this investment generated material revenues.

(2) On 15 March 20X2, a fire occurred in the eastern branch factory which destroyed a material amount of inventory. It is estimated that it will cost $505,000 to repair the significant damage done to the factory.

(3) On 17 March 20X2, a customer of Overexposure Co went into liquidation. Overexposure has been advised that it is unlikely to receive payment for any of the outstanding balances owed by the customer at the year end.

How should these events be reflected in the financial statements at 31 December 20X1?

	Adjust	*Disclose*	*Do nothing*
O	3	2, 3	1
O	2, 3	1	
O	3	1, 2	
O	2	3, 1	

(2 marks)

29.7 Which of the following events between the reporting date and the date the financial statements are authorised for issue must be adjusted in the financial statements?

(1) Declaration of equity dividends

(2) Decline in market value of investments

(3) The announcement of changes in tax rates

(4) The announcement of a major restructuring

- O 1 only
- O 2 and 4
- O 3 only
- O None of them **(2 marks)**

29.8 Which of the following is the correct definition of an adjusting event after the reporting period in accordance with IAS 10 *Events After the Reporting Period*?

- O An event that occurs between the reporting date and the date on which the financial statements are authorised for issue that provides further evidence of conditions that existed at the reporting date
- O An event that occurs between the reporting date and the date on which the financial statements are authorised for issue that provides evidence of conditions that arose subsequent to the reporting date
- O An event that occurs after the date the financial statements are authorised for issue that provides further evidence of conditions that existed at the reporting date
- O An event that occurs after the date the financial statements are authorised for issue that provides evidence of conditions that arose subsequent to the reporting date

(2 marks)

29.9 If a material event occurs after the reporting date but before the financial statements are authorised for issue outside the organisation, and this event does **NOT** require adjustment, what information should be disclosed in the financial statements?

- O The nature of the event and an estimate of the financial effect (or a statement that such an estimate cannot be made)
- O The nature of the event only
- O An estimate of the financial effect (or a statement that such an estimate cannot be made) only
- O No disclosure required **(2 marks)**

(Total = 18 marks)

30 Statements of cash flows (51 mins)

30.1 Which of the following items appear in a company's statement of cash flows?

(1) Surplus on revaluation of non-current assets

(2) Proceeds of issue of shares

(3) Proposed dividend

(4) Irrecoverable debts written off

(5) Dividends received

- O 1, 2 and 5 only
- O 2, 3, 4, 5 only
- O 2 and 5 only
- O 3 and 4 only

(2 marks)

30.2 Part of the process of preparing a company's statement of cash flows is the calculation of cash inflow from operating activities.

Which of the following statements about that calculation (using the indirect method) are correct?

(1) Loss on sale of non-current assets should be deducted from profit before interest and tax.

(2) Increase in inventory should be deducted from profit before interest and tax.

(3) Increase in payables should be added to profit before interest and tax.

(4) Depreciation charges should be added to profit before interest and tax.

- O 1, 2 and 3
- O 1, 2 and 4
- O 1, 3 and 4
- O 2, 3 and 4

(2 marks)

30.3 In the course of preparing a company's statement of cash flows, the following figures are to be included in the calculation of net cash from operating activities.

	$
Depreciation charges	980,000
Profit on sale of non-current assets	40,000
Increase in inventories	130,000
Decrease in receivables	100,000
Increase in payables	80,000

What will the net effect of these items be in the statement of cash flows?

	$
O Addition to operating profit	890,000
O Subtraction from operating profit	890,000
O Addition to operating profit	1,070,000
O Addition to operating profit	990,000

(2 marks)

30.4 Part of a company's draft statement of cash flows is shown below:

	$'000
Profit before tax	8,640
Depreciation charges	(2,160)
Proceeds of sale of non-current assets	360
Increase in inventory	(330)
Increase in trade payables	440

The following criticisms of the above extract have been made:

(1) Depreciation charges should have been added, not deducted.

(2) Increase in inventory should have been added, not deducted.

(3) Increase in trade payables should have been deducted, not added.

(4) Proceeds of sale of non-current assets should not appear in this part of the statement of cash flows.

Which of these criticisms are valid?

O 2 and 3 only

O 1 and 4 only

O 1 and 3 only

O 2 and 4 only

(2 marks)

30.5 In preparing a company's statement of cash flows complying with IAS 7 *Statement of Cash Flows*, which, if any, of the following items could form part of the calculation of cash flow from financing activities?

(1) Proceeds of sale of premises

(2) Dividends received

(3) Bonus issue of shares

- O 1 only
- O 2 only
- O 3 only
- O None of them

(2 marks)

30.6 Which of the following assertions about statements of cash flows is/are correct?

(1) A statement of cash flows prepared using the direct method produces a different figure for operating cash flow from that produced if the indirect method is used.

(2) Rights issues of shares do not feature in statements of cash flows.

(3) A surplus on revaluation of a non-current asset will not appear as an item in a statement of cash flows.

(4) A profit on the sale of a non-current asset will appear as an item under Cash Flows from Investing Activities in a statement of cash flows.

- O 1 and 4
- O 2 and 3
- O 3 only
- O 2 and 4

(2 marks)

30.7 An extract from a statement of cash flows prepared by a trainee accountant is shown below.

Cash flows from operating activities

	$m
Profit before taxation	28
Adjustments for: Depreciation	(9)
Operating profit before working capital changes	19
Decrease in inventories	13
Increase in receivables	(4)
Increase in payables	(8)
Cash generated from operations	10

Which **TWO** of the following criticisms of this extract are correct?

- ☐ Depreciation charges should have been added, not deducted.
- ☐ Decrease in inventories should have been deducted, not added.
- ☐ Increase in receivables should have been added, not deducted.
- ☐ Increase in payables should have been added, not deducted.

(2 marks)

30.8 Which of the following items could appear in a company's statement of cash flows?

(1) Proposed dividends

(2) Rights issue of shares

(3) Bonus issue of shares

(4) Repayment of loan

- O 1 and 3
- O 2 and 4
- O 1 and 4
- O 2 and 3

(2 marks)

30.9 IAS 7 *Statement of Cash Flows* requires the statement of cash flows to open with the calculation of net cash from operating activities, arrived at by adjusting profit before taxation.

Which one of the following lists consists only of items which could appear in such a calculation?

- O Depreciation, increase in receivables, decrease in payables, proceeds from sale of equipment, increase in inventories
- O Increase in payables, decrease in inventories, profit on sale of plant, depreciation, decrease in receivables
- O Increase in payables, proceeds from sale of equipment, depreciation, decrease in receivables, increase in inventories
- O Depreciation, interest paid, proceeds from sale of equipment, decrease in inventories

(2 marks)

30.10 The following extract is from the financial statements of Pompeii, a limited liability company at 31 October:

	20X9	*20X8*
	$'000	$'000
Equity and liabilities		
Share capital	120	80
Share premium	60	40
Retained earnings	85	68
	265	188
Non-current liabilities		
Bank loan	100	150
	365	338

What is the cash flow from financing activities to be disclosed in the statement of cash flows for the year ended 31 October 20X9?

- O $60,000 inflow
- O $10,000 inflow
- O $110,000 inflow
- O $27,000 inflow

(2 marks)

30.11 A draft statement of cash flows contains the following calculation of cash flows from operating activities:

	$m
Profit before tax	13
Depreciation	2
Decrease in inventories	(3)
Decrease in trade and other receivables	5
Decrease in trade payables	4
Net cash inflow from operating activities	21

Which of the following corrections need to be made to the calculation?

(1) Depreciation should be deducted, not added.

(2) Decrease in inventories should be added, not deducted.

(3) Decrease in receivables should be deducted, not added.

(4) Decrease in payables should be deducted, not added.

- O 1 and 3
- O 2 and 3
- O 1 and 4
- O 2 and 4

(2 marks)

30.12 The following extract is taken from a draft version of company's statement of cash flows, prepared by a trainee accountant.

	$'000
Net cash flow from operating activities	
Profit before tax	484
Depreciation charges	327
Profit on sale of property, plant and equipment	35
Increase in inventories	(74)
Decrease in trade and other receivables	(41)
Increase in trade payables	29
Cash generated from operations	760

Four possible mistakes that may have been made by the trainee accountant are listed below.

(1) The profit on sale of property, plant and equipment should be subtracted, not added.

(2) The increase in inventories should be added, not subtracted.

(3) The decrease in trade and other receivables should be added, not subtracted.

(4) The increase in trade payables should be subtracted, not added.

Which of the four mistakes did the trainee accountant make when preparing the draft statement?

- O 1 and 2 only
- O 1 and 3 only
- O 2 and 4 only
- O 3 and 4 only **(2 marks)**

30.13 Which, if any, of the following items could be included in 'cash flows from financing activities' in a statement of cash flows that complies with IAS 7 *Statement of Cash Flows*?

(1) Interest received

(2) Taxation paid

(3) Proceeds from sale of property

- O 1 only
- O 2 only
- O 3 only
- O None of them **(2 marks)**

30.14 Which one of the following statements is correct, with regard to the preparation of a statement of cash flows that complies with IAS 7 *Statement of Cash Flows*?

- O A statement of cash flows prepared using the direct method produces the same figure for net cash from operating activities as a statement produced by the indirect method.
- O An increase in a bank overdraft during the accounting period is included within cash flows from financing activities.
- O A profit on the sale of equipment is included within cash flows from investing activities.
- O A surplus on the revaluation of property will appear within cash flows from investing activities. **(2 marks)**

30.15 The following information is available about the plant, property and equipment of Lok Co, for the year to 31 December 20X3.

	$'000
Carrying amount of assets at beginning of the year	462
Carrying amount of assets at end of the year	633
Increase in revaluation surplus during the year	50
Disposals during the year, at cost	110
Accumulated depreciation on the assets disposed of	65
Depreciation charge for the year	38

Based on this information, what amount will be included for purchases of property, plant and equipment for the year, in a statement of cash flows that complies with IAS 7 *Statement of Cash Flows?*

$ [ ]

(2 marks)

30.16 A company sold warehouse premises at a loss during a financial period. How would this transaction be included in a statement of cash flows for the period that complies with IAS 7 *Statement of Cash Flows* and that uses the indirect method to present cash flows from operating activities?

	Loss on disposal	***Proceeds from sale***
O	Deduct as an adjustment in the calculation of cash flows from operating activities	Include in cash flows from investing activities
O	Deduct as an adjustment in the calculation of cash flows from operating activities	Include in cash flows from operating activities
O	Add as an adjustment in the calculation of cash flows from operating activities	Include in cash flows from investing activities
O	Add as an adjustment in the calculation of cash flows from operating activities	Include in cash flows from operating activities

(2 marks)

30.17 Big Time Co had the following transactions during the year.

Using the direct method, what is Big Time Co's cash flow from operating activities?

- Purchases from suppliers were $18,500, of which $2,550 was unpaid at the year end. Brought forward payables were $1,000.
- Wages and salaries amounted to $9,500, of which $750 was unpaid at the year end. The financial statements for the previous year showed an accrual for wages and salaries of $1,500.
- Interest of $2,100 on a long-term loan was paid in the year.
- Sales revenue was $33,400, including $900 receivables at the year end. Brought forward receivables were $400.

$ [ ]

(2 marks)

30.18 Which one of the following statements is correct?

- If a business makes a profit, it has positive cash flow.
- If a business makes a loss, it has negative cash flow.
- A business may make a profit but have negative cash flow.
- A business that breaks even has cash inflows equal to cash used. **(2 marks)**

30.19 Toots Co has made healthy profits for the past year, although at times the company has been close to running out of cash. Because Toots Co is profitable, Adam – their accountant – is unconcerned by the cash shortage. Jo, the financial controller at Toots Co, is concerned. Jo tells Adam, 'profits are fine on paper, but in the real world cash is king'. Jo believes Toots Co needs to take a more proactive approach to cash flow management.

Adam and Jo have two different views. Who is correct, and why?

- Adam is correct. A profitable business should not waste management time on cash flow issues.
- Adam is correct. A profitable business will always survive and prosper.
- Jo is correct. Proactive cash flow management is required under IAS 7 *Statement of Cash Flows*.
- Jo is correct. A business that does not have cash available to fund operations is likely to fail. **(2 marks)**

30.20 Which one of the following statements correctly identifies a valid disadvantage to users of financial statements of the statement of cash flows?

- Under IAS 7 *Statement of Cash Flows*, an entity may use any format for their statement.
- There is an opportunity to reclassify some cash outflows that might have been reported in the operating section as investing cash outflows.
- Under IAS 7 *Statement of Cash Flows* the statement of cash flows may cover a different period of time to the other financial statements.
- Cash flow figures are more open to manipulation than the profit figure. **(2 marks)**

30.21 The accountant of F Co is preparing the statement of cash flows using the direct method for reporting cash flows from operating activities. The following information is available at 31 March 20X7.

	$
Sales	750,000
Purchases	400,000
Receivables at 31 March 20X7	184,000
Receivables at 1 April 20X6	163,000
Payables at 31 March 20X7	102,000
Payables at 1 April 20X6	111,000

What will be disclosed as cash receipts from customers in the statement of cash flows for the year ended 31 March 20X7?

- O $320,000
- O $771,000
- O $750,000
- O $729,000 **(2 marks)**

(Total = 42 marks)

31 Swing and cat (18 mins)

Swing purchased 80% of Cat's equity on 1 January 20X7 for $120,000 when Cat's retained earnings were $50,000. The fair value of the non-controlling interest on that date was $40,000. During the year, Swing sold goods which cost $80,000 to Cat, at an invoiced cost of $100,000. Cat had 50% of the goods still in inventories at the year end. The two companies' draft financial statements as at 31 December 20X8 are shown below.

STATEMENTS OF PROFIT OR LOSS FOR THE YEAR ENDED 31 DECEMBER 20X8

	Swing	*Cat*
	$'000	$'000
Revenue	5,000	1,000
Cost of sales	2,900	600
Gross profit	2,100	400
Other expenses	1,700	320
Profit before tax	400	80
Income tax	130	25
Profit for the year	270	55

STATEMENTS OF FINANCIAL POSITION AT 31 DECEMBER 20X8

	Swing	*Cat*
	$'000	$'000
Non-current assets		
Investment in Cat	120	–
Tangible non-current assets	1,880	200
	2,000	200
Current assets		
Inventory	500	120
Trade receivables	650	40
Bank and cash	390	35
	1,540	195
	3,540	395
Equity and liabilities		
Equity		
Share capital	2,000	100
Retained earnings	400	200
	2,400	300

	Swing	Cat
	$'000	$'000
Current liabilities		
Trade payables	910	30
Tax	230	65
	1,140	95
	3,540	395

31.1 Complete the following to determine goodwill at acquisition. **(3 marks)**

	$'000	$'000
Fair value of consideration transferred		☐
Plus fair value of non-controlling interest at acquisition		☐
Less fair value of net assets acquired as represented by:		
Ordinary share capital	☐	
Retained earnings	☐	
		☐
Goodwill		☐

31.2 What is the amount of the adjustment for unrealised profit on inventory?

$ ☐ **(1.5 marks)**

31.3 What will be consolidated cost of sales at 31 December 20X8?

$ ☐ **(2.5 marks)**

31.4 Which **TWO** of the following statements concerning the non-controlling interest are correct?

- ☐ Non-controlling interest describes shares in the consolidated entity not held by the parent.
- ☐ Non-controlling interest describes shares in the subsidiary not held by the parent.
- ☐ 20% of Swing's consolidated retained earnings will be allocated to the non-controlling interest.
- ☐ 20% of Cat's profit for the year will be allocated to the non-controlling interest.

(2 marks)

31.5 Complete the following to determine consolidated retained earnings. **(6 marks)**

	Swing	*Cat*
	$'000	$'000
Per question	[ ]	[ ]
Adjustment	[ ]	
Pre-acquisition retained earnings		[ ]
Total		[ ]
Group share of Cat	[ ]	
Group retained earnings	[ ]	

(Total = 15 marks)

32 Black and Bury **(18 mins)**

The following are the financial statements relating to Black, a limited liability company, and its subsidiary company Bury.

STATEMENTS OF PROFIT OR LOSS FOR THE YEAR ENDED 31 OCTOBER 20X5

	Black	*Bury*
	$'000	$'000
Sales revenue	245,000	95,000
Cost of sales	(140,000)	(52,000)
Gross profit	105,000	43,000
Distribution costs	(12,000)	(10,000)
Administrative expenses	(55,000)	(13,000)
Dividend income from Bury	7,000	
Profit before tax	45,000	20,000
Tax	(13,250)	(5,000)
Profit for the year	31,750	15,000

STATEMENTS OF FINANCIAL POSITION AS AT 31 OCTOBER 20X5

		Black		Bury
	$'000	$'000	$'000	$'000
Assets				
Non-current assets				
Property, plant and equipment		110,000		40,000
Investments				
21,000,000 $1 ordinary shares in Bury at cost		21,000		
		131,000		40,000
Current assets				
Inventory, at cost	13,360		3,890	
Trade receivables and dividend receivable	14,640		6,280	
Bank	3,500		2,570	
Total assets		31,500		12,740
		162,500		52,740
Equity and liabilities				
Equity				
$1 Ordinary shares		100,000		30,000
Retained earnings		33,500		10,280
		133,500		40,280
Current liabilities				
Payables	9,000		2,460	
Dividend payable	20,000		10,000	
Total equity and liabilities		29,000		12,460
		162,500		52,740

Additional information

(1) Black purchased its $1 ordinary shares in Bury on 1 November 20X0. At that date the balance on Bury's retained earnings was $2 million. The fair value of the non-controlling interest at the date of acquisition was $11,800,000. Goodwill on acquisition was $800,000.

(2) During the year ended 31 October 20X5 Black sold goods which originally cost $12 million to Bury. Black invoiced Bury at cost plus 40%. Bury still has 30% of these goods in inventory at 31 October 20X5.

(3) Bury owed Black $1.5 million at 31 October 20X5 for some of the goods Black supplied during the year.

32.1 Black purchased its shares in Bury on 1 November 20X0. Goodwill on acquisition was $800,000.

What was the amount paid by Black to acquire the shares? (see the information in point (1))

$ ____________ **(3 marks)**

32.2 **Task 1**

The dividend due to Black from Bury will be:

- ○ Included in consolidated profit for the year
- ○ Added to the total of non-controlling interest
- ○ Included in consolidated current liabilities
- ○ Eliminated on consolidation

(2 marks)

Task 2

The dividend payable by Black will be:

- ○ Deducted from consolidated profit for the year
- ○ Deducted from consolidated current assets
- ○ Included in consolidated current liabilities
- ○ Eliminated on consolidation

(2 marks)

(Total = 4 marks)

32.3 **Task 1**

What is the amount of the unrealised profit on the intragroup sale?

$ [ ]

(1.5 marks)

Task 2

Show how this is posted:

	DEBIT	CREDIT
Inventory	○	○
Retained earnings	○	○

(1.5 marks)

(Total = 3 marks)

32.4 Bury owed Black $1.5 million for goods supplied. How will this be accounted for in the consolidated financial statements?

	Debit	Credit
Payables	○	○
Receivables	○	○

(1 mark)

32.5 Non-controlling interest will appear in both the consolidated statement of profit or loss (SPL) and the consolidated statement of financial position (SFP).

Task 1

The amount of non-controlling interest in the consolidated SPL is:

$ [ ] **(2 marks)**

Task 2

Fill in the blanks to calculate the amount of non-controlling interest in the consolidated SFP. **(2 marks)**

	$ $'000	Add/Subtract
Fair value at acquisition		
Share of post-acquisition retained earnings (in right hand column, indicate whether to 'Add' or 'Subtract' this)		
Total		

(Total = 4 marks)

(Total = 15 marks)

33 Prestend **(18 mins)**

Prestend is the parent company of Northon. The following are the statements of financial position for both companies as at 31 October 20X7.

		Prestend		Northon
	$'000	$'000	$'000	$'000
Assets				
Non-current assets				
Property, plant and equipment		4,200		3,300
Investments: shares in Northon at cost		3,345		–
Current assets				
Inventory	1,500		800	
Receivables	1,800		750	
Bank	600		350	
		3,900		1,900
Total assets		11,445		5,200

		Prestend		Northon
	$'000	$'000	$'000	$'000
Equity and liabilities				
Equity				
$1 ordinary shares		9,000		4,000
Retained earnings		525		200
		9,525		4,200
Current liabilities				
Payables		1,220		200
Tax		700		800
Total equity and liabilities		11,445		5,200

The following information is also available.

(1) Prestend purchased 2,800,000 shares in Northon a year ago when Northon had retained earnings of $60,000. The fair value of the non-controlling interest at the date of acquisition was $1,415,000.

(2) During the year Prestend sold goods with an invoice value of $240,000 to Northon. These goods were invoiced at cost plus 20%. Half of the goods are still in Northon's inventory at the year end.

(3) Northon owes Prestend $30,000 at 31 October 20X7 for goods it purchased during the year.

33.1 Complete the following to determine goodwill at acquisition: **(3 marks)**

	$ $'000	Add/Subtract
Fair value of consideration transferred		
Fair value of non-controlling interest at acquisition (in right hand column, indicate whether to 'Add' or 'Subtract' this).		
Total A		
Fair value of net assets acquired:		
Ordinary share capital		
Retained earnings		
Total B		

33.2 Select the correct formula for goodwill:

- O A minus 100% B
- O A minus 70% B
- O A plus 100% B
- O A plus 70% B

(2 marks)

33.3 What is the unrealised profit on intragroup sales?

- O $40,000
- O $48,000
- O $20,000
- O $24,000

(2 marks)

33.4 A parent-subsidiary relationship is based on **control**.

Which **TWO** of the following would signify that one entity controls another?

- ☐ Ownership of more than 50% of equity shares
- ☐ Ownership of 40% of equity shares and 80% of preference shares
- ☐ Ability to exert significant influence over policies
- ☐ Power to appoint or remove the majority of board members

(2 marks)

33.5 Fill in the gaps to complete the working for group retained earnings. **(6 marks)**

	Prestend	*Northon*	Add/Subtract
	$'000	$'000	
Per question			
Adjustment for unrealised profit			
Pre-acquisition retained earnings			
Total Northon			
Group share of Northon			
Group retained earnings			

(Total = 15 marks)

34 Liverton and Everpool (18 mins)

The summarised statements of profit or loss of two companies, Liverton and Everpool, for the year ended 31 May 20X6 are provided below. Liverton acquired 3,000,000 ordinary shares in Everpool for $3,500,000 on 1 June 20X4. At that time, the retained earnings of Everpool were $200,000 and the fair value of the non-controlling interest in Everpool was $1,000,000.

STATEMENTS OF PROFIT OR LOSS FOR THE YEAR ENDED 31 MAY 20X6

	Liverton	*Everpool*
	$'000	$'000
Sales revenue	6,400	2,600
Cost of sales	(3,700)	(1,450)
Gross profit	2,700	1,150
Distribution costs	(1,100)	(490)

	Liverton	*Everpool*
	$'000	$'000
Administrative expenses	(700)	(320)
Profit from operations	900	340
Dividends received from Everpool	150	
Profit before tax	1,050	340
Tax	(400)	(80)
Profit for the year	650	260

The following information is also available.

(1) Everpool's total share capital consists of 4,000,000 ordinary shares of $1 each.

(2) During the year ended 31 May 20X6 Liverton sold goods costing $120,000 to Everpool for $200,000. At 31 May 20X6, 60% of these goods remained in Everpool's inventory.

34.1 Complete the following to determine goodwill on acquisition of Everpool. **(3 marks)**

	$
	$'000
Fair value of consideration transferred	
Fair value of non-controlling interest	
Total	
Fair value of net assets acquired:	
Share capital	
Retained earnings	
Total	
Goodwill	

34.2 Calculate the unrealised profit on Liverton's sales to Everpool

$ ☐ **(2 marks)**

34.3 Complete the consolidated statement of profit or loss. **(10 marks)**

	$
	$'000
Sales revenue	
Cost of sales	
Gross profit	
Distribution costs	
Administrative expenses	
Profit before tax	
Income tax expense	
Profit for the year	
Profit attributable to:	
Owners of the parent	
Non-controlling interest	

(Total = 15 marks)

35 Consolidated financial statements (65 mins)

On 1 January 20X0 Alpha Co purchased 90,000 ordinary $1 shares in Beta Co for $270,000. At that date Beta Co's retained earnings amounted to $90,000 and the fair values of Beta Co's assets at acquisition were equal to their carrying amounts.

Three years later, on 31 December 20X2, the statements of financial position of the two companies were:

	Alpha Co	*Beta Co*
	$	$
Sundry net assets	230,000	260,000
Shares in Beta	180,000	
	410,000	260,000
Share capital		
Ordinary shares of $1 each	200,000	100,000
Retained earnings	210,000	160,000
	410,000	260,000

The share capital of Beta Co has remained unchanged since 1 January 20X0. The fair value of the non-controlling interest at acquisition was $42,000.

35.1 What amount should appear in the group's consolidated statement of financial position at 31 December 20X2 for goodwill?

- O $52,000
- O $80,000
- O $122,000
- O $212,000

(2 marks)

35.2 What amount should appear in the group's consolidated statement of financial position at 31 December 20X2 for non-controlling interest?

- O $49,000
- O $58,000
- O $51,000
- O $42,000

(2 marks)

35.3 What should the figure for retained earnings be in the group's consolidated statement of financial position at 31 December 20X2?

$ [ ]

(2 marks)

35.4 Which of the following companies are subsidiaries of Gamma Co?

Zeta Co:	Gamma Co owns 51% of the non-voting preference shares of Zeta Co.
Iota Co:	Gamma Co has three representatives on the board of directors of Iota Co. Each director can cast 10 votes each out of the total of 40 votes at board meetings.
Kappa Co:	Gamma Co owns 75% of the ordinary share capital of Kappa Co, however Kappa Co is located overseas and is subject to tax in that country.

- O Zeta Co, Iota Co and Kappa Co
- O Zeta Co and Kappa Co
- O Iota Co and Kappa Co
- O Zeta Co and Iota Co

(2 marks)

35.5 Hilton Co acquired 80% of the share capital of Shrew Co on 1 January 20X3 for $280,000.

The statements of financial position of the two companies at 31 December 20X3 were as follows:

STATEMENTS OF FINANCIAL POSITION

	Hilton Co	*Shrew Co*
	$	$
Sundry assets	660,000	290,000
Investment in Shrew	280,000	
	940,000	290,000
Issued share capital	400,000	140,000
Share premium account	320,000	50,000
Retained earnings		
As at 1 January 20X3	140,000	60,000
Profit for 20X3	80,000	40,000
	940,000	290,000

There have been no changes in the share capital or share premium account of either company since 1 January 20X3. The fair value of the non-controlling interest on acquisition was $65,000.

What figure for goodwill on consolidation should appear in the consolidated statement of financial position of the Hilton group at 31 December 20X3?

- O $30,000
- O $55,000
- O $95,000
- O $(10,000) **(2 marks)**

35.6 What figure for non-controlling interest should appear in the consolidated statement of financial position of the Hilton group at 31 December 20X3?

- O $77,000
- O $85,000
- O $73,000
- O $105,000 **(2 marks)**

35.7 Fanta Co acquired 100% of the ordinary share capital of Tizer Co on 1 October 20X7.

On 31 December 20X7 the share capital and retained earnings of Tizer Co were as follows:

	$'000
Ordinary shares of $1 each	400
Retained earnings at 1 January 20X7	100
Retained profit for the year ended 31 December 20X7	80
	580

The profits of Tizer Co have accrued evenly throughout 20X7. Goodwill arising on the acquisition of Tizer Co was $30,000.

What was the cost of the investment in Tizer Co?

- O $400,000
- O $580,000
- O $610,000
- O $590,000

(2 marks)

35.8 Evergreen Co owns 35% of the ordinary shares of Deciduous. What is the correct accounting treatment of the revenues and costs of Deciduous for the reporting period in the consolidated statement of profit or loss of the Evergreen group?

- O The revenues and costs of Deciduous are added to the revenues and costs of Evergreen on a line by line basis.
- O 35% of the profit for the year of Deciduous should be added to Evergreen's consolidated profit before tax.
- O 35% of the revenues and costs of Deciduous are added to the revenues and costs of Evergreen on a line by line basis.
- O The revenues and costs of Deciduous are added to the revenues and costs of Evergreen Co on a line by line basis, then 65% of the profit for the year is deducted so that only Evergreen Co's share remains in the consolidated financial statements.

(2 marks)

35.9 Mercedes Co has owned 100% of Benz Co since incorporation. At 31 March 20X9 extracts from their individual statements of financial position were as follows.

	Mercedes Co	*Benz Co*
	$	$
Share capital	100,000	50,000
Retained earnings	450,000	120,000
	550,000	170,000

During the year ended 31 March 20X9, Benz Co had sold goods to Mercedes Co for $50,000. Mercedes Co still had these goods in inventory at the year end. Benz Co uses a 25% mark up on all goods.

What were the consolidated retained earnings of Mercedes Group at 31 March 20X9?

- O $560,000
- O $580,000
- O $570,000
- O $557,500

(2 marks)

35.10 Micro Co acquired 90% of the $100,000 ordinary share capital of Minnie Co for $300,000 on 1 January 20X9 when the retained earnings of Minnie Co were $156,000. At the date of acquisition the fair value of plant held by Minnie Co was $20,000 higher than its carrying amount. The fair value of the non-controlling interest at the date of acquisition was $75,000.

What is the goodwill arising on the acquisition of Minnie Co?

- O $119,000
- O $99,000
- O $139,000
- O $24,000

(2 marks)

35.11 On 1 April 20X7 Possum Co acquired 60% of the share capital of Koala Co for $120,000. During the year Possum Co sold goods to Koala Co for $30,000, including a profit margin of 25%. 40% of these goods were still in inventory at the year end.

The following extract was taken from the financial statements of Possum Co and Koala Co at 31 March 20X8.

	Possum Co	*Koala Co*
	$'000	$'000
Revenue	750	400
Cost of sales	(420)	(100)
Gross profit	330	300

What is the consolidated gross profit of the Possum group at 31 March 20X8?

- O $627,600
- O $633,000
- O $622,500
- O $627,000

(2 marks)

35.12 Which **TWO** of the following statements are correct?

- ☐ Aye Co owns 25% of the ordinary share capital of Bee Co, which means that Bee Co is an associate of Aye Co.
- ☐ Cee Co can appoint 4 out of 6 directors to the board of Dee Co, which means that Cee Co has control over Dee Co.
- ☐ Ear Co has the power to govern the financial and operating policies of Fef Co, which means that Fef Co is an associate of Ear Co.
- ☐ Gee Co owns 19% of the share capital of Hay Co, but by agreement with the majority shareholder, has control over the financial and operating policies of Hay Co, so Hay Co is an associate of Gee Co. **(2 marks)**

35.13 Clementine Co has owned 21% of the ordinary shares of Tangerine Co for several years. Clementine Co does not have any investments in any other companies, and chooses to account for the investment at cost.

How should the investment in Tangerine Co be reflected in the financial statements of Clementine Co?

- O The revenues and costs and assets and liabilities of Tangerine Co are added to the revenues and costs and assets and liabilities of Clementine Co on a line by line basis.
- O An amount is shown in the statement of financial position for 'investment in associate' being the original cost paid for the investment plus Clementine Co's share of the profit for the year of Tangerine Co. 21% of the profit for the year of Tangerine Co should be added to Clementine Co's profit before tax in the statement of profit or loss each year.
- O An amount is shown in the statement of financial position under 'investments' being the original cost paid for the investment, this amount does not change. Dividends received from Tangerine are recognised in the statement of profit or loss of Clementine Co.
- O An amount is shown in the statement of financial position under 'investments' being the original cost paid for the investment, this amount does not change. 21% of the profit for the year of Tangerine Co should be added to Clementine Co's profit for the year in the statement of profit or loss each year. **(2 marks)**

35.14 Which of the following statements relating to parent companies and subsidiaries are correct?

(1) A parent company could consolidate a company in which it holds less than 50% of the ordinary share capital in certain circumstances.

(2) Goodwill on consolidation will appear as an item in the parent company's individual statement of financial position.

(3) Consolidated financial statements ignore the legal form of the relationship between parents and subsidiaries and present the results and position of the group as if it was a single entity.

- O 1 and 2 only
- O 1 and 3 only
- O 2 and 3 only
- O 3 only **(2 marks)**

35.15 P Co, the parent company of a group, owns shares in three other companies. P Co's holdings are:

Q	Shares giving control of 60% of the voting rights in Q Co.
R	Shares giving control of 20% of the voting rights in R Co. P Co also has the right to appoint or remove all the directors of R Co.
S	Shares giving control of 10% of the voting rights in S Co, plus 90% of the non-voting preference shares.

Which of these companies are subsidiaries of P Co?

O Q Co, R Co and S Co

O Q Co and S Co only

O R Co and S Co only

O Q Co and R Co only **(2 marks)**

35.16 Which of the following should be accounted for in the consolidated financial statements of Company A using equity accounting?

(1) An investment in 51% of the ordinary shares of W Co

(2) An investment in 20% of the preference (non-voting) shares of X Co

(3) An investment in 33% of the ordinary shares of Y Co

(4) An investment in 20% of the ordinary shares of Z Co, and an agreement with other shareholders to appoint the majority of the directors to the board of Z Co

O 1 and 4 only

O 2 only

O 3 only

O 3 and 4 only **(2 marks)**

35.17 Breakspear Co purchased 600,000 of the voting equity shares of Fleet Co when the value of the non-controlling interest in Fleet Co is $150,000.

The following information relates to Fleet at the acquisition date.

	At acquisition
	$'000
Share capital, $0.5 ordinary shares	500
Retained earnings	150
Revaluation surplus	50
	700

The goodwill arising on acquisition is $70,000. What was the consideration paid by Breakspear Co for the investment in Fleet Co?

- O $420,000
- O $770,000
- O $620,000
- O $570,000

(2 marks)

35.18 Date Co owns 100% of the ordinary share capital of Prune Co. The following balances relate to Prune Co.

	At acquisition	*At 31.12.X8*
	$'000	$'000
Tangible non-current assets		
Freehold land	500	500
Plant and equipment	350	450
	850	950

At acquisition, the fair value of Prune Co's land was $50,000 more than shown in the financial statements of Prune Co. At 31 December 20X8, Date Co's financial statements show a total tangible non-current asset balance of $1,250,000.

What amount should be included in the consolidated financial statements of the Date group at 31 December 20X8 for tangible non-current assets?

- O $2,250,000
- O $1,000,000
- O $1,850,000
- O $2,200,000

(2 marks)

35.19 Six Co owns 80% of the equity share capital of Seven Co. At 31 December 20X4, the trade receivables and trade payables of the two companies were as follows:

	Six Co	*Seven Co*
Trade receivables	$64,000	$39,000
Trade payables	$37,000	$48,000

These figures include $30,000 that is owed by Seven Co to Six Co for the purchase of goods, for which Six Co has not yet paid. These goods were sold by Six Co for a profit of $15,000 and 50% of them were still held as inventory by Seven Co at 31 December 20X4.

What should be the amounts for trade receivables and trade payables in the consolidated statement of financial position as at 31 December 20X4?

- O Trade receivables $73,000, Trade payables $55,000
- O Trade receivables $88,000, Trade payables $70,000
- O Trade receivables $95,000, Trade payables $77,000
- O Trade receivables $103,000, Trade payables $85,000

(2 marks)

35.20 Donna Co acquired 80% of the equity share capital of Blitsen Co on 1 January 20X4 when the retained earnings of Blitsen Co were $40,000. The fair value of the non-controlling interest at this date was $25,000. At 31 December 20X4, the equity capital of Blitsen Co was as follows:

	$'000
Share capital	40
Share premium	10
Retained earnings	60
	110

During the year Blitsen Co sold goods to Donna Co for $20,000. This price included a mark-up of $12,000 for profit. At 31 December 20X4, 50% of these goods remained unsold in the inventory of Donna Co.

What is the value of the non-controlling interest in the Donna Group at 31 December 20X4, for the purpose of preparing the consolidated statement of financial position?

$ [   ]

(2 marks)

35.21 Volcano Co acquired 75% of the equity share capital of Lava Co on 1 September 20X3. The retained profits of the two individual companies at the beginning and end of their financial year were as follows.

	Volcano Co	*Lava Co*
	$'000	$'000
Retained earnings at 1 January 20X3	596	264
Retained earnings at 31 December 20X3	650	336

What is the parent company's share of consolidated retained earnings that should be reported in the consolidated statement of financial position of the Volcano Group at 31 December 20X3?

- O $668,000
- O $674,000
- O $704,000
- O $722,000

(2 marks)

35.22 Tin Co acquired 90% of the equity share capital of Drum Co on 1 April 20X3. The following information relates to the financial year to 31 December 20X3 for each company.

	Tin Co	*Drum Co*
	$'000	$'000
Retained earnings at 1 January 20X3	840	170
Profit for the year	70	60
Retained earnings at 31 December 20X3	910	230

Neither company paid any dividends during the year.

What profit is attributable to the parent company in the consolidated statement of profit or loss of the Tin Group for the year to 31 December 20X3?

- O $83,500
- O $110,500
- O $115,000
- O $124,000

(2 marks)

35.23 Sand Co acquired 80% of the equity share capital of Sun Co several years ago. In the year to 31 December 20X4, Sand Co made a profit for the year of $120,000 and Sun Co made a profit for the year of $35,000. During the year Sun Co sold goods to Sand Co at a price of $40,000. The profit margin was 40% on the sales price. At 31 December 20X4, 25% of these goods were still held in the inventory of Sand Co.

What profit is attributable to the parent company in the consolidated statement of profit or loss of the Sand Group for the year to 31 December 20X4?

- O $144,000
- O $148,000
- O $144,800
- O $151,000

(2 marks)

35.24 On 1 August 20X7 Patronic purchased 18 million of the 24 million $1 equity shares of Sardonic. The acquisition was through a share exchange of two shares in Patronic for every three shares in Sardonic. The market price of a share in Patronic at 1 August 20X7 was $5.75.

What is the fair value of the consideration transferred for the acquisition of Sardonic?

- O $103.5 million
- O $69 million
- O $155.25 million
- O $92 million

(2 marks)

35.25 X Co acquired 80% of the equity share capital in Y Co on 31 July 20X6. Extracts from the two companies' statements of profit or loss for the year ended 30 September 20X6 were as follows:

	X Co	*Y Co*
	$'000	$'000
Revenue	3,400	2,400
Cost of sales	1,500	1,800

During the year ended 30 September 20X6, Y Co sold goods for $5,000 each month to X Co, at a mark up of 25%. At the end of the year X Co had 50% of these goods left in inventory.

What is the group gross profit for the year ended 30 September 20X6?

- O $1,901,000
- O $1,999,000
- O $2,004,000
- O $1,904,000

(2 marks)

35.26 WX acquired 75% of the equity share capital of YZ several years ago. At 31 March 20X6 WX had goods in inventory valued at a cost of $60,000, that had been purchased from YZ at a mark-up of 20%.

What is the effect on the profit attributable to the non-controlling interest, and the profit attributable to the parent company for the year ended 31 March 20X6?

	Profit attributable to non-controlling interest	***Profit attributable to WX***
O	no effect	decrease by $5,000
O	no effect	decrease by $12,000
O	decrease by $3,000	decrease by $9,000
O	decrease by $2,500	decrease by $7,500

(2 marks)

35.27 P owns 80% of the equity share capital of S. The profit for the year of S for the year ended 31 December 20X6 was $60 million. During 20X6, P sold goods to S for $4 million at cost plus 20%. At the year end 50% of these goods were left in the inventory of S.

What is the non-controlling interest share of the profit for the year of S for the year ended 31 December 20X6?

- $11.36 million
- $11.6 million
- $11.68 million
- $12 million **(2 marks)**

(Total = 54 marks)

36 Binky and Smokey (15 mark question) (18 mins)

36.1 Two companies Binky and Smokey trade in the same market. Their financial statements for the year ended 31 October 20X6 are summarised below:

STATEMENTS OF PROFIT OR LOSS FOR THE YEAR ENDED 31 OCTOBER 20X6

		Binky		Smokey
	$'000	$'000	$'000	$'000
Sales revenue		284		305
Cost of sales		(155)		(151)
Gross profit		129		154
Expenses				
Administrative	24		37	
Selling and distribution	35		53	
Depreciation	9		12	
Loan note interest			5	
		(68)		(107)
Profit for the year		61		47

STATEMENTS OF FINANCIAL POSITION AS AT 31 OCTOBER 20X6

		Binky		Smokey
	$'000	$'000	$'000	$'000
Assets				
Non-current assets				
At cost	320		515	
Accumulated depreciation	(75)		(96)	
		245		419
Current assets				
Inventory	91		293	
Receivables	46		75	
Bank	64		15	
		201		383
		446		802
Equity and liabilities				
Equity				
Share capital		150		250
Retained earnings		108		177

	$'000	Binky $'000	$'000	Smokey $'000
10% Loan note		–		50
Current liabilities		188		325
Total equity and liabilities		446		802

Ratio	Formula
Gross profit %	$\frac{\text{Gross profit}}{\text{Sales}} \times 100$
Net profit %	$\frac{\text{Profit for the year}}{\text{Sales}} \times 100$
Asset turnover	$\frac{\text{Sales}}{\text{CapitalEmployed}}$
Current ratio	$\frac{\text{Current ratio}}{\text{Current liabilities}}$
Quick ratio	$\frac{\text{Current assets} - \text{inventory}}{\text{Current liabilities}}$
Receivables collection period	$\frac{\text{Receivables}}{\text{Sales}} \times 365$

Using the above formulae, complete the following table by calculating the required ratios for Binky and Smokey. **(10 marks)**

Required ratios

Ratio	Binky	Smokey
Gross profit %		
Net profit %		
Asset turnover		
Current ratio		
Quick ratio		
Receivables collection period		

36.2 Fill in the blanks to complete this short comment on the performance of Binkey and Smokey: **(5 marks)**

Of the two companies ________ has the higher net profit percentage.

This is due to ________ expenses.

Both companies have low quick ratios. In Smokey's case this is because much of its working capital is tied up in ________ . This has given rise to ________ problems.

________ needs to improve credit control.

The ________ ratio shows that Binky is making better use of its working capital than Smokey.

(Total = 15 marks)

37 Interpretation of financial statements (24 mins)

37.1 Which one of the following would help a company with high gearing to reduce its gearing ratio?

- O Making a rights issue of equity shares
- O Issuing further long-term loan notes
- O Making a bonus issue of shares
- O Paying dividends on its equity shares **(2 marks)**

37.2 A company's gross profit as a percentage of sales increased from 24% in the year ended 31 December 20X1 to 27% in the year ended 31 December 20X2.

Which of the following events is most likely to have caused the increase?

- O An increase in sales volume
- O A purchase in December 20X1 mistakenly being recorded as happening in January 20X2
- O Overstatement of the closing inventory at 31 December 20X1
- O Understatement of the closing inventory at 31 December 20X1 **(2 marks)**

37.3 Which of the following transactions would result in an increase in capital employed?

- O Selling inventory at a profit
- O Writing off an irrecoverable debt
- O Paying a payable in cash
- O Increasing the bank overdraft to purchase a non-current asset **(2 marks)**

37.4 From the following information regarding the year to 31 August 20X6, what is the accounts payable payment period? You should calculate the ratio using purchases as the denominator.

	$
Sales	43,000
Cost of sales	32,500
Opening inventory	6,000
Closing inventory	3,800
Trade payables at 31 August 20X6	4,750

- O 40 days
- O 50 days
- O 53 days
- O 57 days

(2 marks)

37.5 Quality Co is analysing its financial performance. An extract from its draft statement of financial position at 31 March 20X8 is set out below.

	$	$
Non-current assets		450
Current assets: Inventory	65	
Receivables	110	
Prepayments	30	
	205	
		655
Equity:		
Ordinary share capital	400	
Statement of profit or loss	100	
		500
Non-current liability:		
Loan	75	
Current liabilities:		
Payables	30	
Bank overdraft (note)	50	
	80	
		655

Note. The bank overdraft first occurred on 30 September 20X7.

(2 marks)

In the analysis of the financial and liquidity position of Quality Co, its gearing, current and quick ratios are to be calculated.

Complete the sentences below. You should calculate gearing using the capital employed (debt + equity) as the denominator. **(2 marks)**

Gearing is [ ] %

Quick ratio is [ ] .

Current ratio is [ ] .

37.6 Which of the following is a ratio which is used to measure how much a business owes in relation to its size?

- O Asset turnover
- O Profit margin
- O Gearing
- O Return on capital employed **(2 marks)**

37.7 A business operates on a gross profit margin of $33^1/_3$%. Gross profit on a sale was $800, and expenses were $680.

What is the net profit margin?

- O 3.75%
- O 5%
- O 11.25%
- O 22.67% **(2 marks)**

37.8 A company has the following details extracted from its statement of financial position:

	$'000
Inventories	1,900
Receivables	1,000
Bank overdraft	100
Payables	1,000

The industry the company operates in has a current ratio norm of 1.8. Companies who manage liquidity well in this industry have a current ratio lower than the norm.

Which of the following statements accurately describes the company's liquidity position?

- O Liquidity appears to be well managed as the bank overdraft is relatively low.
- O Liquidity appears to be poorly-controlled as shown by the large payables balance.
- O Liquidity appears to be poorly-controlled as shown by the company's relatively high current ratio.
- O Liquidity appears to be poorly-controlled as shown by the existence of a bank overdraft. **(2 marks)**

37.9 Why is analysis of financial statements carried out?

- O So that the analyst can determine a company's accounting policies
- O So that the significance of financial statements can be better understood through comparisons with historical performance and with other companies
- O To get back to the 'real' underlying figures, without the numbers being skewed by the requirements of IFRS Standards
- O To produce a report that can replace the financial statements, so that the financial statements no longer need to be looked at **(2 marks)**

37.10 In the year ended 31 December 20X1, Jolo Ltd makes profit before interest and tax of $47,000, pays interest of $31,000 and has outstanding loans of $270,000.

What is the interest cover ratio for Jolo Ltd as at 31 December 20X1? (Give your answer to 2 decimal places)

[ ] times **(2 marks)**

(Total = 20 marks)

Mixed banks

38 Mixed bank 1 **(46 mins)**

38.1 The following information is available for a sole trader who keeps no accounting records:

	$
Net business assets at 1 July 20X4	186,000
Net business assets at 30 June 20X5	274,000
During the year ended 30 June 20X5:	
Cash drawings by proprietor	68,000
Additional capital introduced by proprietor	50,000
Business cash used to buy a car for the proprietor's wife, who takes no part in the business	20,000

Using this information, what is the trader's profit for the year ended 30 June 20X5?

$ [ ]

(2 marks)

38.2 Evon, a limited liability company, issued 1,000,000 ordinary shares of 25 cents each at a price of $1.10 per share, all received in cash.

What should be the accounting entries to record this issue?

O	Debit	Bank	$1,100,000
	Credit	Share capital	$250,000
	Credit	Share premium	$850,000
O	Debit	Share capital	$250,000
	Debit	Share premium	$850,000
	Credit	Bank	$1,100,000
O	Debit	Bank	$1,100,000
	Credit	Share capital	$1,100,000
O	Debit	Bank	$1,100,000
	Credit	Share capital	$250,000
	Credit	Retained earnings	$850,000

(2 marks)

38.3 Which of the following statements apply when preparing a consolidated statement of financial position?

(1) All intra-group balances should be eliminated.

(2) Intra-group profit in year-end inventory should be eliminated.

(3) Closing inventory held by subsidiaries needs to be included at fair value.

- O 1 only
- O 1, 2 and 3
- O 1 and 2 only
- O 3 only

(2 marks)

38.4 At 1 July 20X4 a limited liability company's capital structure was as follows:

	$
Share capital 1,000,000 shares of 50c each	500,000
Share premium account	400,000

In the year ended 30 June 20X5 the company made the following share issues:

1 January 20X5

A bonus issue of one share for every four in issue at that date, using the share premium account.

1 April 20X5

A rights issue of one share for every ten in issue at that date, at $1.50 per share.

What will be the balances on the company's share capital and share premium accounts at 30 June 20X5 as a result of these issues?

	Share capital	*Share premium account*
	$	**$**
O	687,500	650,000
O	675,000	375,000
O	687,500	150,000
O	687,500	400,000

(2 marks)

38.5 The trade receivables account below contains several incorrect entries.

TRADE RECEIVABLES

	$		$
Opening balance	138,400	Credit sales	80,660
Receipts from credit customers	78,420	Contras against credit balances in payables ledger	1,000
		Irrecoverable debts written off	4,950
		Dishonoured cheques from credit customers	850
		Closing balance	129,360
	216,820		216,820

What should the closing balance be when all the errors are corrected?

- O $133,840
- O $135,540
- O $137,740
- O $139,840

(2 marks)

38.6 A limited liability company's trial balance does not balance. The totals are:

Debit	$384,030
Credit	$398,580

A suspense account is opened for the difference.

Which of the following pairs of errors could clear the balance on the suspense account when corrected?

- O Debit side of bank general ledger account undercast by $10,000; $6,160 paid for rent correctly entered in the bank general ledger account but entered in the rent account as $1,610.
- O Debit side of bank general ledger account overcast by $10,000; $1,610 paid for rent correctly entered in the bank general ledger account but entered in the rent account as $6,160.
- O Debit side of bank general ledger account undercast by $10,000; $1,610 paid for rent correctly entered in the bank general ledger account but entered in the rent account as $6,160.
- O Debit side of bank general ledger account overcast by $10,000; $6,160 paid for rent correctly entered in the bank general ledger account but entered in the rent account as $1,610.

(2 marks)

38.7 Which **TWO** of the following items could appear in a company's statement of cash flows?

- ☐ Surplus on revaluation of non-current assets
- ☐ Repayment of long-term borrowing
- ☐ Bonus issue of shares
- ☐ Interest received

(2 marks)

38.8 The following information is available for Orset, a sole trader who does not keep full accounting records:

	$
Inventory 1 July 20X4	138,600
Inventory 30 June 20X5	149,100
Purchases made for year ended 30 June 20X5	716,100

Orset makes a standard gross profit of 30% on sales.

Based on these figures, what is Orset's sales figure for the year ended 30 June 20X5?

- O $2,352,000
- O $1,038,000
- O $917,280
- O $1,008,000

(2 marks)

38.9 At 1 July 20X4 a company had prepaid insurance of $8,200. On 1 January 20X5 the company paid $38,000 for insurance for the year to 30 September 20X5.

What figures should appear for insurance in the company's financial statements for the year ended 30 June 20X5?

	Statement of Profit or Loss	*Statement of Financial Position*
O	$27,000	Prepayment $19,000
O	$39,300	Prepayment $9,500
O	$36,700	Prepayment $9,500
O	$55,700	Prepayment $9,500

(2 marks)

38.10 Which of the following statements are correct?

(1) A liability is a present obligation of the entity to transfer an economic resource as a result of past events.

(2) An uncertain liability may be called a provision.

(3) A contingent liability should be disclosed in the notes to the financial statements.

- O 1 only
- O 1 and 2 only
- O 2 and 3 only
- O 1, 2 and 3

(2 marks)

38.11 Alpha buys goods from Beta. At 30 June 20X5 Beta's account in Alpha's records showed $5,700 owing to Beta. Beta submitted a statement to Alpha as at the same date showing a balance due of $5,200.

Which one of the following could account fully for the difference?

- O Alpha has sent a cheque to Beta for $500 which has not yet been received by Beta.
- O The credit side of Beta's account in Alpha's records has been undercast by $500.
- O An invoice for $250 from Beta has been treated in Alpha's records as if it had been a credit note.
- O Beta has issued a credit note for $500 to Alpha which Alpha has not yet received.

(2 marks)

38.12 Which of the following statements about intangible assets are correct?

(1) If certain criteria are met, research expenditure must be recognised as an intangible asset.

(2) The notes to the financial statements should disclose the gross carrying amount and the accumulated amortisation at the beginning and the end of the period for each class of intangible asset.

(3) Intangible assets must be amortised over their useful life.

- O 2 and 3 only
- O 1 and 3 only
- O 1 and 2 only
- O All three statements are correct.

(2 marks)

38.13 Which of the following material events that took place after the reporting date, but before the financial statements were approved, are non-adjusting when applying IAS 10 *Events After the Reporting Period*?

(1) Inventory held at the reporting date was sold for less than cost.

(2) Capital raised by issuing shares at a premium.

(3) A company reorganisation which results in discontinuing a line of activity producing 25% of its profit.

(4) The settlement of a claim for compensation from a former employee wrongly dismissed just before the reporting date.

- O 1 and 2
- O 1, 3 and 4
- O 1 and 3 only
- O 2 and 3

(2 marks)

38.14 A company sublets part of its office accommodation. In the year ended 30 June 20X5 cash received from tenants was $83,700.

Details of rent in arrears and in advance at the beginning and end of the year were:

	In arrears	*In advance*
	$	$
1 July 20X4	3,800	2,400
30 June 20X5	4,700	3,000

All arrears of rent were subsequently received.

What figure should be included for rental income in the company's statement of profit or loss for the year ended 30 June 20X5?

$ [ ] **(2 marks)**

38.15 At 30 June 20X4 a company's allowance for receivables was $39,000. At 30 June 20X5 trade receivables totalled $517,000. It was decided to write off irrecoverable debts totalling $37,000. The allowance for receivables was to be adjusted to the equivalent of 5% of the trade receivables.

What figure should appear in the statement of profit or loss for these items?

- O $61,000
- O $22,000
- O $24,000
- O $23,850 **(2 marks)**

38.16 IAS 2 *Inventories* defines the extent to which overheads are included in the cost of inventories of finished goods.

Which of the following statements about the IAS 2 requirements in this area are correct?

(1) Finished goods inventories may be valued on the basis of labour and materials cost only, without including overheads.

(2) Carriage inwards, but not carriage outwards, should be included in overheads when valuing inventories of finished goods.

(3) Factory management costs should be included in fixed overheads allocated to inventories of finished goods.

- O All three statements are correct
- O 1 and 2 only
- O 1 and 3 only
- O 2 and 3 only **(2 marks)**

38.17 A limited liability company sold a building at a profit.

How will this transaction be treated in the company's statement of cash flows?

	Proceeds of sale	*Profit on sale*
O	Cash inflow under financing activities	Add to profit in calculating cash flow from operating activities
O	Cash inflow under investing activities	Deducted from profit in calculating cash flow from operating activities
O	Cash inflow under investing activities	Added to profit in calculating cash flow from operating activities
O	Cash inflow under financing activities	Deducted from profit in calculating cash flow from operating activities

(2 marks)

38.18 Which of the following items may appear in a company's statement of changes in equity, according to IAS 1 *Presentation of Financial Statements*?

(1) Unrealised revaluation gains

(2) Dividends paid

(3) Proceeds of equity share issue

(4) Profit for the period

O 2, 3 and 4 only

O 1, 3 and 4 only

O All four items

O 1, 2 and 4 only **(2 marks)**

38.19 Sigma's bank statement shows an overdrawn balance of $38,600 at 30 June 20X5. A check against the company's bank general ledger account revealed the following differences:

(1) Bank charges of $200 have not been entered in the bank general ledger account.

(2) Lodgements recorded on 30 June 20X5 but credited by the bank on 2 July $14,700.

(3) Cheque repayments entered in the bank general ledger account but not presented for payment at 30 June 20X5 $27,800.

(4) A cheque payment to a supplier of $4,200 charged to the account in June 20X5 recorded in the bank general ledger account as a receipt.

Based on this information, what was the bank general ledger account balance **before** any adjustments?

O $43,100 overdrawn

O $16,900 overdrawn

O $60,300 overdrawn

O $34,100 overdrawn **(2 marks)**

(Total = 38 marks)

39 Mixed bank 2 (48 mins)

39.1 The plant and machinery cost account of a company is shown below. The company's policy is to charge depreciation at 20% on the straight line basis, with proportionate depreciation in years of acquisition and disposal.

PLANT AND MACHINERY – COST

20X5	$	20X5	$
		30 June Transfer disposal	14,000
1 Jan Balance b/f	280,000		
1 Apr Bank	48,000		
1 Sept Bank	36,000	31 Dec Balance c/f	350,000
	364,000		364,000

What should be the depreciation charge for the year ended 31 December 20X5?

- O $67,000
- O $70,000
- O $64,200
- O $68,600

(2 marks)

39.2 Which of the following are correct?

(1) The statement of financial position value of inventory should be as close as possible to net realisable value.

(2) The valuation of finished goods inventory must include production overheads.

(3) Production overheads included in valuing inventory should be calculated by reference to the company's normal level of production during the period.

(4) In assessing net realisable value, inventory items must be considered separately, or in groups of similar items, not by taking the inventory value as a whole.

- O 1 and 2 only
- O 3 and 4 only
- O 1 and 3 only
- O 2, 3 and 4

(2 marks)

39.3 A business sublets part of its office accommodation.

The rent is received quarterly in advance on 1 January, 1 April, 1 July and 1 October. The annual rent has been $24,000 for some years, but it was increased to $30,000 from 1 July 20X5.

What amounts for this rent should appear in the company's financial statements for the year ended 31 January 20X6?

	Statement of Profit or Loss	*Statement of Financial Position*
O	$27,500	$5,000 in accrued income
O	$27,000	$2,500 in accrued income
O	$27,000	$2,500 in deferred income
O	$27,500	$5,000 in deferred income

(2 marks)

39.4 The figures shown in the table below are an extract from the financial statements of Ridgeway (capital employed is $1.5 million).

	$
Revenue	1 000,000
Cost of sales	400,000
Gross profit	600,000
Distribution expenses and administration cost	300,000
Profit before interest and tax	300,000
Finance cost	50,000
Profit before tax	250,000
Income tax expense	100,000
Profit for the year	150,000

What is the return on capital employed (ROCE)?

- O 7%
- O 10%
- O 40%
- O 20%

(2 marks)

39.5 Which of the following events after the reporting period would normally qualify as adjusting events according to IAS 10 *Events After the Reporting Period*?

(1) The bankruptcy of a credit customer with a balance outstanding at the end of the reporting period

(2) A decline in the market value of investments

(3) The declaration of an ordinary dividend

(4) The determination of the cost of assets purchased before the end of the reporting period

- O 1, 3, and 4
- O 1 and 2 only
- O 2 and 3 only
- O 1 and 4 only

(2 marks)

39.6 Ordan received a statement from one of its suppliers, Alta, showing a balance due of \$3,980. The amount due according to the payables ledger account of Alta in Ordan's records was only \$230. Comparison of the statement and the ledger account revealed the following differences:

(1) A cheque sent by Ordan for \$270 has not been allowed for in Alta's statement.

(2) Alta has not allowed for goods returned by Ordan \$180.

(3) Ordan made a contra entry, reducing the amount due to Alta by \$3,200, for a balance due from Alta in Ordan's receivables ledger. No such entry has been made in Alta's records.

What is the remaining difference between the two companies' records after adjusting for these items?

\$ [ ] **(2 marks)**

39.7 A company's trial balance failed to agree, and a suspense account was opened for the difference.

Subsequent checking revealed that sales returns of \$130 had been credited to the purchases returns account and an entry on the credit side of the bank general ledger account for the purchase of some machinery \$18,000 had not been posted to the plant and machinery account.

Which **TWO** of the following journal entries would correct the errors?

☐ DEBIT: Sales return \$130, CREDIT: Purchase returns \$130

☐ DEBIT: Sales returns \$130, Purchase returns \$130, CREDIT: Suspense account \$260

☐ DEBIT: Suspense account \$260, CREDIT: Sales returns \$130, Purchase returns \$130

☐ DEBIT: Plant and machinery \$18,000, CREDIT: Suspense account \$18,000

☐ DEBIT: Suspense account \$18,000, CREDIT: Plant and machinery \$18,000 **(2 marks)**

39.8 A company's draft financial statements for 20X5 showed a profit of \$630,000. However, the trial balance did not agree, and a suspense account appeared in the company's draft statement of financial position. Subsequent checking revealed the following errors:

(1) The cost of an item of plant \$48,000 had been entered in the bank general ledger account and in the plant register as \$4,800. Depreciation at the rate of 10% per year (\$480) had been charged.

(2) Bank charges of \$440 appeared in the bank statement in December 20X5 but had not been entered in the company's records.

(3) One of the directors of the company paid \$800 due to a supplier in the company's payables ledger by a personal cheque. The bookkeeper recorded a debit in the supplier's ledger account but did not complete the double entry for the transaction.

(4) The payments side of the bank general ledger account had been understated by \$10,000.

Which of the above items would require an entry to the suspense account in correcting them?

○ All four items

○ 3 and 4 only

○ 2 and 3 only

○ 1, 2 and 4 only **(2 marks)**

39.9 What will the company's profit be after the correction of the above errors?

- O $634,760
- O $624,760
- O $624,440
- O $625,240

(2 marks)

39.10 Which of the following statements are correct?

(1) A company might make a rights issue if it wished to raise more equity capital.

(2) A rights issue might increase the share premium account whereas a bonus issue is likely to reduce it.

(3) A bonus issue will generate cash for a company.

(4) A rights issue will always increase the number of shareholders in a company whereas a bonus issue will not.

- O 1 and 2
- O 1 and 3
- O 2 and 3
- O 2 and 4

(2 marks)

39.11 Which of the following statements are correct?

(1) Contingent assets are included as assets in financial statements if it is probable that they will arise.

(2) Contingent liabilities must be provided for in financial statements if it is probable that they will arise.

(3) Material non-adjusting events are disclosed by note in the financial statements.

- O 1 only
- O 1 and 3
- O 2 and 3
- O 3 only

(2 marks)

39.12 At 1 January 20X5 a company had an allowance for receivables of $18,000.

At 31 December 20X5 the company's trade receivables were $458,000.

It was decided:

- To write off debts totalling $28,000 as irrecoverable
- To adjust the allowance for receivables to the equivalent of 5% of the remaining receivables

What figure should appear in the company's statement of profit or loss for the total of debts written off as irrecoverable and the movement in the allowance for receivables for the year ended 31 December 20X5?

- O $49,500
- O $31,500
- O $32,900
- O $50,900

(2 marks)

39.13 The following trade payables account contains some errors. All goods are purchased on credit.

TRADE PAYABLES

	$		$
Purchases	963,200	Opening balance	384,600
Discounts received	12,600	Purchases returns	17,400
Contras with amounts receivable in receivables ledger	4,200	Bank payments to suppliers	988,400
Closing balance	410,400		
	1,390,400		1,390,400

What should the closing balance be when the errors have been corrected?

- O $325,200
- O $350,400
- O $358,800
- O $376,800

(2 marks)

39.14 Which one of the following journal entries is required to record goods taken from inventory by the owner of a business?

- O DEBIT Drawings
  CREDIT Purchases
- O DEBIT Sales
  CREDIT Drawings
- O DEBIT Drawings
  CREDIT Inventory
- O DEBIT Purchases
  CREDIT Drawings

(2 marks)

39.15 The following information is available about the transactions of Razil, a sole trader who does not keep proper accounting records:

	$
Opening inventory	77,000
Closing inventory	84,000
Purchases	763,000

Gross profit as a percentage of sales: 30%

Based on this information, what is Razil's sales revenue for the year?

- O $982,800
- O $1,090,000
- O $2,520,000
- O $1,080,000 **(2 marks)**

39.16 Which of the following statements are correct?

(1) All non-current assets must be depreciated.

(2) If property accounted for in accordance with *IAS 16 Property, Plant and Equipment* is revalued, the gain on revaluation is shown in the statement of profit or loss.

(3) If a tangible non-current asset is revalued, all tangible assets of the same class should be revalued.

(4) In a company's published statement of financial position, tangible assets and intangible assets must be shown separately.

- O 1 and 2
- O 2 and 3
- O 3 and 4
- O 1 and 4 **(2 marks)**

39.17 The following bank reconciliation statement has been prepared by a trainee accountant at 31 December 20X5.

	$
Balance per bank statement (overdrawn)	38,640
Add: lodgements not credited	19,270
	57,910
Less: unpresented cheques	14,260
Balance per bank general ledger account	43,650

What should the final bank general ledger account balance be when all the above items have been properly dealt with?

- O $43,650 overdrawn
- O $33,630 overdrawn
- O $5,110 overdrawn
- O $72,170 overdrawn **(2 marks)**

39.18 On 1 January 20X5 a company purchased some plant.

The invoice showed:

	$
Cost of plant	48,000
Delivery to factory	400
One year warranty covering breakdown during 20X5	800
	49,200

Modifications to the factory building costing $2,200 were necessary to enable the plant to be installed.

What amount should be capitalised for the plant in the company's records?

- O $51,400
- O $48,000
- O $50,600
- O $48,400

(2 marks)

39.19 A business had an opening inventory of $180,000 and a closing inventory of $220,000 in its financial statements for the year ended 31 December 20X5.

Which **TWO** of the following entries for these opening and closing inventory figures are made when completing the financial records of the business?

- ☐ DEBIT: Inventory account $180,000, CREDIT: Statement of profit or loss (SPL) $180,000
- ☐ DEBIT: Statement of profit or loss (SPL) $220,000, CREDIT: Inventory account $220,000
- ☐ DEBIT: Statement of profit or loss (SPL) $180,000, CREDIT: Inventory account $180,000
- ☐ DEBIT: Inventory account $220,000, CREDIT: Statement of profit or loss (SPL) $220,000
- ☐ DEBIT: Inventory account $40,000, CREDIT: Purchases account $40,000
- ☐ DEBIT: Purchases account $40,000, CREDIT: Inventory account $40,000

(2 marks)

39.20 Tinsel Co has 5 million $1 issued ordinary shares. At 1 May 20X0 Fairy Co purchased 60% of Tinsel Co's $1 ordinary shares for $4,000,000. At that date Tinsel Co had net assets with a fair value of $4,750,000 and a share price of $1.10. Fairy Co valued the non-controlling interest in Tinsel Co at acquisition as $2,200,000.

What is the total goodwill on acquisition at 1 May 20X0?

- O $1,150,000
- O $1,750,000
- O $750,000
- O $1,450,000

(2 marks)

(Total = 40 marks)

40 Mixed bank 3 (46 mins)

40.1 On 1 September 20X6, a business had inventory of $380,000. During the month, sales totalled $650,000 and purchases $480,000. On 30 September 20X6 a fire destroyed some of the inventory. The undamaged goods in inventory were valued at $220,000. The business operates with a standard gross profit margin of 30%.

Based on this information, what is the cost of the inventory destroyed in the fire?

- O $185,000
- O $140,000
- O $405,000
- O $360,000

(2 marks)

40.2 Which of the following should appear as separate items in a company's statement of changes in equity?

(1) Profit for the financial year

(2) Income from investments

(3) Dividends paid on redeemable preference shares

(4) Dividends paid on equity shares

- O 1, 3 and 4
- O 1 and 4 only
- O 2 and 3 only
- O 1, 2 and 3

(2 marks)

40.3 The following information is available about a company's dividends:

			$
20X5	Sept.	Final dividend for the year ended 30 June 20X5 paid (declared August 20X5)	100,00 0
20X6	March	Interim dividend for the year ended 30 June 20X6 paid	40,000
20X6	Sept.	Final dividend for the year ended 30 June 20X6 paid (declared August 20X6)	120,000

What figures, if any, should be disclosed in the company's statement of profit or loss and other comprehensive income (SPLOCI) for the year ended 30 June 20X6 and its statement of financial position (SOFP) as at that date?

	SPLOCI for the period	***SOFP liability***
O	$160,000 deduction	$120,000
O	$140,000 deduction	nil
O	nil	$120,000
O	nil	nil

(2 marks)

40.4 Goose Co has a 49% shareholding in each of the following three companies.

- Turkey Co: Goose Co has the right to appoint or remove a majority of the directors of Turkey Co.
- Duck Co: Goose Co has more than half the voting rights in Duck Co as a result of an agreement with other investors.
- Partridge Co: Goose Co has the power to govern the financial and operating policies of Partridge Co.

Which of these companies are subsidiaries of Goose Co for financial reporting purposes?

○ Turkey Co and Duck Co only

○ Partridge Co and Duck Co only

○ Partridge Co and Turkey Co only

○ Partridge Co, Turkey Co and Duck Co **(2 marks)**

40.5 At 1 July 20X5 a company's allowance for receivables was $48,000.

At 30 June 20X6, trade receivables amounted to $838,000. It was decided to write off $72,000 of these debts and adjust the allowance for receivables to $60,000.

What are the final amounts for inclusion in the company's statement of financial position at 30 June 20X6?

	Trade receivables	Allowances for receivables	Net balance
	$	**$**	**$**
○	838,000	60,000	778,000
○	766,000	60,000	706,000
○	766,000	108,000	658,000
○	838,000	108,000	730,000

(2 marks)

40.6 Which **TWO** of the following statements about inventory valuation for statement of financial position purposes are correct?

☐ According to IAS 2 *Inventories*, average cost and FIFO (first in, first out) are both acceptable methods of arriving at the cost of inventories.

☐ Inventories of finished goods may be valued at labour and materials cost only, without including overheads.

☐ Inventories should be valued at the lowest of cost, net realisable value and replacement cost.

☐ It may be acceptable for inventories to be valued at selling price less estimated profit margin. **(2 marks)**

40.7 A business received a delivery of goods on 29 June 20X6, which was included in inventory at 30 June 20X6. The invoice for the goods was recorded in July 20X6.

What effect will this have on the business?

(1) Profit for the year ended 30 June 20X6 will be overstated.

(2) Inventory at 30 June 20X6 will be understated.

(3) Profit for the year ending 30 June 20X7 will be overstated.

(4) Inventory at 30 June 20X6 will be overstated.

- O 1 and 2
- O 2 and 3
- O 1 only
- O 1 and 4

(2 marks)

40.8 Based on the information below, what is the acid test ratio for Edward Co?

EDWARD CO TRIAL BALANCE (EXTRACT)

	$
Receivables	176,000
Inventories	20,000
Trade payables	61,000
Bank overdraft	79,000
Long term loan	10,000
Retained earnings	5,000

- O 1.13:1
- O 1.40:1
- O 1.35:1
- O 1.26:1

(2 marks)

40.9 Which of the following characteristics of financial information are included in the IASB's *Conceptual Framework*?

(1) Comparability

(2) Relevance

(3) Timeliness

(4) Faithful representation

- O All four items
- O 1, 2 and 3 only
- O 1, 2 and 4 only
- O 2, 3 and 4 only

(2 marks)

40.10 Details of a company's insurance policy are shown below:

Premium for year ended 31 March 20X6 paid April 20X5	$10,800
Premium for year ending 31 March 20X7 paid April 20X6	$12,000

What figures should be included in the company's financial statements for the year ended 30 June 20X6?

	Statement of Profit or Loss	*Statement of Financial position SOFP*
	$	$
O	11,100	9,000 prepayment (DEBIT)
O	11,700	9,000 prepayment (DEBIT)
O	11,100	9,000 accrual (CREDIT)
O	11,700	9,000 accrual (CREDIT)

(2 marks)

40.11 Which of the following statements about bank reconciliations are correct?

- In preparing a bank reconciliation, unpresented cheques must be deducted from the bank balance shown in the bank statement.
- A cheque from a customer paid into the bank but dishonoured must be corrected by making a debit entry in the bank general ledger account.
- An overdraft is a debit balance in the bank statement.

O 1 and 2

O 2 and 3

O 1 and 3

O 3 only **(2 marks)**

40.12 At 30 June 20X5 the equity of Meredith, a limited liability company, was:

	$m
Share capital	
Ordinary shares of $1 each	100
Share premium account	80

During the year ended 30 June 2006, the following transactions took place:

1 September 20X5	A bonus issue of one ordinary share for every two held, using the share premium account.
1 January 20X6	A fully subscribed rights issue of two ordinary shares for every five held at that date, at $1.50 per share.

What would the balances on each account be at 30 June 20X6?

	Share capital	*Share premium*
	$m	**$m**
O	210	110
O	210	60
O	240	30
O	240	80

(2 marks)

40.13 Which of the following statements about the requirements of IAS 37 *Provisions, Contingent Liabilities and Contingent Assets* are correct?

(1) Contingent assets and liabilities should not be recognised in the financial statements.

(2) A contingent asset should only be disclosed in the notes to a financial statement where an inflow of economic benefits is probable.

(3) A contingent liability may be ignored if the possibility of the transfer of economic benefits is remote.

O All three statements are correct

O 1 and 2 only

O 1 and 3 only

O 2 and 3 only **(2 marks)**

40.14 Which of the following errors would cause a trial balance not to balance?

(1) An error in the addition in the bank general ledger account.

(2) Failure to record a transaction at all.

(3) Cost of a motor vehicle debited to motor expenses account. The bank entry was correctly made.

(4) Goods taken by the proprietor of a business recorded by debiting purchases and crediting drawings account.

O 1 only

O 1 and 2 only

O 3 and 4 only

O All four items **(2 marks)**

40.15 Manchester has 10 million $1 issued ordinary shares. At 1 May 20X9 Bristol purchased 70% of Manchester's $1 ordinary shares for $8,000,000. At that date Manchester had net assets with a fair value of $8,750,000 and its share price was $1.20. The non-controlling interest is valued using the share price at the date of acquisition.

What was the total goodwill arising on acquisition at 1 May 20X9?

$ [ ] **(2 marks)**

40.16 All the sales made by a retailer are for cash, and her sale prices are fixed by doubling cost. Details recorded of her transactions for September 20X6 are as follows:

		$
1 Sept	Inventories	40,000
30 Sept	Purchases for month	60,000
	Cash banked for sales for month	95,000
	Inventories	50,000

Which **TWO** of the following conclusions could separately be drawn from this information?

(1) $5,000 cash has been stolen from the sales revenue prior to banking.

(2) Goods costing $5,000 have been stolen.

(3) Goods costing $2,500 have been stolen.

(4) Some goods costing $2,500 had been sold at cost price.

- O 1 and 2
- O 1 and 3
- O 2 and 4
- O 3 and 4

(2 marks)

40.17 A company owns a number of properties which are rented to tenants. The following information is available for the year ended 30 June 20X6:

	Rent in advance	*Rent in arrears*
	$	$
1 July 20X5	134,600	4,800
30 June 20X6	144,400	8,700

Cash received from tenants in the year ended 30 June 20X6 was $834,600.

All rent in arrears was subsequently received.

What figure should appear in the company's statement of profit or loss for rent receivable in the year ended 30 June 20X6?

- O $840,500
- O $1,100,100
- O $569,100
- O $828,700

(2 marks)

40.18 The following trade receivables account has been prepared by a trainee accountant:

TRADE RECEIVABLES

	$		$
20X3		*20X3*	
1 Jan Balance b/d	284,680	31 Dec Bank receipts from credit customers	179,790
31 Dec Credit sales	189,120	Contras against amounts owing by company in payables ledger	800
Irrecoverable debts written off	5,460		
Sales returns	4,920	Balance c/d	303,590
	484,180		484,180

What should the closing balance on the account be when the errors in it are corrected?

- O $290,150
- O $286,430
- O $282,830
- O $284,430

(2 marks)

40.19 The carrying amount of a company's non-current assets was $200,000 at 1 August 20X0. During the year ended 31 July 20X1, the company sold non-current assets for $25,000 on which it made a loss of $5,000. The depreciation charge for the year was $20,000.

What was the carrying amount of non-current assets at 31 July 20X1?

- O $150,000
- O $155,000
- O $170,000
- O $175,000

(2 marks)

(Total = 38 marks)

41 Mixed bank 4 (41 mins)

41.1 A company issued one million ordinary $1 shares at a premium of 50c per share. The proceeds were correctly recorded in the bank general ledger account, but were incorrectly credited to the sales account.

Which one of the following journal entries will correct the error?

		DEBIT	*CREDIT*
		$	$
O	Sales	1,500,000	
	Share capital		1,000,000
	Share premium		500,000
O	Share capital	1,000,000	
	Share premium		500,000
	Sales		1,500,000
O	Sales	1,500,000	
	Share capital		1,500,000
O	Share capital	1,500,000	
	Sales		1,500,000

(2 marks)

41.2 After proposing a final dividend, Kenilworth Co has a current ratio of 2.0 and a quick ratio of 0.8.

If the company now uses its positive cash balance to pay that final dividend, what will be the effect upon these two ratios?

- O Increase current ratio and decrease quick ratio
- O Increase current ratio and increase quick ratio
- O Decrease current ratio and decrease quick ratio
- O Decrease current ratio and increase quick ratio **(2 marks)**

41.3 A property company received cash for rent totalling $838,600 in the year ended 31 December 20X6.

Figures for rent in advance and in arrears at the beginning and end of the year were:

	1 January 20X6	*31 December 20X6*
	$	$
Rent received in advance	102,600	88,700
Rent in arrears (all subsequently received)	42,300	48,400

What amount should appear in the company's statement of profit or loss for the year ended 31 December 20X6 for rental income?

- O $818,600
- O $738,000
- O $939,200
- O $858,600

(2 marks)

41.4 Which one of the following journal entries is correct according to its narrative?

		Debit	**Credit**
		$	**$**
O	Mr Smith personal account	100,000	
	Directors' remuneration		100,000
	Bonus allocated to account of managing director (Mr Smith)		
O	Purchases	14,000	
	Wages	24,000	
	Repairs to buildings		38,000
	Transferring cost of repairs to buildings carried out by company's own employees, using materials from inventory.		
O	Sales returns	2,800	
	Purchases returns		2,800
	Correction of error: sales returns incorrectly debited to purchases returns account		
O	Suspense account	20,000	
	Rent receivable		10,000
	Rent payable		10,000
	Correction of error: rent received credited in error to rent payable account.		

(2 marks)

41.5 IAS 37 *Provisions, Contingent Liabilities and Contingent Assets* deals with accounting for contingencies. What is the correct accounting treatment for the following?

(1) A probable loss (a constructive obligation exists, for which the amount can be reliably estimated)

(2) A probable gain

	Probable loss	*Probable gain*
O	Accrued	Disclosed
O	Accrued	Not disclosed
O	Disclosed, but not accrued	Disclosed
O	Disclosed, but not accrued	Not disclosed

(2 marks)

41.6 A company has occupied rented premises for some years, paying an annual rent of $120,000. From 1 April 20X6 the rent was increased to $144,000 per year. Rent is paid quarterly in advance on 1 January, 1 April, 1 July and 1 October each year.

What figures should appear for rent in the company's financial statements for the year ended 30 November 20X6?

	SPLOCI	*SOFP*
	$	**$**
O	136,000	Prepayment 12,000
O	136,000	Prepayment 24,000
O	138,000	Nil
O	136,000	Accrual 12,000

(2 marks)

41.7 At 1 January 20X6 a company had an allowance for receivables of $49,000.

At 31 December 20X6 the company's trade receivables were $863,000 and it was decided to write off balances totalling $23,000. The allowance for receivables was to be adjusted to the equivalent of 5% of the remaining receivables.

What total figure should appear in the company's statement of profit or loss for receivables expense?

O $16,000

O $65,000

O $30,000

O $16,150 **(2 marks)**

41.8 At 1 January 20X6, a company's capital structure was as follows:

	$
Ordinary share capital	
2,000,000 shares of 50c each	1 000,000
Share premium account	1,400,000

In January 20X6 the company issued 1,000,000 shares at $1·40 each.

In September 20X6 the company made a bonus issue of one share for every three held using the share premium account.

What were the balances on the company's share capital and share premium accounts after these transactions?

	Share capital	***Share premium***
	$	**$**
O	4,000,000	800,000
O	3,200,000	600,000
O	2,000,000	1,800,000
O	2,000,000	1,300,000

(2 marks)

41.9 Which of the following statements about the treatment of inventory and work in progress in financial statements are correct?

(1) Inventory should be valued at the lowest of cost, net realisable value and replacement cost.

(2) In valuing work in progress, materials costs, labour costs and variable and fixed production overheads must be included.

(3) Inventory items can be valued using either first in, first out (FIFO) or weighted average cost.

(4) A company's financial statements must disclose the accounting policies used in measuring inventories.

O All four statements are correct.

O 1, 2 and 3 only

O 2, 3 and 4 only

O 1 and 4 only **(2 marks)**

41.10 The plant and equipment account in the records of a company for the year ended 31 December 20X6 is shown below.

PLANT AND EQUIPMENT – COST

20X6	$	20X6	$
1 Jan Balance b/d	960,000		
1 July Bank	48,000	30 Sept Transfer disposal account	84,000
		31 Dec Balance c/d	924,000
	1,008,000		1,008,000

The company's policy is to charge depreciation on the straight line basis at 20% per year, with proportionate depreciation in the years of purchase and sale.

What should be the charge for depreciation in the company's statement of profit or loss for the year ended 31 December 20X6?

$ [ ] **(2 marks)**

41.11 The trial balance of a company did not balance, and a suspense account was opened for the difference.

Which **TWO** of the following errors would require an entry to the suspense account in correcting them?

☐ A bank payment to purchase a motor van had been correctly entered in the bank general ledger account but had been debited to the motor expenses account.

☐ The debit side of the wages account had been undercast.

☐ Sales returns had been credited to the purchases returns account.

☐ A cash refund to a customer had been recorded by debiting the bank general ledger account and crediting the customer's account in the receivables ledger. **(2 marks)**

41.12 A trader took goods that had cost $2,000 from inventory for personal use.

Which one of the following journal entries would correctly record this?

		DEBIT	*CREDIT*
		$	**$**
O	Drawings	2,000	
	Inventory		2,000
O	Purchases	2,000	
	Drawings		2,000
O	Sales	2,000	
	Drawings		2,000
O	Drawings	2,000	
	Purchases		2,000

(2 marks)

41.13 Nasty is a wholly owned subsidiary of Ugly. Inventories in their individual statements of financial position at the year end are shown as:

Ugly	$40,000
Nasty	$20,000

Sales by Ugly to Nasty during the year were invoiced at $15,000 which included a profit by Ugly of 25% on cost. Two thirds of these goods were included in inventories at the year end.

At what value should inventories appear in the consolidated statement of financial position?

- O $50,000
- O $57,000
- O $57,500
- O $58,000

(2 marks)

41.14 Where in the financial statements should tax on profit for the current period, and profit for the period, be separately disclosed?

	Statement of profit or loss and other comprehensive income	*Statement of changes in equity*
O	Tax on profit and profit for the period	Tax on profit
O	Profit for the period	Tax on profit and profit for the period
O	Tax on profit	Profit for the period
O	Tax on profit and profit for the period	Profit for the period

(2 marks)

41.15 When is the diminishing balance method of depreciating non-current assets more appropriate than the straight line method?

- O When the expected life of the asset is short
- O When the asset is expected to decrease in value by a fixed percentage of cost each year
- O When the expected life of the asset is not capable of being estimated accurately
- O When the asset is expected to decrease in value less in later years than in the early years of its life

(2 marks)

41.16 A draft statement of cash flows contains the following:

	$m
Profit before tax	22
Depreciation	8
Increase in inventories	(4)
Decrease in receivables	(3)
Increase in payables	(2)
Net cash inflow from operating activities	21

Which of the following corrections need to be made to the calculation?

(1) Depreciation should be deducted, not added

(2) Increase in inventories should be added, not deducted

(3) Decrease in receivables should be added, not deducted

(4) Increase in payables should be added, not deducted

- O 1 and 2
- O 1 and 3
- O 2 and 4
- O 3 and 4 **(2 marks)**

41.17 Your inexperienced colleague, Paul Jones, has attempted to extract and total the individual balances in the receivables ledger. He provides you with the following listing which he has prepared.

	$
Bury Inc	7,500
P Fox & Son (Swindon) Co	2,000
Frank Wrendlebury & Co	4,297
D Richardson & Co	6,847
Ultra Co	783
Lawrenson Co	3,765
Walkers Inc	4,091
P Fox & Son (Swindon) Co	2,000
Whitchurch Co	8,112
Ron Bradbury & Co	5,910
Anderson Co	1,442
	46,747

Subsequent to the drawing up of the list, the following errors have so far been found.

(1) Paul Jones had forgotten to draw up a sales invoice for $267 to be sent to Whitchurch Co, therefore this has been incorrectly omitted from the receivables ledger.

(2) Paul Jones omitted the $2,435 balance of Rectofon Co from the list.

(3) A credit note for $95 sent to Bury Co was entered in the account in the receivables ledger as $75.

What is the revised balance of the receivables ledger after correcting these errors?

- O $45,665
- O $47,449
- O $47,429
- O $45,645 **(2 marks)**

(Total = 34 marks)

42 Mixed bank 5 **(46 mins)**

42.1 A firm has the following transactions with its product R.

1 January 20X1	Opening inventory: nil
1 February 20X1	Buys 10 units at $300 per unit
11 February 20X1	Buys 12 units at $250 per unit
1 April 20X1	Sells 8 units at $400 per unit
1 August 20X1	Buys 6 units at $200 per unit
1 December 20X1	Sells 12 units at $400 per unit

The firm uses FIFO to value its inventory. What is the inventory value at the end of the year?

- O $nil
- O $1,700
- O $2,400
- O $2,007.20

(2 marks)

42.2 Which of the following provides advice to the International Accounting Standards Board (the Board) as well as informing the Board of the implications of proposed IFRS Standards for users and preparers of financial statements?

- O The IFRS Advisory Council
- O The IFRS Interpretations Committee
- O The IFRS Foundation
- O The Trustees of the IFRS

(2 marks)

42.3 Samantha has extracted a trial balance and created a suspense account with a credit balance of $759 to make it balance.

Samantha found the following:

(1) A sales invoice for $4,569 had accidently not been drawn up and therefore has not been entered in the accounting records.

(2) A payment of $1,512 has been posted correctly to the trade payables account but no other entry has been made.

(3) A credit sale of $131 has only been credited to the sales account.

What is the remaining balance on the suspense account after these errors have been corrected?

- O $3,810 DEBIT
- O $2,140 CREDIT
- O $890 CREDIT
- O $622 DEBIT

(2 marks)

42.4 Carol had receivables of $598,600 at 30 November 20X8. Her allowance for receivables at 1 December 20X7 was $12,460. She wished to change it to the equivalent of 2% of receivables at 30 November 20X8. On 29 November 20X8 she received $635 in full settlement of a debt that she had written off in the year ended 30 November 20X7.

What total amount should be recognised for receivables in the statement of profit or loss for the year ended 30 November 20X8?

- O $488 CREDIT
- O $11,972 DEBIT
- O $1,123 CREDIT
- O $147 DEBIT

(2 marks)

42.5 Joanna has prepared her draft financial statements for the year ended 30 April 20X8, and needs to adjust them for the following items:

(1) Rent of $10,500 was paid and recorded on 2 January 20X7 for the period 1 January to 31 December 20X7. The landlord has advised that the annual rent for 20X8 will be $12,000 although it has not been invoiced or paid yet.

(2) Property and contents insurance is paid annually on 1 March. Joanna paid and recorded $6,000 on 1 March 20X8 for the year from 1 March 20X8 to 28 February 20X9.

What should the net effect on profit be in the draft financial statements for the year ended 30 April 20X8 of adjusting for the above items?

- O $1,000 decrease
- O $1,500 increase
- O $1,000 increase
- O $1,500 decrease

(2 marks)

42.6 Carter, a limited liability company, has non-current assets with a carrying amount of $2,500,000 on 1 December 20X7.

During the year ended 30 November 20X8, the following occurred:

(1) Depreciation of $75,000 was charged to the statement of profit or loss.

(2) Land and buildings with a carrying amount of $1,200,000 were revalued to $1,700,000.

(3) An asset with a carrying amount of $120,000 was disposed of for $150,000.

(4) The carrying amount of non-current assets at 30 November 20X8 was $4,200,000.

In accordance with IAS 7 *Statement of Cash Flows*, what are the net cash flows from the above transactions to be included in 'net cash flows from investing activities' for the year ended 30 November 20X8?

- O $(1,395,000)
- O $(1,365,000)
- O $150,000
- O $(1,245,000)

(2 marks)

42.7 A bookkeeper has found several errors in the accounting records.

(1) A sales invoice has been entered as $895 rather than $859.

(2) An invoice for rent has been incorrectly posted to the office expenses account (the bank payment entry is correct)

(3) A contra of $400 between the receivables and purchases ledger has only been entered in the receivables account.

Which of the following errors will need to be adjusted through the suspense account?

- O 3 only
- O 1 and 3 only
- O 1 and 2 only
- O 1, 2 and 3

(2 marks)

42.8 Luis sold goods to Pedro in May 20X9 with a list price of $98,000. Luis allowed a trade discount of 10%. Pedro returned goods with a list price of $3,000 on 31 May and returned a further $5,000 of goods at list price on 6 June as they were found to be unsuitable.

How much should Luis record in the sales returns account at 31 May?

- O $2,700
- O $3,000
- O $8,000
- O $7,200

(2 marks)

42.9 A newly-registered company is considering the accounting policies it should adopt.

Policies under consideration are:

(1) Research and development expenditure should be capitalised and amortised over the years in which the resultant product is sold or used.

(2) Inventory should be valued at the lower of cost and net realisable value.

(3) Goodwill arising in a business combination should be written off immediately to the statement of profit or loss.

Which of these possible accounting policies would, if adopted, contravene IFRS Standards?

- O 1 and 2 only
- O 2 and 3 only
- O 1 and 3 only
- O 1, 2 and 3

(2 marks)

42.10 You have recently been appointed as assistant accountant of PQR Co. You have assisted in preparing a forecast set of financial statements for the company whose year end is 31 December 20X7. The forecast shows that the company is expected to make a loss during the year to 31 December 20X7.

The managing director is concerned that the company's shareholders would be unhappy to hear that the company had made a loss. He is determined to avoid making a loss if at all possible. He has made the following suggestions in order to remedy the situation.

(1) Value inventory using the LIFO basis as prices are rising so this will reduce inventory costs in the statement of profit or loss.

(2) Create a provision against future losses in case this happens again in the future.

(3) Stop amortising all capitalised development expenditure.

Which of these suggestions do you agree with?

- O 1 and 2 only
- O 3 only
- O 2 only
- O None of the statements

(2 marks)

42.11 Which of the following journal entries may be accepted as being correct according to their narratives?

			DEBIT $	**CREDIT** $
1	Wages account Purchases account Buildings account		38,000 49,000	 87,000
	Labour and materials used in construction of extension to factory			
2	Directors' personal accounts: Directors' remuneration	A B	30,000	 40,000 70,000
	Directors' bonuses transferred to their accounts			
3	Suspense account Sales account		10,000	 10,000
	Correction of error in addition – total of credit side of sales account $10,000 understated			

- O 1 and 3
- O 1 and 2
- O 3 only
- O 2 and 3

(2 marks)

42.12 Which of the following costs should be included in valuing inventories of finished goods held by a manufacturing company, according to IAS 2 *Inventories*?

(1) Carriage inwards

(2) Carriage outwards

(3) Depreciation of factory plant

(4) Accounts department costs relating to wages for production employees

- O All four items
- O 2 and 3 only
- O 1, 3 and 4 only
- O 1 and 4 only

(2 marks)

42.13 Frog acquired 100% of the ordinary share capital of Toad on 1 October 20X7.

On 31 December 20X7 retained earnings of Toad and Frog were as follows:

	Frog	*Toad*
	$'000	$'000
Retained earnings at 1 January 20X7	500	100
Retained profit for the year ended 31 December 20X7	150	60
	650	160

The profits of Toad have accrued evenly throughout 20X7.

What figure for retained earnings should be included in the consolidated financial statements of the Frog group at 31 December 20X7?

- O $150,000
- O $175,000
- O $665,000
- O $810,000

(2 marks)

42.14 The following extract is from the statement of profit or loss of Gearing Co for the year ended 30 April 20X8.

	$
Profit before tax	68,000
Tax	(32,000)
Profit for the year	36,000

In addition to the profit above:

(1) Gearing Co paid a dividend of $21,000 during the year.

(2) A gain on revaluation of land resulted in a surplus of $18,000.

What total amount will be added to retained earnings at the end of the financial year?

- $36,000
- $33,000
- $47,000
- $15,000

(2 marks)

42.15 What does an increase in the allowance for receivables result in?

- A decrease in current liabilities
- An increase in profit for the year
- An increase in working capital
- A decrease in working capital

(2 marks)

42.16 A company's telephone bill consists of two elements. One is a quarterly rental charge, payable in advance; the other is a quarterly charge for calls made, payable in arrears. At 1 April 20X9, the previous bill dated 1 March 20X9 had included line rental of $90. Estimated call charges during March 20X9 were $80.

During the following 12 months, bills totalling $2,145 were received on 1 June, 1 September, 1 December 20X9 and 1 March 20Y0, each containing rental of $90 as well as call charges. Estimated call charges for March 20Y0 were $120.

What is the amount to be charged to the statement of profit or loss for the year ended 31 March 20Y0?

- $2,185
- $2,205
- $2,155
- $2,215

(2 marks)

42.17 Which **THREE** of the following sets of items all appear on the same side of the trial balance?

(1) Sales, interest received and accruals

(2) Receivables, drawings and discount received

(3) Non current assets, cost of sales and carriage outwards

(4) Capital, trade payables and other operating expenses

(5) Sundry expenses, prepayments and purchases

- 1, 4 and 5
- 1, 3 and 5
- 1, 2 and 3
- 3, 4 and 5

(2 marks)

42.18 A sole trader's accounts show an increase in net assets over a year of $173,000. Drawings were $77,000 and capital introduced was $45,000.

What was the profit for the year?

$ [ ] **(2 marks)**

42.19 Capital introduced is $50. Profits brought forward at the beginning of the year amount to $100 and liabilities are $70. Assets are $90.

What is the retained profit for the year?

- O $130 profit
- O $130 loss
- O $10 profit
- O $10 loss **(2 marks)**

(Total = 38 marks)

43 Mixed bank 6 (43 mins)

43.1 If there is a debit balance of $1,250 on X's account in the accounting records of Y, what does this mean?

- O X owes $1,250 to Y
- O Y owes $1,250 to X
- O X has returned goods worth $1,250 to Y
- O X is owed $1,250 by Y **(2 marks)**

43.2 You are an employee of Exelan Co and have been asked to help prepare the end of year statements for the period ended 30 November 20X9 by agreeing the figure for the total receivables.

The following figures, relating to the financial year, have been obtained from the accounting records.

	$
Purchases for the year	361,947
Sales	472,185
Returns inwards	41,226
Returns outwards	16,979
Irrecoverable debts written off	4,586
Discounts received	1,864
Payments to suppliers	342,791
Bank receipts from customers	429,811
Customer cheques dishonoured	626

You discover that at the close of business on 30 November 20X8 the total of the receivables amounted to $50,241.

What is the balance on the receivables account at 30 November 20X9?

- O $47,429
- O $56,601
- O $46,177
- O $71,676

(2 marks)

43.3 Sandilands Co uses a computer package to maintain its accounting records. A printout of its bank general ledger account for the month of May 20X3 was extracted on 31 May and is summarised below.

	$		$
Balance b/d	546	Payments	5,966
Receipts	6,293	Balance c/d	873
	6,839		6,839

The company's chief accountant provides you with the following information.

(1) Bank charges of $630 shown on the bank statement have not been entered in the company's bank general ledger account.

(2) Three standing orders entered on the bank statement have not been recorded in the company's bank general ledger account : a subscription for trade journals of $52, an insurance premium of $360 and a business rates payment of $2,172.

(3) A cheque drawn by Sandilands Co for $693 and presented to the bank on 26 May has been incorrectly entered in the bank general ledger account as $936.

After correcting the errors above, what is the revised balance on the bank general ledger account?

- O $2,098 DEBIT
- O $2,584 DEBIT
- O $3,868 CREDIT
- O $3,382 CREDIT

(2 marks)

43.4 A company purchases a machine for $9,000. The machine is depreciated at 30% per year on the diminishing balance basis. A full year's depreciation is charged in the year of purchase, with none in the year of sale. During Year 4, it is sold for $3,000.

What is the profit or loss on disposal?

- O $1,000 profit
- O $87 loss
- O $1,410 profit
- O $840 profit

(2 marks)

43.5 Which one of the following does a business aim to ensure by charging depreciation in the financial statements?

- O The cost of non-current assets is spread over the accounting periods which benefit from their use.
- O There are sufficient funds set aside to replace the assets when necessary.
- O Profits are not understated.
- O Assets are shown at their realisable value **(2 marks)**

43.6 A business purchased an asset on 1 January 20X1 at a cost of $160,000. The asset had an expected life of eight years and a residual value of $40,000. The straight line method is used to measure depreciation. The financial year ends on 31 December.

At 31 December 20X3, the estimated remaining life of the asset from that date is now expected to be only three more years, but the residual value is unchanged.

What will be the carrying amount of the asset as at 31 December 20X3, for inclusion in the statement of financial position?

- O $97,500
- O $100,000
- O $107,500
- O $115,000 **(2 marks)**

43.7 The debit side of a trial balance totals $400 more than the credit side.

Which one of the following errors would fully account for the difference?

- O $200 paid for building repairs has been correctly entered in the bank general ledger account and credited to the building non-current asset account.
- O Purchases returns of $200 were debited to the sales returns account.
- O A receipt of $400 for commission receivable has been omitted from the records.
- O A purchase invoice for $400 has been omitted from the records. **(2 marks)**

43.8 Under IAS 1 *Presentation of Financial Statements*, which of the following **must** be disclosed on the **face** of the statement of profit or loss and other comprehensive income?

- O Profit before tax
- O Gross profit
- O Revenue
- O Dividends **(2 marks)**

43.9 The following bank reconciliation has been prepared:

	$
Balance per bank statement (overdrawn)	73,680
Add: Outstanding lodgements	102,480
Less: Unpresented cheques	(87,240)
Balance per bank general ledger account (credit)	88,920

Assuming the amounts stated for items other than the bank general ledger account balance are correct, what should the bank general ledger account balance be?

- O $88,920 credit (as currently stated)
- O $120,040 credit
- O $58,440 debit
- O $58,440 credit

(2 marks)

43.10 In relation to statements of cash flows, which, if any, of the following are correct?

(1) The direct method of calculating net cash from operating activities leads to a different figure from that produced by the indirect method, but this is balanced elsewhere in the statement of cash flows.

(2) A company making high profits must necessarily have a net cash inflow from operating activities.

(3) Profits and losses on disposals of non-current assets appear as items under cash flows from investing activities in the statement of cash flows or a note to it.

- O Item 1 only
- O Items 2 and 3 only
- O None of the items
- O All of the items

(2 marks)

43.11 Which of the following items could appear on the credit side of a trade receivables account?

(1) Receipts from customers

(2) Irrecoverable debts written off

(3) Increase in the allowance for receivables

(4) Sales

(5) Credits for goods returned by customers

(6) Cash refunds to customers

- O 1, 2 and 5
- O 1, 2 and 6
- O 3, 4 and 5
- O 3, 4, 5 and 6

(2 marks)

43.12 A business has compiled the following information for the year ended 31 October 20X2:

	$
Opening inventories	386,200
Purchases	989,000
Closing inventories	422,700

The gross profit percentage of sales is 40%

What is the sales revenue for the year?

- O $1,333,500
- O $1,587,500
- O $2,381,250
- O The sales revenue is impossible to calculate from this information. **(2 marks)**

43.13 On 30 September 20X1 part of the inventory of a company was completely destroyed by fire.

The following information is available:

- Inventory at 1 September 20X1 at cost $49,800
- Purchases for September 20X1 $88,600
- Sales for September 20X1 $130,000
- Inventory at 30 September 20X1 – undamaged items $32,000
- Standard gross profit percentage on sales 30%

Based on this information, what is the cost of the inventory destroyed?

- O $17,800
- O $47,400
- O $15,400
- O $6,400 **(2 marks)**

43.14 Catt sells goods at a margin of 50%. During the year to 31 March 20X3 the business made purchases totalling $134,025 and sales totalling $240,000. Inventories in hand at 31 March 20X3, valued at cost, was $11,385 higher than the corresponding figure at 1 April 20X2.

What was the cost of the goods Catt had drawn out?

- O $2,640
- O $14,590
- O $25,410
- O $37,360 **(2 marks)**

43.15 Thatch plc's current ratio this year is 1.33:1 compared to that of 1.25:1 last year. Which of the following would be possible explanations?

(1) Thatch made an unusually large sale immediately prior to the year end.

(2) Thatch paid its payables earlier than usual out of a bank overdraft.

(3) Thatch made an unusually large purchase of goods for cash immediately prior to the year end and these goods remain in inventory.

(4) Thatch paid its payables earlier than usual out of a positive cash balance.

- O 1 and 2 only
- O 2 and 3 only
- O 1 and 3 only
- O 1 and 4 only

(2 marks)

43.16 Lexus owns 60% of the voting equity of Nexus. The following information relates to the results of Lexus and Nexus for the year.

	Lexus	*Nexus*
	$'000	$'000
Revenue	350	150
Cost of sales	200	60
Gross profit	150	90

During the year, Nexus sold goods to Lexus for $50,000. Lexus still had 40% of these goods in inventory at the year end. Nexus uses a 25% mark up on all goods.

What were the consolidated sales and cost of sales of the Lexus group at the year end?

	Sales	*Cost of sales*
O	$500,000	$210,000
O	$500,000	$214,000
O	$450,000	$210,000
O	$450,000	$214,000

(2 marks)

43.17 At 1 July 20X0 the share capital and share premium account of a company were as follows:

	$
Share capital – 300,000 ordinary shares of 25c each	75,000
Share premium account	200,000

During the year ended 30 June 20X1 the following events took place:

(1) On 1 January 20X1 the company made a rights issue of one share for every five held, at $1.20 per share.

(2) On 1 April 20X1 the company made a bonus (capitalisation) issue of one share for every three in issue at that time, using the share premium account to do so.

What are the correct balances on the company's share capital and share premium accounts at 30 June 20X1?

	Share capital	*Share premium account*
O	$460,000	$287,000
O	$480,000	$137,000
O	$120,000	$137,000
O	$120,000	$227,000

(2 marks)

43.18 A statement of cash flows prepared in accordance with IAS 7 *Statement of Cash Flows* opens with the calculation of cash flows from operating activities from the profit before taxation.

Which of the following lists of items consists only of items that would be **added** to profit before taxation in that calculation?

- O Decrease in inventories, depreciation, profit on sale of non-current assets
- O Increase in trade payables, decrease in trade receivables, profit on sale of non-current assets
- O Loss on sale of non-current assets, depreciation, increase in trade receivables
- O Decrease in trade receivables, increase in trade payables, loss on sale of non-current assets

(2 marks)

(Total = 36 marks)

44 Mixed bank 7 (43 mins)

44.1 The following information was disclosed in the financial statements of Highfield Co for the year ended 31 December 20X2.

	20X1	*20X2*
	$	$
Plant & equipment cost	255,000	235,000
Accumulated depreciation	(100,000)	(110,000)

During 20X2, the following occurred in respect of plant & equipment:

	$
Purchases of plant and equipment	10,000
Depreciation charged on plant and equipment	25,000
Loss on disposal of plant and equipment	8,000

What were the sales proceeds received on disposal of the plant and equipment?

- O $7,000
- O $15,000
- O $25,000
- O $8,000

(2 marks)

44.2 The issued share capital of Maelstrom Co is as follows:

Ordinary shares of 10c each	$1,000,000
8% Preferred shares of 50c each (redeemable)	$500,000

In the year ended 31 October 20X2, the company has paid the preferred dividend for the year and an interim dividend of 2c per share on the ordinary shares. A final ordinary dividend of 3c per share is declared on 30 October 20X2.

What is the total amount of dividends recognised in the financial statements relating to the year ended 31 October 20X2?

- O $580,000
- O $90,000
- O $130,000
- O $500,000

(2 marks)

44.3 When a company makes a rights issue of equity shares which of the following effects will the issue have?

(1) Working capital is increased

(2) Liabilities are increased

(3) Share premium account is reduced

(4) Investments are increased

- O 1 only
- O 1 and 2
- O 3 only
- O 1 and 4

(2 marks)

44.4 Which of the following may appear as current liabilities in a company's statement of financial position?

(1) A revaluation surplus

(2) Loan due for repayment within 1 year

(3) Income tax payable

(4) Preferred dividends payable on redeemable preference shares

- O 1, 2 and 3
- O 1, 2 and 4
- O 1, 3 and 4
- O 2, 3 and 4

(2 marks)

44.5 If a trial balance does not balance, which of the following errors might have caused this?

(1) The discounts received balance was overstated both in the discounts received account and in the trade payables account

(2) Cash paid for the purchase of office furniture was debited to the general expenses account.

(3) Returns inwards were included on the credit side of the trial balance.

- O 1 only
- O 1 and 2
- O 3 only
- O 2 and 3

(2 marks)

44.6 The following information is available about a company's dividends:

		$
20X5		
September	Final dividend for the year ended 30 June 20X5 paid (declared August 20X5)	100,000
20X6		
March	Interim dividend for the year ended 30 June 20X6 paid	40,000
September	Final dividend for the year ended 30 June 20X6 paid (declared August 20X6)	20,000

What figures, if any, should be disclosed in the company's statement of profit or loss and other comprehensive income for the year ended 30 June 20X6 and its statement of financial position as at that date?

	SPLOCI for the period	*SOFP liability*
O	$160,000 deduction	$120,000
O	$140,000 deduction	nil
O	nil	$120,000
O	nil	nil

(2 marks)

44.7 Which, if any, of the following statements about intangible assets are correct?

(1) Deferred development expenditure must be amortised over a period not exceeding five years.

(2) If the conditions specified in IAS 38 *Intangible Assets* are met, development expenditure may be capitalised, if the directors decide to do so.

(3) Trade investments must appear in a company's statement of financial position under the heading of intangible assets.

- O 1 and 2
- O 2 and 3
- O 1 and 3
- O None of the statements are correct

(2 marks)

44.8 A company owns a number of properties which are rented to tenants. The following information is available for the year ended 30 June 20X6:

	Rent in advance	*Rent in arrears*
	$	$
30 June 20X5	134,600	4,800
30 June 20X6	144,400	8,700

The rent income recognised in the company's statement of profit and loss for the year ended 30 June 20X6 was $828,700.

All rent in arrears was subsequently received.

What was the cash received from tenants in the year ended 30 June 20X6?

$ [ ]

(2 marks)

44.9 Which of the following transactions is an asset transaction?

- O Depreciation of plant and equipment
- O Expenditure on rent
- O Payment of interest on loan stock
- O Buying shares as an investment

(2 marks)

44.10 Which of the following transactions would be shown as an expense in the statement of profit or loss?

- O Expenditure resulting in improvements to property
- O Expenditure on heat and light
- O Purchasing non-current assets
- O Repaying a bank overdraft

(2 marks)

44.11 The trade payables account below contains a number of errors:

TRADE PAYABLES

	$		$
Opening balance (amounts owed to suppliers)	318,600	Purchases	1 268,600
Payment to suppliers	1,364,300	Contras against debt balances in receivables ledger	48,000
Purchases returns	41,200	Discounts received	8,200
Refunds received from suppliers	2,700	Closing balance	402,000
	1,726,800		1,726,800

All items relate to credit purchases.

What should the closing balance be when all the errors are corrected?

- O $128,200
- O $509,000
- O $224,200
- O $144,600

(2 marks)

44.12 What are the journal entries for an accrual of rent expenses of $500?

- O DEBIT prepayments $500, CREDIT rent $500
- O DEBIT accrual $500, CREDIT rent $500
- O DEBIT rent $500, CREDIT accruals $500
- O DEBIT rent $500, CREDIT prepayments $500

(2 marks)

44.13 An electrical store and a cake shop both have the same mark up on cost. However, the gross profit margin of the electrical store is significantly higher than that of the cake shop.

Which of the following is a possible reason for this?

- O The cake shop has a higher turnover of inventory than the electrical store.
- O The electrical store takes advantage of trade-discounts for bulk buying.
- O The cake shop has a higher level of wastage of inventory than the electrical store.
- O The cake shop's revenue is increasing, while that of the electrical store is decreasing.

(2 marks)

44.14 Analysis of the statement of financial position of Charon for the year ended 20X9 reveals the following relationships:

Current ratio	2:1
Sales: current assets	5:1
Acid test ratio	1.5:1

If the sales for the year were $30 million, what is the value of inventory that will appear in the statement of financial position?

- O $1.5m
- O $10.5m
- O $3.0m
- O $4.5m **(2 marks)**

44.15 Which of the following statements are correct?

(1) If company A has an investment in company B that gives it control over the company B, then company B is classified as a subsidiary in the consolidated financial statements of company A.

(2) If a company has associates, but not subsidiaries, it will not prepare consolidated financial statements.

(3) If a company has a 21% investment in the voting equity of another company, it will account for its investment using the equity method in the consolidated financial statements.

- O 1 and 2
- O 2 and 3
- O All three statements are correct
- O None of the statements are correct **(2 marks)**

44.16 XYX Co's non-current assets had carrying amounts of $368,400 and $485,000 at the beginning and end of the year respectively. Depreciation for the year was $48,600. Assets originally costing $35,000, with a carrying amount of $18,100 were sold in the year for $15,000.

What were the additions to non-current assets in the year?

- O $183,300
- O $200,200
- O $49,900
- O $180,200 **(2 marks)**

44.17 At 1 November 20X9, Telway Co had an allowance for receivables of $90,000. At 31 October 20X0, its trade receivables were $1,232,000 of which $60,000 was identified as unrecoverable and was written off. Telway Co's allowance for receivables has now been adjusted to the equivalent of 5% of remaining trade receivables.

What amount should be recorded in the statement of profit or loss for the receivables expense for the year ended 31 October 20X0?

- O $58,600 debit
- O $28,600 debit
- O $31,400 credit
- O $118,600 debit

(2 marks)

44.18 Why do we prepare a trial balance?

- O To test the accuracy of the double entry bookkeeping records
- O To prepare management accounts
- O To prepare financial statements
- O To clear the suspense account

(2 marks)

(Total = 36 marks)

BPP

Answers

Part A: The context and purpose of financial reporting

1 The context and purpose of financial reporting

1.1 The correct answer is: The International Accounting Standards Board (the Board)

The role of the Board is to develop and publish IFRS Standards.

1.2 The correct answer is: 2 and 3 only

A sole trader does not have any shareholders. The financial statements are unlikely to be of interest to a financial analyst as they are more usually interested in the financial statements of public companies.

1.3 The correct answers are:

A supplier of goods on credit is interested only in the statement of financial position, ie an indication of the current state of affairs.		**FALSE**
The objective of financial statements is to provide financial information about the reporting entity's assets, liabilities, equity, income and expenses that is useful to users of the financial statements in assessing the prospects for future net cash flows to the reporting entity and in accessing management's stewardship of the entity's economic resources.	**TRUE**	

The first statement is false – although the supplier needs to know the current situation, the supplier also needs to be able to assess future prospects to ensure the entity has the ability to pay and to support an ongoing relationship.

The second statement is true.

1.4 The correct answer is: 1 only

Statement 2 is incorrect – shareholders are only liable for the debts of the business up to the amount they have invested in shares, whereas sole traders are liable for all of the debts of the business.

1.5 The correct answer is: Corporate governance is the system by which companies and other entities are directed and controlled.

1.6 The correct answer is: 1 only

The responsibility of the financial statements rests with the directors, whether or not those financial statements are audited. Some of the duties of directors are statutory duties, laid down in law, including the duty to act within their powers, promote the success of the company and exercise reasonable skill and care.

1.7 The correct answer is: A list of all the assets owned and all the liabilities owed by a business

The statement of financial position contains a list of all the assets owned and all the liabilities owed by a business.

1.8 The correct answer is: A record of income generated and expenditure incurred over a given period

The statement of profit or loss contains a record of income generated and expenditure incurred over a given period.

1.9 The correct answer is: 3 only

Unless a partnership is a limited liability partnership, the partners' individual exposure to debt is not limited because the partnership is not a separate legal entity from the partners themselves. Financial records must be maintained by a partnership, but there is no requirement to make them publicly available unless the partnership is a limited liability partnership.

1.10 The correct answer is: 1, 2 and 3

All three statements are true.

1.11 The correct answer is: 3 only

The IFRS Advisory Council is a forum for the Board to consult with the outside world. The Board produces IFRS Standards and is overseen by the IFRS Foundation.

1.12 The correct answer is: Formulate IFRS Standards

The role of the Board is to develop and publish IFRS Standards.

1.13 The correct answer is: Ensure IFRS Standards focus primarily on the needs of global, multi-national organisations

The IFRS Foundation does not focus primarily on the needs of global, multi-national organisations. One of the objectives of the Foundation is to take account of the financial reporting needs of emerging economies and small and medium-sized entities (SMEs).

1.14 The correct answer is: To provide examples of best financial reporting practice for national bodies who develop their own requirements

One of the ways IFRS Standards are used is as an international benchmark for those countries which develop their own requirements.

1.15 The correct answer is: In the event that the business generates a profit, this is due to the sole trader only.

1.16 The correct answer is: The company's shareholders are not personally liable for the debts of the business.

1.17 The correct answers are:

Sole traders and partnerships are unincorporated businesses. This means there is a legal distinction between the business and their owners.		**FALSE**
When a sole trader takes money from the business for personal use, this is known as drawings.	**TRUE**	

Statement 1 is false as in the case of unincorporated businesses, there is no legal distinction between the business and their owners.

Part B: The qualitative characteristics of financial information

2 The qualitative characteristics of financial information

2.1 The correct answer is: The business entity concept

2.2 The correct answer is: The accruals basis

2.3 The correct answer is: The materiality concept

2.4 The correct answer is: 1 and 4

Information has the quality of faithful representation when it is complete, neutral and free from material error.

2.5 The correct answer is: Consistency

To maintain consistency, the presentation and classification of items in the financial statements should stay the same from one period to the next, unless a change is required by an IFRS Standard or unless there is a significant change in the nature of operations or a review of the accounts indicates a more appropriate presentation.

2.6 The correct answer is: 1 and 3

Relevance and faithful representation.

2.7 The correct answer is: Financial information should be complete, neutral and free from error.

The first option describes accruals.

The second option describes timeliness.

The third option describes consistency.

2.8 The correct answer is: 1 only

2.9 The correct answer is: 2 only

Information is material if its omission or misstatement could influence the economic decisions of users taken on the basis of the financial statements. Statement 1 describes the opposite of the accruals basis. Statement 3 is also incorrect, faithful representation does not prevent estimates being made.

2.10 The correct answer is: Relevance, Faithful representation, Comparability, Verifiability, Timeliness and Understandability

2.11 The correct answer is: Accruals

The accruals basis is not a qualitative characteristic of financial information.

2.12 The correct answer is: Providing reliable investment advice

Providing information regarding the financial position and performance of a business are primary objectives of financial statements. All classes of users require information for decision making.

2.13 The correct answers are:

Companies should never change the presentation or classification of items in their financial statements, even if there is a significant change in the nature of operations.		**INCORRECT**
Companies should create provisions in times of company growth to be utilised in more difficult times, to smooth profits.		**INCORRECT**

The first option is incorrect. The presentation or classification can be changed if there is a significant change in the nature of operations, if an IFRS Standard requires it, or if a review of the accounts indicates a more appropriate presentation.

ANSWERS

The second option is incorrect. Companies should not make provisions in order to smooth profits. Provisions should only be made in accordance with IAS 37 *Provisions, Contingent Liabilities and Contingent Assets.*

2.14 The correct answer is: Prudence does not allow for overstatement of liabilities.

The other options are incorrect. Prudence is a component of neutrality. It does not allow for overstatement or understatement of assets, liabilities, income or expenses.

2.15 [Timeliness] means having information available to decision makers in time to be capable of influencing their decisions.

2.16 The correct answer is: Classifying, characterising and presenting information clearly and concisely makes it understandable.

The first statement is from the *Conceptual Framework for Financial Reporting* and describes understandability. The second statement is incorrect as providing users of the financial statements with details of all transactions the entity has entered into would make the financial statements very difficult to understand. Statement 3 refers to the enhancing characteristic of timeliness. Statement 4 refers to the enhancing characteristic of faithful representation.

2.17 The correct answer is: Capable of making a difference to decisions made by users and having a predictive value, confirmatory value or both

Relevant information is capable of making a difference to decisions made by users and has a predictive value. Faithful representation has the characteristics of being:

- complete
- neutral
- free from error

2.18 [Historical cost] for an asset is the cost that was incurred when the asset was acquired or created and, for a liability, is the value of the consideration received when the liability was incurred.

2.19 The accounting concept described above is known as [substance over form].

2.20 This describes the enhancing characteristic of [comparability].

2.21 'The financial statements are normally prepared on the assumption that an entity is a [going concern] and will continue in operation for the foreseeable future.'

2.22 The correct answer is: 1, 2 and 3

2.23 The qualitative characteristic being described here is [verifiability].

2.24 In the general ledger, for every debit entry there is a corresponding credit entry. This is relevant to the [duality] concept of accounting.

2.25 The accounting concept is [offsetting].

Part C: The use of double entry and accounting systems

3 Double entry bookkeeping I

3.1 The correct answer is: Assets – liabilities – opening capital + drawings = profit

Phrased another way, assets – liabilities = opening capital + profits – drawings

3.2 The correct answer is: Closing capital – opening capital + drawings – capital introduced

This show the increase in net assets and is the correct form of the accounting equation.

3.3 The correct answer is: $180,000

Increase in net assets = profit + new capital - drawings

= $(72,500 + 8,000 – 2,200)

= $78,300

Therefore, closing net assets = $(101,700 + 78,300) = $180,000.

3.4 $ 55,500

Increase in net assets = profit + new capital – drawings

= $(35,400 + 10,200 – 6,000)

= $39,600

Opening capital = opening net assets = $(95,100 – 39,600) = $55,500.

3.5 The correct answer is:

	Debit ($)	Credit ($)
Drawings account	800	
Purchases account		800

The selling price is not relevant to this adjustment.

3.6 The correct answer is: The lengthening of the period of credit given to customers

This will mean less cash coming into the bank.

Option 1: Sale of an asset will bring in cash; whether it was sold at a profit or loss is irrelevant.

Option 2: Depreciation reduces profit but has no cash effect.

Option 4: Slowing down payments to suppliers will increase bank balances.

3.7 The correct answer is: $54,000 profit

Increase in net assets	= Capital introduced + profit – drawings
184,000 – 128,000	= 50,000 + profit – 48,000
Profit	= 56,000 – 50,000 + 48,000
	= $54,000

3.8 The correct answer is:

	Debit ($)	Credit ($)
Debit purchases	400	
Debit trade payables	250	
Credit bank		650

A payment is a credit to the bank general ledger account. The payment to J Bloggs is a cash purchase and so the double entry is DEBIT Purchases, CREDIT bank. Remember that the purchase from J Doe has already been recorded as DEBIT Purchases, CREDIT Trade

Payables, so the payment of cash to clear the invoice should now be recorded as DEBIT Trade Payables, CREDIT bank.

3.9 The correct answer is:

	Debit ($)	Credit ($)
Debit receivables	150	
Debit sales returns	300	
Credit sales		150
Credit bank		300

The double entry for the sale of goods on credit is DEBIT Receivables, CREDIT Sales $150. The return of goods previously sold for cash is DEBIT Sales Returns, CREDIT Bank $300.

3.10 The correct answer is: Debit note

A debit note is sent to a supplier with a return of goods. A debit note is in effect a request for a credit note.

3.11 The correct answer is: $186,450 DEBIT

The balance carried down from the previous period shows debits exceed credits and so it is a debit balance brought down for the new period.

3.12 The correct answer is: $14,000 CREDIT

The opening balance on the ledger is $14,000 CREDIT. This is the amount that would have appeared in the trial balance at 1 October 20X0.

3.13 The correct answer is: Sales invoices

Details of sales invoices can be found in the receivables ledger. A quotation provides information on the proposed amount to be charged for goods or services but is not evidence of a sale or purchase. Credit notes received are recorded in the payables ledger. Trade discounts are given at the point of sale and are not recorded in the accounting records.

3.14 The correct answers are:

A debit records an increase in liabilities		**FALSE**
A debit records a decrease in assets		**FALSE**
A credit records an increase in liabilities	**TRUE**	
A credit records a decrease in capital		**FALSE**

A debit records an increase in assets or a decrease in liabilities. A credit records an increase in liabilities and/or capital. Therefore, only the third statement is true.

3.15 The correct answer is: Debit purchases, Credit trade payables

Remember that only credit purchases are listed in the trade payables account.

3.16 The correct answer is: An imprest system for petty cash helps with management of small cash expenditures and reduces the risk of fraud.

The amount paid in to replenish petty cash at the beginning of each period should be the amount of petty cash spending in the previous period, which is the total of expenditures shown by petty cash vouchers for the previous period. The amount of petty cash at any time is the maximum petty cash balance minus the value of the petty cash vouchers for the period.

3.17 The correct answer is: Petty cash voucher

The petty cash voucher is a record that cash has been issued for an approved item of expense. The receipt is evidence of the amount of the expense. The petty cash record is a list of petty cash transactions and not evidence of them.

3.18

Description	Business document
A document sent by a business to a credit customer requesting payment for goods or services provided.	Sales invoice
A request for payment sent by the supplier to the credit customer.	Supplier (purchase) invoice
A document sent by a supplier to a customer in respect of goods returned or overpayments made by the customer.	Credit note

3.19 [1, 2 and 4 only]

The customer and supplier names and addresses, details of the amount due and the date by which invoice must be settled are shown on supplier (purchase) invoices. The amount currently outstanding in respect of previous purchases is not normally shown on supplier invoices. This would instead be shown on a supplier statement.

3.20 A [goods received note] provides confirmation that goods have been received from a supplier. It is prepared by the [customer] .

3.21 The correct answer is: Debit note

A debit note is a document sent by a customer to a supplier formally requesting that the supplier issues them with a credit note.

4 Double entry bookkeeping II

4.1 £ [534]

RECEIVABLES LEDGER

20X9		$
1 May	P Dixon	160
4 May	M Maguire ($80 × 87.5%)	70
5 May	M Donald	304
		534

4.2 £ [823]

PAYABLES LEDGER

20X9		$
2 May	A Clarke (W1)	323
4 May	D Daley	400
6 May	G Perkins	100
		823

Working

$$\$380 \times \frac{85}{100} = \$323$$

ANSWERS

4.3 The correct answer is:

	Debit ($)	Credit ($)
Debit purchases	450	
Debit trade payables	250	
Credit purchase returns		700

The purchase of goods on credit is recorded as DEBIT Purchases, CREDIT Trade Payables $450. The return of goods which were purchased on credit is recorded as DEBIT Trade Payables, CREDIT Purchase Returns. Combining both entries gives the answer above.

4.4 The correct answer is:

Debit bank
Credit sales
Credit trade receivables

Money received is a debit to the bank general ledger account. The cash received from R Singh is offset against the trade receivable balance due from R Singh: DEBIT Bank, CREDIT Trade Receivables. The cash received from S Kalu is a cash sale: DEBIT Bank, CREDIT Sales.

4.5 The correct answer is:

Debit	Credit
Trade receivables	Sales

An increase in trade receivables is a debit entry as this is an increase in an asset. Sales are an increase in income and therefore a credit entry.

4.6 The correct answers are:

A debit entry in the bank general ledger account will increase an overdraft in the accounts		**FALSE**
A debit entry in the bank general ledger account will increase a bank balance in the accounts	**TRUE**	

When money is received by a business, a debit entry is made in the bank general ledger account. A bank receipt decreases an overdraft and increases a bank balance.

4.7 The correct answer is: $474,485 CREDIT

TRADE PAYABLES

	$		$
Bank	100,750	Balance b/d	250,225
Balance c/d	474,485	Purchases	325,010
	575,235		575,235

4.8 The correct answer is: $79,000

Credit sales = $80,000 – $10,000 + $9,000 = $79,000.

4.9 The correct answer is: DEBIT purchases $100, CREDIT payables $50, CREDIT bank $50

The first option is incorrect as the debits and credits don't equal each other, the second option is incorrect as the debits and credits are the wrong way round and the fourth option is incorrect as the credit purchase has been ignored.

4.10 To record this transaction, debit receivables $250 and credit sales $250.

You are recording the transaction in Steel Co's accounting records – Steel Co is the seller, so the double entry is debit receivables, credit sales.

4.11 The correct answer is: $22,000

	$	$
Sales		40,000
Returns inwards		(2,000)
		38,000
Opening inventory	3,000	
Purchases	20,000	
Returns outwards	(4,000)	
Closing inventory	(3,000)	
		(16,000)
Gross profit		22,000

4.12 The correct answer is: An asset of $71,192

The receivables allowance is deducted from trade receivables and the net figure of $71,192 ($75,943 – $4,751) is reported in the statement of financial position.

4.13 The correct answer is: Assets are represented by debit balances.

The first option is incorrect because some debit balances are assets.

The third and fourth options are incorrect because income and liabilities are credit balances.

4.14 The correct answer is: CREDIT $8,500 and DEBIT $678

The two balances must be separately disclosed. The bank account balance is an asset and the loan is a non-current liability.

4.15 The correct answer is: $284,931

The debits are as follows:

	$
Opening inventory	9,649
Purchases	142,958
Expenses	34,835
Non-current assets	63,960
Receivables	31,746
Bank (asset)	1,783
	284,931

4.16 The correct answer is: $17,649

(5,754 + 11,745 + 150)

4.17 The correct answer is: By preventing transactions from being processed inaccurately

No system can prevent a transaction being processed inaccurately, for example being posted to an incorrect but valid account code (although an effective system can reduce the likelihood of this).

4.18 The correct answer is: Controls

Accounting systems have controls in place to ensure that information is input, processed and output completely and accurately.

4.19 Businesses make [sales] to their customers. When credit customers settle the amount due to the business, they will be provided with a document confirming that the payment has been received. This document is known as a [receipt].

Businesses also make [purchases] from their suppliers. When businesses make a payment to settle the amount due to their suppliers, they will receive a [payment] confirmation.

4.20 [Bank general ledger account]

The trade receivables account is normally an asset account. The trade payables account is normally a liability account and the electricity expense account is normally an expense account. The bank general ledger account can either be an asset or a liability, depending on whether there is a positive bank balance or an overdraft.

4.21 [Sales returns]

The sales returns account is used to record credit notes issued to credit customers. The capital account is used to record transactions with the owners of the business. The non-current asset account is an asset account and carriage outwards is an expense account.

4.22 The correct answer is: Sales (an income account)

4.23 The correct answers are:

- The accounting system can be used to provide financial reports which show whether individual departments are controlling their expenditure effectively.
- The accounting system can be used to provide financial reports which show sales volumes for individual product lines.
- The accounting system can be used to provide information on the amount owed to each individual credit customer at any point in time.

An organisation's accounting system cannot be used to provide information on the organisation's competitors. The other statements are all benefits of an accounting system to the organisation.

4.24 The correct answers are:

In a computerised accounting system, sales invoices are manually input into the accounting system by the accounts assistant		**FALSE**
In a computerised accounting system, sales credit notes are manually input in the accounting system by the accounts assistant		**FALSE**

Both statements are false. In a computerised account system, both sales invoices and sales credit notes are created in the receivables ledger. Both the receivables ledger and the trade receivables general ledger account are then automatically updated from the details on the sales invoices or the sales credit notes.

4.25 Purchase invoices and purchase credit notes received from a supplier are [manually] entered into the computerised accounting system by the accounts assistant.

Purchase invoices and purchase credit notes are not created within a business's accounting system as they are received from external suppliers. Therefore, they have to be entered manually into the accounting system.

4.26 Journal entries are used to record business transactions in the accounting records. A journal entry must have a debit entry and a corresponding credit entry.

The fact that all journals have both a debit and a credit entry is a feature of duality.

4.27 The correct answers are:

Date	**YES**	
Amount	**YES**	
General ledger account names and codes	**YES**	
Trial balance		**NO**

Standard features of journal entries are the date of the transaction, the amount concerned (sometimes split into the net amount, income tax amount and the gross amount). The general ledger account names and codes are also selected as part of the journal entry.

The trial balance is not a journal entry but instead is a separate listing.

4.28 The correct answers are:

- The accounts assistant enters details of the amount per the purchase invoice and the invoice date into the computerised accounting system
- The invoice must be coded both to the relevant payables ledger account and the purchases expense account

Purchase invoices have to be manually keyed into the accounting system by the accounts assistant as they are received from outside the business. Income tax must be recorded correctly where relevant.

The invoice must be coded correctly both to the relevant payables ledger account and the purchases expense account. Once the invoice has been posted to the relevant payables account, the trade payables account in the general ledger will be automatically updated.

4.29 The correct answers are:

In a computerised accounting system, the total of the receivables ledger balances and the trade receivables balance must be reconciled on a regular basis		**FALSE**
The trade receivables general ledger account is used to establish the amount due from each individual credit customer		**FALSE**

In a computerised accounting system, the total of the receivables ledger balances and the trade receivables balance do not need to be reconciled. They are automatically updated from the same information, therefore, a reconciliation is not required. The individual receivables ledger accounts and not the trade receivables general ledger account are used to establish the amounts due from each individual credit customer.

4.30

Description	Term
A computer software package tailor made for the accounting requirements of a particular client	Bespoke accounting software package
A computer software package that can be used by multiple organisations	Off the shelf accounting software package

4.31 The data and software can be held remotely on the computer servers of the service provider hosting the service. This is known as cloud accounting.

Alternatively, the data and software can be installed locally on the computers of its accounting staff. In this situation the accounting staff will access the accounting software and data through the organisation's local file sharing drives.

4.32 This type of information is known as standing data.

5 Sales tax

5.1 The correct answer is: The company sold some products to businesses not registered for sales tax.

The first, second and third options could all be reasons why the output tax does not equal 20% of sales. The fourth option is incorrect as it makes no difference whether the customer is registered for sales tax or not.

5.2 $ 11,910

SALES TAX ACCOUNT

	$		$
		Balance b/d	4,540
Purchases ($64,000 × 15%)	9,600	Sales ($109,250 × 15%/115%)	14,250
∴ Cash paid	11,910	Balance c/d	2,720
	21,510		21,510

5.3 The correct answer is: DEBIT Purchases $575, CREDIT Payables $575

Alana is not registered for sales tax purposes and therefore cannot reclaim the input sales tax of $75.

5.4 The correct answer is: $7,000

SALES TAX ACCOUNT

	$		$
Purchases ($65,000 × 20%)	13,000	Sales ($120,000 × 20% / 120%)	20,000
∴ Paid to tax authority	7,000		
	20,000		20,000

5.5 The correct answer is: Assets $2,600 less Liabilities $1,000 equals Capital $1,600

	$
Assets	
Opening cash	1,000
Cash received $(1,000 + 200 sales tax)	1,200
Closing cash	2,200
Inventory $(800 – 400)	400
	2,600
Liabilities	
Opening liabilities	0
Sales tax payable $(200 – 160)	40
Purchase inventory $(800 + 160 sales tax)	960
Closing liabilities	1,000

	$
Capital	
Opening capital	1,000
Profit on sale of inventory $(1,000 – 400)	600
Closing capital	1,600

5.6 The correct answer is: Inclusive of sales tax in the statement of financial position

Receivables and payables include sales tax where applicable.

5.7 The correct answer is: Credited with the total of sales made, excluding sales tax

The sales tax element of the invoices will go to the sales tax account in the statement of financial position.

5.8 The correct answer is: $962.50 CREDIT

Workings are as follows:

	$
Output sales tax $\$27,612.50 \times \frac{17.5}{117.5}$	4,112.50
Input sales tax $\$18,000 \times \frac{17.5}{100}$	3,150.00
∴ Balance on sales tax a/c (credit)	962.50

6 Inventory

6.1 $ 952,750

950,000 – 11,750 + 1,500 + (14,950 × 100/115) = $952,750

6.2 The correct answer is: 1, 3 and 5 only

Carriage outwards and storage are distribution costs.

6.3 The correct answer is: $281,200

	$
Original value	284,700
Coats	
– Cost 400 × $80	(32,000)
– NRV ($75 × 95%) × 400	28,500
	281,200

At 31 January 20X3 the skirts were correctly valued at costs incurred to date of $20 per skirt which was lower than the NRV of $22. Therefore, no adjustment is required for the value of the skirts.

6.4 The correct answer is: $188,500

	$
50 @ $190	9,500
500 @ $220	110,000
300 @ $230	69,000
	188,500

6.5 The correct answers are:

Inventory items are normally to be valued at the higher of cost and net realisable value.		**INCORRECT**
The cost of goods manufactured by an entity will include materials and labour only. Overhead costs cannot be included.		**INCORRECT**
LIFO (last in, first out) cannot be used to value inventory.	**CORRECT**	
First in first out (FIFO) and Average cost (AVCO) are acceptable methods that can be used to value inventory.	**CORRECT**	

Statement (1) is incorrect because inventory should be valued at the lower of cost and NRV, not the higher.

Statement (2) is incorrect because production overheads based on a normal level of production should be included.

6.6 The correct answer is: $461,500

	$
Inventory check balance	483,700
Less: goods from suppliers	(38,400)
Add: goods sold	14,800
Less: goods returned	(400)
Add: goods returned to supplier	1,800
	461,500

6.7 The correct answer is: The current year's profit will be understated and next year's profit will be overstated.

If closing inventory is understated, cost of sales will be overstated. Next year opening inventory will be understated and cost of sales will be understated.

6.8 The correct answer is: $529,200

	$
Inventory count, 4 January 20X2	527,300
Purchases since end of year	(7,900)
Cost of sales since end of year (15,000 × 60%)	9,000
Purchase returns since end of year	800
Inventory at 31 December 20X1	529,200

6.9 The correct answer is: Production overheads should be included in cost on the basis of a company's normal level of activity in the period.

IAS 2 emphasises that production overheads must be allocated to items of inventory on the basis of the normal capacity of the production facilities. Although trade discounts should be deducted, selling costs must not be included in the cost of inventories. IAS 2 does not allow the use of LIFO. Production overheads are part of the costs of conversion of finished goods, and so do form part of the valuation.

6.10 The correct answer is: $40,755

	$
Original inventory valuation	41,875
Cost of damaged items	(1,960)
NRV of damaged items (1,200 – 360)	840
	40,755

6.11 The correct answer is: $4,700

	Cost	*Net realisable value*	*Lower of cost & NRV*	*Units*	*Value*
	$	$	$		$
Basic	6	8	6	200	1,200
Super	9	8	8	250	2,000
Luxury	18	10	10	150	1,500
					4,700

6.12 The correct answer is: $2,950

$2,950 (10 units @ $45 and 50 units @ $50)

6.13 The correct answer is: Plant depreciation, carriage inwards, raw materials, supervisor's wages

Carriage outwards (in the first and fourth options) is a selling expense, so should not be included in the cost of the inventory.

IAS 2 states that storage costs should not be included in the cost of inventory unless they are necessary in the production process before a further production stage. As such, storage of finished goods (in the second option) should not be included in the cost of inventory.

6.14 The correct answer is: $122,900

	$
Balance as initially calculated	116,400
Line 1: (400 × $3) – $200	1,000
Line 2: (200 × $35) – $300 – $1,200	5,500
	122,900

6.15 The correct answer is: $838,100

	$
Inventory count value	836,200
Less: purchases	(8,600)
Add: sales (14,000 × 70/100)	9,800
Add: goods returned	700
Inventory figure	838,100

6.16 The correct answer is: $132,900

The cost of materials used should be based on opening and closing valuations of inventory at AVCO.

	$
Opening inventory	56,200
Purchases	136,500
	192,700
Less: Closing inventory	(59,800)
Cost of materials used	132,900

6.17 The correct answer is: A continuous inventory system removes the need for periodic physical inventory counts.

Continuous inventory reduces the need for physical inventory counts, but in practice periodic counts are needed to ensure that the recorded quantities of inventory match the physical quantities that are held (and, for example, there have not been significant losses of inventory due to theft).

6.18 The correct answer is: $1,800

Date	*Units*	*Unit cost*	*Cost of issues*	*Balance in inventory*
		$	$	$
1 March	50	40		2,000
17 March	50	50		2,500
	100	45*		4,500
31 March	(60)	45	2,700	
	40	45		1,800

Note. * 4,500 / 100

6.19 $ 2,007.20

Date		*Units*	*Cost per unit*		*Average cost per unit*	*Total Cost*
			$		$	$
1 Jan 20X1	Bal b/f	0	0			
1 Feb 20X1	Buy	10	300		300	3,000
11 Feb 20X1	Buy	12	250			3,000
		22		(W1)	272.73	6,000
1 Apr 20X1	Sell	(8)	272.73		272.73	(2,182)
1 Aug 20X1	Buy	6	200			1,200
		20		(W2)	250.90	5,018
1 Dec 20X1	Sell	(12)	250.90		250.90	(3,011)
Closing		8			250.90	2,007.20

$$W1 = \frac{6{,}000}{22 \text{ units}} = \$272.73$$

$$W2 = \frac{5{,}018}{20 \text{ units}} = \$250.90$$

6.20 $ 2,057.12

Calculations as follows.

$$\frac{\text{Total cost}}{\text{Total units}} = \text{periodic weighted AVCO}$$

$$\frac{(10 \times \$300) + (12 \times \$250) + (6 \times \$200) =}{10 + 12 + 6}$$

$$\frac{\$7{,}200}{28 \text{ units}} = \$257.14 \text{ per unit}$$

Closing inventory = (10 + 12 – 8 + 6 – 12) = 8 units

Value of closing inventory $2,057.12 ($257.14 × 8 units)

6.21 The correct answers are:

Opening inventory is automatically shown in the initial trial balance, however, this figure needs to be updated for goods which have been purchased and sold during the year, to calculate closing inventory.	**TRUE**	
Inventory is often a small balance in the financial statements, therefore a late journal entry is appropriate.		**FALSE**
Posting closing inventory as a journal entry ensures that it is correctly accounted for both as a reduction in cost of sales (statement of profit or loss) and as an asset (statement of financial position).	**TRUE**	
The quantity of each line of inventory is often counted during a year end inventory count; once this information is known, inventory can be valued and a closing inventory figure posted to the adjusted trial balance as a journal entry.	**TRUE**	

Statement 2 is false. Where companies hold inventory, it is often a significant balance in the financial statements and therefore must be accurately calculated and recorded in the accounting records.

6.22 An advantage of the [continuous inventory system] is that at any point in time an organisation will know the quantity of each line of inventory held in the warehouse.

6.23 Gross profit for the year using the FIFO method is $ [111,900]

Gross profit for the year using the AVCO method is $ [111,100]

Which method give a higher gross profit for the year (FIFO or AVCO? [FIFO]

Under FIFO, Cost of sales is 35,500 + 70,200 - $33,600 = $72,100; Sales $184,000 - $72,100 = gross profit $111,900

Under AVCO, Cost of sales is 35,500 + 70,200 - $32,800 = $72,900; Sales $184,000 - $72,900 = gross profit $111,100

7 Tangible non-current assets I

7.1 The correct answer is: To allocate the cost of a non-current asset over the accounting periods expected to benefit from its use

It is **never** the second option as funds are not set aside, nor the third option, this is revaluation, nor the fourth – depreciation has nothing to do with the wearing out of assets. Depreciation is an application of the matching concept and allocates the cost of the asset over the accounting periods expected to benefit from its use.

7.2 The correct answer is: An internal control to ensure information relating to non-current assets in the general ledger and the financial statements is correct

7.3 $ 62,210

	$
Balance b/d	67,460
Less: Carrying amount of non-current asset sold	
(4,000 + 1,250)	5,250
	62,210

7.4 The correct answer is: Asset with disposal proceeds of $15,000 and a profit on disposal of $5,000

If disposal proceeds were $15,000 and profit on disposal is $5,000, then the carrying amount must be $10,000, the difference between the asset register figure and the non-current asset account in the general ledger.

7.5 The correct answer is: An overstatement of profit and an overstatement of non-current assets

An expense has been posted as a non-current asset.

7.6 The correct answer is: Assets which are intended to be used by the business on a continuing basis, including both tangible and intangible assets that do not meet the IAS 1 *Presentation of Financial Statements* definition of a current asset

The first option describes current assets.

The third option describes intangible assets.

The fourth option describes inventory.

7.7 The correct answer is: $74,000

	$
Valuation	210,000
Carrying amount (170,000 × 16/20)	(136,000)
Revaluation surplus	74,000

7.8 The correct answer is: Understated by $18,400

	$
Repairs cost overstated	20,000
Depreciation understated ((20,000 – 4,000) × 20% × 6/12)	(1,600)
Profit understated	18,400

7.9 The correct answer is: $43,000

	$
Plant held all year (200,000 – 40,000) × 20%	32,000
Disposal 40,000 × 20% × 9/12	6,000
Additions 50,000 × 20% × 6/12	5,000
	43,000

7.10 The correct answer is: $55,000

	$
Plant held all year (240,000 – 60,000) × 20%	36,000
Addition 160,000 × 20% × 6/12	16,000
Disposal 60,000 × 20% × 3/12	3,000
	55,000

7.11 The correct answer is: $23,375

Cost less 4 months depreciation = 25,500 – 2,125 = $23,375.

7.12 $ 86,000

	$
Purchase price of machine	80,000
Installation	5,000
Testing	1,000
	86,000

Staff training cannot be capitalised as part of the cost of the asset.

7.13 The correct answer is:

Debit	**Credit**
Non-current assets – cost	Payables

The correct answer is: DEBIT Non-current assets – cost, CREDIT Payables.

7.14 The correct answer is:

DEBIT Accumulated depreciation	$35,000	
	$15,000	
DEBIT Loss on disposal (SPL)	$50,000	
DEBIT Bank		$100,000
CREDIT Non-current assets – cost		

Using T-accounts:

PLANT AND MACHINERY ACCOUNT

	$		$
Balance b/d	100,000	Plant and machinery disposals a/c	100,000

PLANT AND MACHINERY ACCUMULATED DEPRECIATION

	$		$
Plant and machinery disposals	35,000	Balance b/d	35,000

PLANT AND MACHINERY DISPOSALS

	$		$
Plant and machinery account	100,000	Accumulated depreciation	35,000
		Bank	50,000
		SPL (loss on sale)	15,000
	100,000		100,000

7.15 The correct answers are:

IAS 16 Property, Plant and Equipment requires entities to disclose the purchase date of each asset.		**FALSE**
The carrying amount of a non-current asset is the cost or valuation of that asset less accumulated depreciation.	**TRUE**	
IAS 16 Property, Plant and Equipment permits entities to make a transfer from the revaluation surplus to retained earnings for excess depreciation on revalued assets.	**TRUE**	
Once decided, the useful life of a non-current asset should not be changed.		**FALSE**

IAS 16 does not require the purchase date of each asset to be disclosed. The carrying amount of an asset = cost/valuation – accumulated depreciation. The useful life of an asset is determined upon acquisition and should be reviewed at least annually and depreciation rates adjusted for the current and future periods if expectations vary significantly from the original estimates. When an asset is revalued, IAS 16 permits entities to make a transfer from the revaluation surplus to retained earnings of the excess depreciation arising due to the revaluation.

7.16 The correct answer is: $50,000

The depreciation charge is calculated based on the remaining useful life at the date of the revaluation: 1,000,000/20 years = $50,000

7.17 Retained earnings $20,000 – Credit entry

Revaluation surplus $20,000 – Debit entry

Revaluation surplus $12,500 – Neither

Retained earnings $12,500 – Neither

The excess deprecation is the new depreciation amount of $50,000 less the old depreciation charge of $30,000 ($750,000/25 years) which is $20,000. This amount should be debited from the revaluation surplus and credited to retained earnings each year. Remember that both retained earnings and the revaluations surplus are credit balances in the trial balance.

7.18 The correct answer is: 1, 2, 3 and 4

The disclosure requirements in IAS 16 are comprehensive, particularly in relation to revalued assets.

7.19 The correct answer is:

Debit	Credit
Revaluation surplus $2,000	Retained earnings $2,000

In this question the consequence of the revaluation to $432,000 is a higher annual depreciation charge. The difference between the new depreciation charge based on the revalued carrying amount and the old depreciation charge based on £400,000 original cost is known as the excess depreciation.

IAS16 allows entities to transfer an amount equal to the excess depreciation from the revaluation surplus to retained earnings in the equity section of the statement of financial position. As X Co wishes to make the transfer, the calculations are as follows:

Old depreciation = $400,000/40 years = $10,000 New depreciation = $432,000/36 years = S12,000

Excess depreciation = $12,000 – $10,000 = $2,000

An amount of $2,000 which represents the excess depreciation can be transferred each year from the revaluation surplus to retained earnings.

The correct accounting entries would be:

Debit Revaluation surplus $2,000 Credit Retained earnings $2,000

8 Tangible non-current assets II

8.1 S 781 profit

	$
Cost	10,000
20X0 Depreciation (25% diminishing balance)	2,500
	7,500
20X1 Depreciation	1,875
	5,625
20X2 Depreciation	1,406
	4,219
20X3 Part exchange	5,000
Profit	781

Note. The road tax is an expense. It does not form part of the cost of the car.

ANSWERS

8.2 The correct answer is: $150,000

	$	$
Carrying amount at 1 August 20X0		200,000
Less depreciation		(20,000)
Less carrying amount of assets disposed of		
Proceeds	25,000	
Loss	5,000	
		(30,000)
Therefore, carrying amount		150,000

8.3 The correct answer is: Understated by $36,100

Debit	Property, plant and equipment	$38,000
Credit	Plant repairs	$38,000
Debit	Depreciation expense	$1,900
Credit	Accumulated depreciation	$1,900

Profit is understated by $38,000 – $1,900 = $36,100

8.4 The correct answer is: $2,500

$$\frac{\$30{,}000-\$6{,}000}{4\text{years}} \times \frac{5\text{months}}{12\text{months}} = \$2{,}500$$

8.5 The correct answer is:

Depreciation charge for year ended 31 December 20X4 (statement of profit or loss)	**Revaluation surplus as at 31 December 20X3 (statement of financial position)**
$	**$**
25,000	360,000

Depreciation of 2% per year indicates the building has a useful economic life of 50 years. At the date of the revaluation, the building has a remaining useful life of 40 years and therefore is depreciated over this period.

Depreciation charge – (1,000,000/40) = $25,000

Revaluation surplus – (1,000,000 – (800,000 – (800,000 × 2% × 10))) = $360,000

8.6 The correct answer is: Expenditure relating to the acquisition or improvement of non-current assets

Improvements are asset expenditure, repairs and maintenance are not.

8.7 The correct answer is: An illuminated sign advertising the business name

An illuminated sign advertising the business name will provide long-term benefits for the business and is therefore a non-current asset, ie asset expenditure. A replacement for a broken window is a repair, so it is expenditure in the statement of profit or loss. Repainting the restaurant is a repair and renewal expense so it would be likely to be treated as an expense in the statement of profit or loss. Cleaning of the kitchen floors is a maintenance cost and is therefore shown as an expense in the statement of profit or loss.

8.8 The correct answer is: Road tax

Number plates, stereo and delivery costs are included in the non-current asset cost of the car. Road tax is an annual expense in the statement of profit or loss.

8.9 The correct answer is: $40,900

	$
Water treatment equipment	39,800
Delivery	1,100
	40,900

8.10 The correct answer is: A computer used in the office

The first option is a receivable, the second and fourth options are inventory.

8.11 The correct answer is: 3 only

Items 1 and 2 are non-current assets. Only item 3 is a current asset.

8.12 The correct answer is: Assets which are expected to be converted into cash in the short-term

8.13 The correct answer is:

Purchase of motor vehicle on 30.9.X1			**Depreciation charge for year ended 30.11.X1**
DEBIT Non-current assets –cost	$15,000		$375
CREDIT Payables		$15,000	

Depreciation charge is 15,000 × 15% × 2/12 = $375

8.14 The correct answer is: $585,000

The revaluation surplus at 30 June 20Y8 was $600,000 ($1,600k – $1,000k). The old deprecation charge was $25,000 ($1,250,000/50 years) per year. The new depreciation charge is $40,000 ($1,600,000/40 years), so the excess depreciation is $15,000 per year. The balance on the revaluation surplus is therefore $600,000 – $15,000 = $585,000 at 30 June 20Y9.

8.15 The correct answer is: A profit on disposal $500

	$
Carrying amount at disposal (15,000 – 10,000)	5,000
Trade-in allowance	5,500
Profit on disposal	500

8.16 The correct answer is: $52,500

Carrying amount at 1.1.X3 = 100,000 – (100,000 × 2/5) = $60,000

New depreciation charge = Carrying amount/Revised useful life = $60,000/8 years = $7,500

Carrying amount at 31.12.X3 = $60,000 – $7,500 = $52,500

8.17 The correct answer is: $7,000

Carrying amount at 1.10.X8: 34,000 – ((34,000 – 4,000) × 3/5) = $16,000

Revised depreciation charge: (Carrying amount – revised residual value)/remaining useful life

= (16,000 – 2,000)/2 = $7,000.

8.18 The correct answer is:

DEBIT Depreciation charge	$6,000	
CREDIT Accumulated depreciation		$6,000

8.19 $ 792,000

In the 5 years to 31 December 20X5, accumulated depreciation on the building is $1,600,000 ×2% × 5 years = $160,000.

On revaluation on 1 January 20X6:

	DEBIT	*CREDIT*
	$	$
Building (2,250,000 – 1,600,000)	650,000	
Accumulated depreciation	160,000	
Revaluation surplus		810,000

The annual depreciation charge from 1 January 20X6 = $2,250,000/45 years remaining = $50,000. This is $18,000 more than the annual depreciation charge based on the historical cost of the asset.

This excess depreciation charge is transferred each year from revaluation surplus to retained earnings, and the revaluation surplus at 31 December 20X6 = $810,000 – $18,000 = $792,000.

8.20 The correct answer is: Profit of $7,500

Annual depreciation was initially $1,000,000/50 years = $20,000.

After revaluation, annual depreciation is $1,200,000/48 years = $25,000.

		$
Valuation, 1 January 20X5		1,200,000
Accumulated depreciation to 30 June 20X5	(6/12 × $25,000)	12,500
Carrying amount at 30 June 20X5		1,187,500
Sale/disposal price		1,195,000
Profit on disposal in statement of profit or loss		7,500

Note. The balance on the revaluation surplus at 30 June will be transferred to retained earnings, but this will not be reported as profit in the statement of profit or loss.

8.21 The correct answer is: $110,000

	$	$
Disposal proceeds		800,000
Carrying amount at 1 January 20X7	750,000	
Depreciation ((750,000/25) × 2)	(60,000)	
		(690,000)
Profit on disposal		110,000

The $50,000 held in the revaluation surplus will be transferred to retained earnings on disposal.

8.22 The correct answer is: $Nil

	$	$
Disposal proceeds		450,000
Carrying amount at 1 January 20X4	600,000	
Depreciation ((600,000/30) × 2)	(40,000)	
		(560,000)
Shortfall		(110,000)

There is no loss to be charged to profit or loss. The shortfall of $110,000 will be set against the $200,000 held in the revaluation surplus in respect of the building. The balance remaining in the revaluation surplus ($90,000) is transferred to retained earnings on disposal.

9 Intangible non-current assets

9.1 The correct answers are:

Research expenditure, other than asset expenditure on research facilities, should be recognised as an expense as incurred.	**TRUE**	
In deciding whether development expenditure qualifies to be recognised as an asset, it is necessary to consider whether there will be adequate finance available to complete the project.	**TRUE**	
Development expenditure recognised as an asset must be amortised over a period not exceeding five years.		**FALSE**

There is no requirement that development expenditure should be amortised over a period not exceeding five years.

9.2 The correct answer is: 2 and 4 only

In statement (1): Development expenditure must be capitalised if the criteria are met.

In statement (3): There is no time scale given by IAS 38 for amortisation.

9.3 The correct answer is: 2 and 3

Development costs are amortised over the useful life of the project. This is not confined to five years.

9.4 The correct answer is: GHK spent $12,000 researching a new type of product. The research is expected to lead to a new product line in three years' time.

Research expenditure can never be capitalised and must be recognised as an expense in the statement of profit or loss in accordance with IAS 38.

9.5 The correct answer is: 1, 2 and 3 only

A factory is a tangible asset as it has physical form. The others are intangible assets.

9.6 The correct answer is: $56,000

The $12,000 spent on converting seaweed does not meet the recognition criteria for an intangible asset and so must be recognised as an expense in profit or loss.

The $60,000 relating to the headache pill must be capitalised. Amortisation must start once commercial production begins and amortisation is $1,000 per month ($60,000/5 years).

The value at the year end represents $60,000 less four months' amortisation.

9.7 The correct answer is: $35,000

The $27,000 research costs are not directed towards a confirmed outcome and so should be recognised as an expense. The $8,000 market research costs suggest that the commercial viability of the product has not yet been determined and so the capitalisation criteria have not yet been satisfied.

9.8 The correct answer is: 2 and 3

The benefits flowing from the completed development are expected to be less than its cost.

Funds are unlikely to be available to complete the development.

A project that is not commercially viable would not be capitalised.

The company must have adequate resources to fund the project for it to be capitalised.

9.9 $ 25,000

The patent should be amortised over its useful life of ten years. (250,000/10) = $25,000

9.10 The correct answer is:

DEBIT Expenses	$5,000	
CREDIT Accumulated amortisation		$5,000

The amortisation charge is $15,000/3 years = $5,000 per annum. The double entry to record the amortisation is DEBIT expenses, CREDIT accumulated amortisation.

9.11 The correct answer is: To allocate the cost of an intangible non-current asset over its useful life

Amortisation is an application of the matching concept and allocates the cost of the intangible asset over its useful life (over the accounting periods expected to benefit from its use).

9.12 The correct answer is: 3 only

A patent has no physical substance and provides future economic benefits; it is therefore an intangible non-current asset.

Computer hardware is a tangible non-current asset as it is physical in substance and provides future economic benefits.

Operating software that operates the computer hardware on first glance may appear to be an intangible non-current asset. However, since it is an integral part of the computer hardware (which could not function without it), it is classed as part of the computer hardware.

A building extension has physical substance and provides future economic benefits and is therefore a tangible non-current asset.

9.13 The correct answer is: To allocate the cost of the intangible non-current asset over the accounting periods expected to benefit from its use

Amortisation is an example of the accruals concept and allocates the cost of the asset over the accounting periods expected to benefit from its use. Statement 1 is false. Statement 2 and statement 3 are also incorrect as the purpose of charging amortisation is not to establish a value for them in the financial statements.

9.14 The correct answers are:

Development expenditure must be recognised as an intangible asset in the statement of financial position, if the relevant criteria in IAS 38 Intangible Assets have beer met.	**TRUE**	
When a company engages in research, it may be searching for new products or looking to design possible new or improved processes.	**TRUE**	
Research expenditure is recognised as an intangible asset in the statement of financial position.		**FALSE**
The IAS 38 Intangible Assets definition of research includes the intention of the entity to complete the intangible asset and use or sell it, and also the ability to use or sell the intangible asset.		**FALSE**

Statements 1 and 2 are correct.

Statement 3 is incorrect as research expenditure is expensed to the statement of profit or loss.

Statement 4 is also incorrect as both intention of the entity to complete the intangible asset and use or sell it, and also the ability to use or sell the intangible asset are included in the IAS 38 definition of development expenditure, not of research.

10 Accruals and prepayments

10.1 The correct answer is:

Statement of profit or loss	Statement of financial position
$34,000 CREDIT	Rent received in advance (CREDIT) $3,000

	$	
Receipt		
1 October 20X1 ($7,500 × 1/3)	2,500	
30 December 20X1	7,500	
4 April 20X2	9,000	
1 July 20X2	9,000	
1 October 20X2 (9,000 × 2/3)	6,000	(3,000 CREDIT; rent in advance)
CREDIT to statement of profit or loss	34,000	

10.2 The correct answer is:

Rent expense	Accrual
$	**$**
100,000	10,000

	$
February to March 20X2 (22,500 × 2/3)	15,000
April to June	22,500
July to September	22,500
October to December	30,000
January 20X3 (30,000 × 1/3)	10,000
Rent for the year	100,000

Accrual 30,000 × 1/3 = 10,000

10.3 $ 33,100

	$
Payments made	34,600
Add: opening balance	8,200
Less: opening accrual	(3,600)
Less: closing balance	(9,300)
Add: closing accrual	3,200
	33,100

10.4 The correct answer is:

Rent receivable	Statement of financial position
$9,900	$1,000 in sundry payables

	$
Statement of profit or loss	
December to June 8,400 × 7/12	4,900
July to November 12,000 × 5/12	5,000
	9,900

Sundry payables 12,000 × 1/12 = 1,000 (December rent received in advance)

10.5 The correct answer is: $70,000

	$
August to September 60,000 × 2/12	10,000
October to July 72,000 × 10/12	60,000
	70,000

10.6 The correct answer is: $87,700

Diesel fuel payable account	$
Balance b/fwd	(1,700)
Payments	85,400
Balance c/fwd	1,300
Purchases	85,000

Cost of fuel used	$
Opening inventory	12,500
Purchases	85,000
Closing inventory	(9,800)
Transfer to SPL	87,700

ANSWERS

10.7 The correct answer is:

Accrued expense at 30 June 20X1	**Charge to SPL year ended 30 June 20X1**
$560	$3,320

ELECTRICITY ACCOUNT

			Accrued expense balance b/fwd	300
20X0:				
1 August	Paid bank	600		
1 November	Paid bank	720		
20X1:				
1 February	Paid bank	900		
30 June	Paid bank	840		
30 June	Accrued expense balance c/d $840 × $^2/_3$	560	SPL	3,320
		3,620		3,620

10.8 The correct answer is: $6,800

GAS SUPPLIER ACCOUNT

	$			$
Balance b/fwd	200			
Bank $600 × 12	7,200	28 February	Invoice	1,300
		31 May	Invoice	1,400
		31 August	Invoice	2,100
		30 November	Invoice	2,000
		30 November	Balance c/d	600
	7,400			7,400

GAS ACCOUNT

		$			$
28 February	Invoice	1,300			
31 May	Invoice	1,400			
31 August	Invoice	2,100			
30 November	Invoice	2,000	30 November	SPL	6,800
		6,800			6,800

10.9 The correct answer is: $27,500

$$\frac{5\text{months}}{12\text{months}} \text{x} \$24{,}000 = \$10{,}000$$

$$\frac{7\text{months}}{12\text{months}} \text{x } \$30{,}000 = \$17{,}500$$

Total rent: $10,000 + $17,500 = $27,500

10.10 $ 316,200

RENTAL INCOME ACCOUNT

	$		$
Opening rent owing	16,900	Opening rent in advance	24,600
Rent income (balancing figure)	316,200	Cash received	318,600
Closing rent in advance	28,400	Closing rent owing	18,300
	361,500		361,500

10.11 The correct answer is:

Statement of profit or loss	***Statement of financial position***
$	**$**
40,000	10,000 prepayment

Statement of profit or loss = $60,000 × 12/18 = $40,000.

Statement of financial position = $60,000 × 3/18 prepayment = $10,000.

10.12 The correct answer is:

Profit for the year	***Net asset position***
$15,000	$265,000

An accrual should be made for $10,000 ($30,000/3 months). The double entry to record the accrual in the accounts is:

DEBIT expenses (SPL)	$10,000
CREDIT accruals (SOFP)	$10,000

This reduces profit from $25,000 to $15,000

An accrual is a liability and so will reduce the net asset position from $275,000 to $265,000. Remember that net assets = assets – liabilities.

10.13 The correct answer is: A loss of $2,277

	$
Original loss	(1,486)
Accrued expense	(1,625)
Prepaid expense	834
Revised loss	(2,277)

10.14 The correct answer is:

Profit for the year	**Net asset position**
$75,000	$325,000

The double entry to record the accrual in the accounts is:

DEBIT expenses (SPL)	$50,000
CREDIT accruals (SOFP)	$50,000

This reduces profit from $125,000 to $75,000 and the net asset position from $375,000 to $325,000.

10.15 The correct answer is: $14,100

This question is designed to test whether candidates understand prepaid expenses and accrued expenses. The best way to approach the question is to prepare a simple working for the heat and light expenses. Prepaid expenses are those expenses that have already been paid but relate to a future accounting period and accrued expenses are expenses that relate to the current accounting period but have not yet been paid for. Using all the information available in the question, the working would look like:

Heat and light expenses for the year ended 31 March 2017

	$
Gas prepaid expenses 1 April 2016	1,000
Electricity accrued expenses 1 April 2016	(500)
Gas paid during year	5,000
Electricity paid during year	7,800
Gas accrued expenses 1 April 2017	2,000
Electricity prepaid expenses 1 April 2017	(1,200)
Total expense	14,100

10.16 The correct answer is: Debit Sales (marketing income) $2,000, Credit Deferred income $2,000

The income has been received in advance of being earned. Therefore, in the year end financial statement for 31 December 20X2, the journal is to debit sales (reducing income in the statement of profit or loss for this period). And credit deferred income (a liability account on the statement of financial position).

10.17 The correct answer is: Debit Prepaid expenses $5,500, Credit Insurance expense $5,500

The buildings insurance premium of $6,600 is for a period of 12 months. Only 2 months relates to the year ended 30 September 20X3, therefore $5,500 ($6,600 * 10/12) is an expense that relates to the following year.

As the expense has been paid in advance of the year end, there is a debit to prepaid expenses (asset account) and a credit to insurance (reduction in expenses).

10.18 Debit | Accrued expense $3,490 |

Credit | Rent expense $3,490 |

The journal entry to reverse the accrued expense is the opposite debit and credit entries to those required to record the original entry.

10.19 Debit | Accrued income $9,500 |

Credit | Rental income | | $9,500 |

This accrued income of $9,500 has been earned by the business at the year end. There is a debit to the accrued income account (an increase in assets) and a credit to rental income (an increase in income in the statement of profit or loss).

11 Receivables and payables

11.1 The correct answers are:

Payables represent money the business owes.	**TRUE**	
Payables are an asset.		**FALSE**
Receivables represent money owed to the business	**TRUE**	

Payables are a liability, so the second statement is false.

11.2 The correct answer is: $24,200

	$
Closing allowance (400,000 – 38,000) × 10%	36,200
Opening allowance	50,000
Decrease in allowance	(13,800)
Irrecoverable debts written off	38,000
Statement of profit or loss charge	24,200

11.3 The correct answer is: $12,600

	$
Irrecoverable debts written off	14,600
Reduction in allowance	(2,000)
	12,600

11.4 $ | 32,500 |

	$
Irrecoverable debt written off	28,500
Increase in allowance ((868,500 – 28,500) × 5% – 38,000)	4,000
	32,500

11.5 The correct answer is: $281,000

$146,000 + ($218,000 – $83,000) = $281,000

11.6 The correct answer is:

Debit	***Credit***
Bank	Irrecoverable debts expense

Because the debt has been previously written off, there is no receivable for which to offset the cash, therefore the double entry is DEBIT Cash, CREDIT Irrecoverable debts expense.

11.7 The correct answer is:

Statement of profit or loss	***Statement of financial position***
$	**$**
7,550	808,450

	$
Allowance required (5% × (864,000 – 13,000))	42,550
Existing allowance	(48,000)
Reduction in allowance	(5,450)
Irrecoverable debts written off	13,000
Statement of profit or loss charge	7,550

Net trade receivables = $864,000 – 13,000 – 42,550

= $808,450

11.8 The correct answer is: An increase in profit for the year

A decrease in the allowance is written back to profit or loss.

11.9 The correct answer is:

Debit	**Credit**
Allowance for receivables	Receivables

The debt needs to be fully written out of the books. An allowance was already made, so the SPL has already been charged ie:

DEBIT Irrecoverable debts (SPL)	X
CREDIT Allowance for receivables (SOFP)	X

Therefore, you only need to clear the balances from Receivables and Allowances for receivables, which the third option will do.

11.10 The correct answer is: rofit for the year is overstated by $16,000, receivables overstated by $16,000

An increase in the allowance for receivables will reduce profits and receivables. Gross profit will not be affected since allowances for receivables are dealt with below the gross profit line.

11.11 $ 1,800

Please enter whether it is CREDIT or DEBIT: CREDIT

		SPL charge
	$	$
Receivables allowance at 31.12.X1 (5% of $20,000)	1,000	
Receivables allowance at 1.1.X1	3,000	
Decrease in allowance		2,000
Irrecoverable debts written off		(1,000)
Debt recovered		800
Total credit to statement of profit or loss		1,800

11.12 The correct answer is:

Debit	***Credit***
Irrecoverable debts	Allowance for receivables

When a business first establishes an allowance for receivables the full amount of the allowance should be debited to Irrecoverable debts (statement of profit or loss) and credited to Allowance for receivables (statement of financial position).

11.13 The correct answer is: $650

		SPL charge
	$	$
Receivables allowance at year end	1,000	
Receivables allowance at beginning of year	850	
Increase in allowance		(150)
Irrecoverable debts written off		(500)
Total charge to statement of profit or loss		650

11.14 The correct answers are:

- An aged receivables analysis shows how long invoices for each customer have been outstanding
- Receivables are included in the statement of financial position net of the receivables allowance

An aged receivables analysis shows the outstanding balances owed by each customer analysed by how long they have been outstanding, usually 30, 60 and 90+ days. The receivables allowance is deducted from the receivables balance in the statement of financial position.

A credit limit is set by the credit control department of the business and is the maximum amount of credit each customer of that business can have. Credit limits are not applied to cash sales.

11.15 The correct answer is: $38,020

The trade payables are due to be paid within 12 months, the overdraft is repayable on demand.

11.16 The correct answer is: Fewer irrecoverable debts

Offering credit facilities will not reduce the level of irrecoverable debts.

11.17 The correct answer is:

Debit	**Credit**
Trade payables	Discounts received (income)

11.18 The correct answer is: 4 only

A payable is a person or institution to whom a business owes money. Statements 1 to 3 are examples of where money is owed to the business from others, so these are receivables. In the case of 2, if a company makes a loan or advance to an employee, this creates a receivable, being the repayment due from the employee.

Statement 4 is an example of where money is owed by the business to others, so this is a payable.

11.19 The correct answer is: 2 only

A payable is a person or institution to whom a business owes money eg, a supplier. The amount of money owed will be known exactly as it will have been billed or invoiced by the supplier. Therefore, the liability of $500 for invoiced goods (2) is a payable.

The amount owed to the tax authorities (1) is an accrual rather than a payable. An accrual or accrued expense is an expense which is charged against the profit or loss for a particular period, with a corresponding liability, even though it has not yet been paid for. The amount and timing of money owed will not be known exactly as it will not yet have been billed or invoiced. However, timing is virtually certain and a close estimate is usually known. This is recorded as the accrual.

The amount owed for the warranty claims (3) is a provision rather than a payable. A provision is a liability of uncertain timing or amount. The timing and/or amount are less certain than for an accrual – as is the estimate for the warranty claim.

11.20 The correct answer is: 3 and 6 only

The reconciling items are 3 and 6.

The supplier statement reconciliation would read as follows with items 3 and 6 as reconciling items. All the other transactions appear both in the ledger and the supplier statement.

Balance per supplier's statement 31 March 20X1	520
Less reconciling items:	
Payment (30 March) not on statement (3)	(385)
Invoice (#533) on statement, not on payables ledger (6)	(35)
Balance per payables ledger 31 March 20X1	100

Invoice #533 would then need to be investigated with the supplier to ensure it is not an error on their part. Once it is established it is a valid invoice, the ledger should be corrected to record this invoice.

11.21 The correct answers are:

An aged receivables analysis often analyses customers by the age of their invoices.	**TRUE**	
In an aged receivables analysis, customer invoices are often analysed in terms of the balances being due for 30+ days, 60+ days and 90+ days.	**TRUE**	
An aged receivables analysis is a useful tool when a business reviews the credit limits that should be offered to existing customers.	**TRUE**	
A year-end aged receivables analysis is included in the financial statements.		**FALSE**

An aged receivables analysis is a management tool used to identify credit customers at risk of non-payment of their debts. The aged receivables analysis does not form part of the financial statements. The trade receivables balance is included as a current asset on the statement of financial position, however, this balance is derived from the balance brought down in the general ledger.

11.22 The correct answers are:

- Offering credit facilities to customers is an administrative expense as a receivables function is required to monitor and chase overdue debts.
- Where credit customers are given a period of time to settle their debts, the business offering the credit is providing finance to them and during this time, is unable to use this money elsewhere in the business.

Statement 2 is not a cost of offering credit facilities to customers. Statement 3 is a benefit of offering credit facilities to customers.

12 Provisions and contingencies

12.1 The correct answers are:

A company should disclose details of the change in carrying amount of a provision from the beginning to the end of the year.	**TRUE**	
Contingent assets must be recognised in the financial statements in accordance with the prudence concept.		**FALSE**
Contingent liabilities must be treated as actual liabilities and provided for if it is probable that they will arise.	**TRUE**	

Contingent assets should not be recognised in the financial statements. However, they should be disclosed if it is probable that the economic benefits associated with the asset will flow to the entity. If it becomes probable that the transfer of economic benefits associated with a contingent liability will happen, then the contingent liability is no longer contingent and a liability should be recognised in the financial statements.

12.2 The correct answer is: 1 and 4 only

A possible transfer of economic benefits should be disclosed. Where transfer is probable a provision should be made.

12.3 The correct answer is: Disclose a provision of $50,000 and a contingent liability of $500,000

As the claim is unlikely to succeed, the potential settlement of $500,000 should be disclosed as a contingent liability note. However, given that the legal costs of $50,000 must be paid whether the claim is successful or not, this amount should be provided for in the company's financial statements.

12.4 The correct answers are:

The company gives warranties on its products at no extra cost to the customer. The company's statistics show that about 5% of sales give rise to a warranty claim.	**CREATE A PROVISION**		
The company has guaranteed the overdraft of another company. The likelihood of a liability arising under the guarantee is assessed as possible.		**DISCLOSURE NOTE ONLY**	

A provision is required for the products sold with a warranty and it should be calculated using the expected value approach. The guarantee is a contingent liability because it is possible that the company will have to pay out, if it was probable, then a provision would be required. If it was remote, no disclosure would be needed.

12.5 The correct answer is: All three statements are correct

12.6 The correct answer is: A charge of $1,086

The provision should be increased by $1,086, the double entry is therefore DEBIT Expenses, CREDIT Provision.

12.7 The correct answer is: A credit of $500

Doggard Co needs to reduce the provision by $500 ie a credit to the statement of profit or loss.

12.8 The correct answer is: A provision is a liability of uncertain timing or amount

A provision is a liability of uncertain timing or amount. A contingent liability is a **possible** obligation of uncertain timing or amount.

12.9 The correct answer is: A contingent liability

The statement is the definition of a contingent liability.

12.10 $ 3,000

Montague should include a provision of $3,000 in his year-end financial statements as this is the best estimate of the amount he will probably have to pay out.

12.11 The correct answer is: $150,000

Mobiles Co should provide on the basis of the expected cost. The expected cost would be calculated as (2.5% × 100,000 × $50) + (2.5% × 100,000 × $10) = $125,000 + $25,000 = $150,000.

12.12 The correct answer is: Each possible outcome weighted according to the probability of each outcome happening

The expected value approach to calculating a provision takes each possible outcome (ie the amount of money that will need to be paid under each circumstance) and weights it according to the probability of that outcome happening. The total amount of each weighted value is the provision.

12.13 The correct answer is: $18,500

	$'000
Provision required at 31.12.X1 = (0.05 × 150) + (0.20 × 25) + (0.75 × 60)	57.5
Provision b/f at 31.12.X0	64
Utilised during year	(25)
Increase required – charge to SPL	18.5
Provision c/f at 31.12.X1	57.5

13 Capital structure and finance costs

13.1 S 200,000

Paid ordinary dividend only: 10m × 2c = $200,000. The dividend paid on the redeemable preference shares will be recognised in the financial statements as a finance cost. Note. The Ordinary shares are 10c shares, not $1 each. Therefore, Alpha's share capital of $1,000,000 means it has $10 million shares in issue (at 10 cents each).

The proposed ordinary dividend will not be recognised in the financial statements, as this arose after the reporting date, and does not provide further evidence of conditions that existed at the reporting date. However, it should be disclosed in the notes to the financial statements.

Only the paid interim ordinary dividend will be recognised as a deduction from equity reserves in the statement of financial position.

13.2 The correct answer is: 1 only

A rights issue will increase cash and therefore assets. Retained earnings remain the same and the share premium account will be increased.

13.3 The correct answer is:

	Debit	**Credit**
	$	**$**
Bank	800,000	
Share capital		500,000
Share premium		300,000

Share capital will be credited with the nominal value of the shares – the balance goes to share premium.

ANSWERS

13.4 The correct answer is:

Ordinary share capital	*Share premium account*
$	**$**
105,000	173,000

	$
Ordinary shares at start of year	50,000
Add: bonus issue 50,000 × 50c	25,000
Add: new issue 60,000 × 50c	30,000
	105,000
Share premium at start of year	180,000
Less: bonus issue 50,000 × 50c	(25,000)
Add: new issue 60,000 × 30c	18,000
	173,000

13.5 The correct answer is:

SPL	**SOFP**
$9,000	$3,000

$9,000 is payable (SPL), but only $6,000 has been paid (April and July).

13.6 The correct answers are:

Dividends paid on ordinary shares should be included in the statement of profit or loss and other comprehensive income.		**FALSE**
Dividends paid on redeemable preference shares are treated in the same way as dividends paid on ordinary shares.		**FALSE**
The statement of profit or loss and other comprehensive income shows the gain on revaluation of non-current assets for the period.	**TRUE**	

Dividends paid on ordinary shares are included in the statement of changes in equity, not the statement of profit or loss and other comprehensive income. Dividends paid on redeemable preference shares are treated like interest on loans and are shown in the statement of profit or loss and other comprehensive income as a finance charge. The gain on revaluation of non-current assets is shown in the statement of profit or loss and other comprehensive income, as other comprehensive income.

13.7 The correct answer is:

Ordinary share capital	***Share premium account***
$	**$**
225,000	250,000

The correct answer is: Ordinary share capital 225,000, Share premium account 250,000.

		$
Ordinary shares		
Opening balance		125,000
Rights issue	250,000 × 25c	62,500
Bonus issue	150,000 × 25c	37,500
		225,000
Share premium		
Opening balance		100,000
Rights issue	250,000 × 75c	187,500
Bonus issue	150,000 × 25c	(37,500)
		250,000

13.8 $ 73,750

		$
July – September	1,000,000 × 8% × 3/12	20,000
October – March	750,000 × 8% × 6/12	30,000
April – June	750,000 × 8% × 3/12	15,000
	500,000 × 7% × 3/12	8,750
		73,750

13.9 The correct answer is:

	Debit	**Credit**
	$	**$**
Share capital account	25,000	
Share premium account		25,000

This is the transfer of the premium to the share premium account.

13.10 The correct answer is:

	Debit	**Credit**
	$	**$**
Share premium	100,000	
Ordinary share capital		100,000

A bonus issue does not involve cash but can be financed from the share premium account.

13.11 The correct answer is: 3 only

A bonus issue does not raise any funds, instead other reserves are capitalised and reclassified as share capital. A rights issue is an issue of shares for cash, the right to buy the shares are initially offered to existing shareholders. If the existing shareholders do not take up their right to buy the shares, then their shareholding will be diluted.

13.12 The correct answer is:

Ordinary share capital	***Share premium account***
$750,000	$310,000

	$
Share capital @ 1.1.20X0	500,000
Issue on 1.4.20X0 (200,000 @ 50c)	100,000
Bonus issue (1.2m ÷ 4) @ 50c	150,000
Share capital as at 31.12.20X0	750,000
Share premium @ 1.1.20X0	300,000
1.4.20X0 200,000 shares @ (130c – 50c)	160,000
Bonus issue (as above)	(150,000)
	310,000

13.13 The correct answer is: Statement of changes in equity

13.14 The correct answer is: Yellow has received a 20% interim dividend

From the information given we can see that Yellow has a credit against Dividends of $5,000 and a debit against Bank, which means that the company has received dividend income. The options for the correct answer are therefore narrowed down to the second or third option. We can now calculate the return from the investment in Blue as follows:

$5,000 Dividend/50,000 shares = 10c Dividend per share

10c Dividend/50c Share = 20% return

Part E: Preparing a trial balance

14 Trial balance (15 mark question)

14.1 **Task 1**

The correct answers are:

- Sales – $138,078 - **Credit**
- Purchases – $82,350 - **Debit**
- Carriage – $5,144 - **Debit**
- Drawings – $7,800 - **Debit**
- Rent and insurance – $6,622 - **Debit**
- Postage and stationery – $3,001 - **Debit**
- Advertising – $1,330 - **Debit**
- Salaries and wages – $26,420 - **Debit**
- Irrecoverable debts – $877 - **Debit**
- Allowance for receivables – $130 - **Credit**
- Receivables – $12,120 - **Debit**
- Payables – $6,471 - **Credit**
- Cash on hand – $177 - **Debit**
- Bank – $1,002 - **Debit**
- Inventory as at 1 June 20X5 – $11,927 - **Debit**
- Equipment at cost – $58,000 - **Debit**
- Accumulated depreciation – $19,000 - **Credit**
- Capital at 1 June 20X5 – $53,091 - **Credit**

Task 2

$ 82,937

	$
Opening inventory	11,927
Purchases	82,350
Carriage inwards	2,211
Closing inventory	(13,551)
	82,937

Task 3

Profit for the year will be decreased by the rent accrual and increased by the insurance prepayment.

ANSWERS

Task 4

$ 51,179

	$
Capital at 1 June 20X5	53,091
Profit for the year	5,888
Drawings	(7,800)
	51,179

Task 5

$ 30,300

	$
Equipment at cost	58,000
Accumulated depreciation at 1 June 20X5	(19,000)
Depreciation for the year (58,000 × 15%)	(8,700)
	30,300

15 Trade receivables and trade payables

15.1 $ 79,000

Credit sales = $80,000* – $10,000 + $9,000 = $79,000.

Note. *Total receipts of $85,000 include $5,000 in relation to cash sales. Therefore, receipts in relation to credit sales are $80,000.

15.2 The correct answer is: The supplier has allowed you $150 cash discount which you had omitted to enter in your ledgers

The first, third and fourth options would make the supplier's statement $150 **higher**.

15.3 The correct answer is: $38,100

	$
Opening balance	34,500
Credit purchases	78,400
Discounts	(1,200)
Payments	(68,900)
Purchase returns	(4,700)
	38,100

15.4 The correct answer is: $7,700 DEBIT

$8,500 – (2 × $400) = $7,700.

15.5 The correct answer is: 1, 2, and 5

Sales and refunds are posted on the **debit** side, changes in the allowance for receivables do not appear in the trade receivables account.

15.6 The correct answer is: $129,200

TRADE RECEIVABLES

	$		$
Opening balance	180,000	Bank receipts from credit customers	232,200
Credit sales	190,000	Irrecoverable debts written off	1,500
Refunds to credit customers	3,300	Sales returns	8,000
		Contras	2,400
		Closing balance (β)	129,200
	373,300		373,300

15.7 The correct answer is: $128,200

TRADE PAYABLES

	$		$
Purchases returns	41,200	Balance b/f	318,600
Bank payments to suppliers	1,364,300	Purchases	1,268,600
Discounts received	8,200	Refunds received from suppliers	2,700
Contras	48,000		
Balance c/f β	128,200		
	1,589,900		1,589,900

15.8 $ 307,100

TRADE RECEIVABLES

	$		$
Opening balance	308,600	Bank receipts from credit customers	148,600
Credit sales	154,200	Contras	4,600
Interest charged on overdue accounts	2,400	Irrecoverable debts written off	4,900
		Closing balance β	307,100
	465,200		465,200

ANSWERS

15.9 The correct answer is: $561,550

TRADE RECEIVABLES

	$		$
Opening balance	614,000	Bank receipts from credit customers	311,000
Credit sales	301,000	Irrecoverable debts written off	35,400
Interest charged on overdue accounts	1,600	Contras	8,650
		Closing balance β	561,550
	916,600		916,600

15.10 The correct answer is:

	Debit	**Credit**
	$	**$**
Trade receivables		608
Sales		608
Bank	608	
Trade receivables	608	

	DEBIT	*CREDIT*	$
Sales price			800
Less: 20% trade discount			120
Less: 5% settlement discount			32
Sale	PQ Co	Sales	608
Cash payment	Bank	PQ Co	608
			608

Goods are sold with a trade discount of 20% ($120) so this is deducted from the sales price. Therefore $640 ($800 – $120) is invoiced to the customer.

The invoice also offers a settlement discount of 5% of the invoiced amount ($32) for early payment. Although it is uncertain if the customer will take advantage of this, you expect that they will, and so the settlement discount must be reflected in the amount recognised as revenue when recording the sale. Therefore, $608 ($640 – $32) is recorded in sales, with a corresponding amount for trade receivables.

Since the customer did pay the discounted amount of $608, this amount is debited to bank and credited to the trade receivables.

The second option represents a situation where the customer was not expected to take up the discount at the time of the sale (and so revenue was recorded at the full invoiced amount), and did not take up the discount when they paid.

The third option represents a situation where the customer was expected to take up the discount at the time of the sale (and so revenue was recorded at the discounted invoiced amount), but did not take up the discount when they paid (and so the discount not taken was credited to revenue).

The fourth option represents a situation where the customer was not expected to take up the discount at the time of the sale (and so revenue was recorded at the full invoiced amount), but did take up the discount when they paid (and so the discount taken was debited to revenue).

15.11 The correct answers are:

- A payment was made by Bees Co to Nicholas Co but has not yet been received by Nicholas Co.
- Goods have been despatched by Nicholas Co to Bees Co but have not yet been received into Bees Co's warehouse

Both of the timing issues shown in options 1 and 2 could result in the balance per the supplier statement being higher than the balance per Bees Co's payables ledger account.

In respect of the transposition error, Bees Co has overstated the invoice in the payables ledger, making the balance per Nicholas Co's payables ledger higher. Therefore this does not explain why the balance per the supplier statement is higher than the balance per the payables ledger account.

The omission of a settlement discount in the payables ledger account would result in the balance per the payables ledger being higher than the balance per the supplier statement. Therefore, this does not explain the balances stated in the scenario.

15.12 The correct answer is: Bank receipts from customers, sales returns, irrecoverable debts written off, contras against amounts due to suppliers in the payable ledger

15.13 The correct answer is: $295,420

TRADE RECEIVABLES

	$		$
Balance b/d	318,650	Bank receipts from customers	181,140
Credit sales	163,010	Irrecoverable debts written off	1,390
Interest on overdue accounts	280	Sales returns	3,990
		Balance c/d β	295,420
	481,940		481,940

15.14 The correct answer is: $130,585

TRADE PAYABLES

	$		$
Returns outwards	27,490	Balance b/f	142,320
Payments to payables	196,360	Credit purchases (183,800 × 1.175)	215,965
Discount received	1,430		
Contra	2,420		
Balance c/f β	130,585		
	358,285		358,285
		Balance b/f	130,585

ANSWERS

15.15 The correct answer is: $32,123

Balance per ledger	$31,554	CREDIT
Discount	$53	DEBIT
Invoice	$622	CREDIT
Corrected balance	$32,123	

15.16 The correct answer is: An invoice received from a different supplier being allocated against Lima's account in the payables ledger

The balance per the payables ledger account is higher than the balance per the supplier statement. This could be caused by an invoice received from a different supplier being allocated against Lima's account in the payables ledger.

A contra entry being omitted from the supplier statement would result in the balance per the supplier statement being overstated. An invoice recorded on the debit side of the payables ledger would reduce the balance per the payables ledger below the balance per the supplier statement. Likewise, a bank payment duplicated on the payables ledger would reduce the amount shown as outstanding on the payables ledger. Therefore, options 1, 2 and 4 are incorrect.

15.17 The correct answer is: As a current liability

Trade payables are a current liability.

15.18 The correct answer is: DEBIT trade receivables $4,900, CREDIT sales $4,900, DEBIT bank $2,850, DEBIT sales $150, CREDIT trade receivables $3,000

Sales invoices:

Invoices amounting to $2,000 should be recorded net of the 5% settlement discount (ie, $1,900), since Y Ltd expects X to take the discount on these. The remaining $3,000 of invoices should be recorded at the full amount.

Therefore, sales = ($1,900 + $3,000) = $4,900, with a corresponding amount for receivables.

Payment received:

Y Ltd did not expect Z to take the settlement discount on invoices of $3,000, so these would have been originally recorded in sales and receivables at the full amount of $3,000.

However, Customer Z has paid £2,850 against receivables of $3,000. The difference of $150 is debited to sales and credited to receivables, thereby accounting for the discount.

15.19 The correct answer is:

	Debit	Credit
	$	**$**
Trade receivables	1,000	
Sales		1,000
Bank	950	
Sales	50	
Trade receivables		1,000

The invoice offers a settlement discount of 5% of the invoiced amount ($50) for early payment. Although it is uncertain if the customer will take advantage of this, you expect that they will not, therefore the full sales amount must be recognised as revenue when recording the sale, ie, $1,000.

As the customer did pay the discounted amount of $950, this amount is debited to bank, however this is against a receivable of $1,000, so the difference of $50 is debited to sales, to account for the fact that revenue has been reduced by the discount.

The first option represents a situation where the customer was expected to take up the discount at the time of the sale (and so revenue was recorded at the discounted invoiced amount), and took up the discount when they paid.

In the second option, the entry for the sale is correct. However, the entry for the payment is incorrect as the discount (which was not accounted for at the time of the sale) has still not been accounted for.

In the fourth option, the entry for the payment is correct. However, the entry for the sale is incorrect as it records the sale at the discounted amount, even though the customer was not expected to take the discount at the time of the sale.

15.20 The correct answer is: $517,500

The irrecoverable receivable has not been adjusted in the list of balances so will need to be written off. The early settlement discount was not expected to be taken at the time the invoice was raised and therefore the sale and receivable would have been recorded at the gross amount in accordance with IFRS 15 *Revenue from Contracts with Customers*. The correct adjustment for this discount when taken would be to DEBIT Revenue $12,500 CREDIT Receivables $12,500 in the general ledger. In a computerised accounting system and with the correct coding, this will automatically be adjusted in the relevant receivables ledger account too.

The calculation is as follows:

	$
Total list of receivables ledger balances	560,000
Irrecoverable debt write off	(30,000)
Settlement discounts	(12,500)
Adjusted total list of receivables ledger balances	517,500

15.21 The trade payables account shows the total of the amount owed to all [credit suppliers].

The trade payables account forms part of the [general ledger] and therefore is part of the [double entry] system.

15.22 The correct answers are:

- It is important that transactions with suppliers are recorded completely and accurately in the accounting records.
- The reconciliation enables the accounts assistant to verify to an independent source that the balances on the individual supplier accounts are accurate.

Where suppliers do not send supplier statements, the balances on individual supplier accounts cannot be reconciled to external documents. Having items in transit means that there will be differences between the balances on individual supplier accounts and the relevant supplier statement. However, so long as these items can be identified, a supplier statement reconciliation provides a useful verification of the completeness and accuracy of the payables ledger balances.

16 Bank reconciliations

16.1 The correct answer is: $657 overdrawn

$(565)o/d – $92 dishonoured cheque = $(657) o/d

16.2 $ 6,450 overdrawn

	$	
Balance b/d	5,675	o/d
Less duplicated standing order	(125)	
Add dishonoured cheque (450 × 2)	900	
	6,450	o/d

16.3 The correct answer is: $1,970

	$
Opening bank balance	2,500
Payment ($1,000 – $200) × 90%	(720)
Receipt ($200 – $10)	190
Closing bank balance	1,970

16.4 The correct answer is: $880 overdrawn

	$
Balance per bank statement	(800)
Unpresented cheque	(80)
Dishonoured cheque (affects bank general ledger account only)	
	(880)

16.5 The correct answer is: $11,200 overdrawn

Bank general ledger account	$	Bank statement	$
Balance	(8,970)	Balance b/f (bal fig)	(11,200)
Bank charges	(550)	Credit in error	(425)
		Unpresented cheques	(3,275)
		Outstanding deposits	5,380
	(9,520)		(9,520)

16.6 The correct answer is: $29,220 CREDIT

	$
Bank statement	(36,840)
Deposits credited after date	51,240
Unpresented cheques	(43,620)
Balance per bank general ledger account (o/d)	(29,220)

16.7 The correct answers are:

- Cheque paid in, subsequently dishonoured
- Bank charges

Dishonoured cheques and bank charges must be entered in the bank general ledger account.

16.8 The correct answer is: 1,4 and 5

Bank charges, direct debits and dishonoured cheques will all be entered into the bank general ledger account.

16.9 The correct answer is: $3,670 balance at bank

	$
Overdraft	(3,860)
Unpresented cheques	(9,160)
	(13,020)
Outstanding lodgements	16,690
Bank general ledger account	3,670

16.10 The correct answer is: 2 and 4

1 – The difference between the bank statement and the bank general ledger account is resolved by means of the reconciliation. 3 – Bank charges not entered in the bank general ledger account should be entered and the bank general ledger account balance corrected.

16.11 $ 11,200 overdrawn

Bank general ledger account	$	Bank statement	$
Balance	(8,970)	Balance	(11,200)
Bank charges	(550)	Credit in error	(425)
		Unpresented cheques	(3,275)
		Outstanding lodgements	5,380
	(9,520)		(9,520)

16.12 The correct answer is: $700 overdrawn

The bank is overdrawn.

	$
Overdraft	(38,600)
Outstanding lodgements	41,200
	2,600
Unpresented cheques	(3,300)
Overdraft	(700)

ANSWERS

16.13 The correct answer is: 1, 2, 5 and 6

The other two items are part of the bank reconciliation.

16.14 The correct answer is: $19,900 overdrawn

	$
Overdraft per bank statement	39,800
Less: deposits credited after date	(64,100)
Add: unpresented cheques	44,200
Overdraft per bank general ledger account	19,900

16.15 The correct answer is:

Bank general ledger account entry	**Bank reconciliation**
2, 4	1, 3

17 Correction of errors

17.1 The correct answer is: Credit note issued to a customer of $400 has been debited to trade receivables.

The credit note should have been **credited** to trade receivables, so the effect is doubled.

17.2 The correct answer is:

	Debit	**Credit**
	$	**$**
Sales returns	88	
Purchases returns	88	
Suspense accounts		176

Start by posting the adjustment in full:

	DEBIT	*CREDIT*
	$	$
Sales returns	384	296
Purchases returns	384	296
Suspense account		176

17.3 The correct answer is: The purchases returns total of $3,591 was included in the trial balance as a debit balance.

Purchases returns are returns to suppliers, which should therefore reduce the purchases balance – ie it should be a credit balance.

The first option would result in credits being higher than debits in the trial balance. The second and third options would not cause an imbalance.

17.4 The correct answer is: A purchase of goods for $50 being omitted from the trade payables account.

The second and third options would make the credit side $50 higher. The fourth option would have no effect.

17.5 The correct answer is: Plant and machinery purchased was debited to the purchases account.

This has debited a non-current asset to cost of sales which is an error of principle as it has broken the principles of accounting – ie that non-current assets should be capitalised and shown as assets on the statement of financial position.

17.6 The correct answer is: An error where one side of a transaction has been recorded in the wrong account, and that account is of the same class as the correct account.

A transaction has been posted to the wrong account, but not the wrong class of account.

17.7 The correct answer is: An error of original entry

This is an error of original entry.

17.8 $ 97,100

	$
Draft profit for the year	83,600
Add: purchase price	18,000
Less: additional depreciation (18,000 × 25%)	(4,500)
Adjusted profit for the year	97,100

17.9 The correct answer is: The trial balance being $10 higher on the credit side

The bank general ledger account was credited with $210 reimbursement of petty cash. However, the general ledger was posted with only $200 of expenditure (debits). Therefore, the credits are $10 higher than the debits.

17.10 The correct answer is: $14,600

$10,200 + $3,000 + $1,400 = $14,600.

17.11 The correct answer is: Understatement of gross profit by $40,000 and understatement of profit for the year by $30,000

Both errors will affect cost of sales and therefore gross profit, making a net effect of $40,000. Profit for the year will be further reduced by $10,000 missing from stationery expense.

17.12 The correct answer is: The debit side to be $96 more than the credit side

Debits will exceed credits by 2 × $48 = $96.

17.13 The correct answer is:

Errors of principle	Errors of transposition
Will not be revealed	Will be revealed

Errors of principle, such as recording an asset expenditure transaction as expenditure on the statement of profit or loss, would not be revealed by a trial balance because it would not create an inequality between total debits and total credits. Transposition errors are errors where figures (digits) are written in the wrong order in either a credit or a debit entry. This would create an imbalance between credits and debits, and so the error would be indicated by extracting a trial balance.

17.14 The correct answer is: $62,000

	DEBIT	*CREDIT*
	$	$
Non-current assets	85,000	
Receivables	7,000	
Trade payables		3,000
Bank loan		15,000
Allowance for depreciation, non-current assets		15,000
Inventory	4,000	
Accruals		1,000
Prepayments	2,000	
Bank overdraft		2,000
Capital (β)		62,000
	98,000	36,000

17.15 $ 46,000

Debit balances	$	$
Purchases	160,000	
Non-current assets	120,000	
Receivables	33,000	
Other expenses	110,000	
Bank	18,000	
		441,000
Credit balances		
Payables	27,000	
Capital	66,000	
Sales	300,000	
Purchase returns	2,000	
		395,000
Bank loan (credit balance)		46,000

17.16 The correct answer is:

Total assets (SOFP)	***Profit for the year***
$600,000	$100,000

$600,000 – $50,000 = $600,000. $150,000 – $50,000 = $100,000.

17.17 The correct answer is:

Statement of financial position	**Statement of profit or loss**
$560	$3,320

Statement of financial position $560, Statement of profit or loss $3,320.

ELECTRICITY ACCOUNT

	$		$
Balance b/fwd 300			
20X9:			
1 August Paid bank	600		
1 November Paid bank	720		
20Y0:			
1 February Paid bank	900		
30 June Paid bank	840		
30 June Accrual c/d $840 × $^2/_3$	560	SPL	3,320
	3,620		3,620

ANSWERS

17.18 The correct answer is:

Item 1	*Item 2*
Credit	Debit

This question tests whether candidates understand the nature of the errors and where the corrections need to be recorded.

Item 1 – there has been a transposition error recorded in the individual ledger, therefore an adjustment must be made on the credit side of the receivables ledger.

Item 2 – The credit note must be credited to the receivables ledger twice (both to remove the original debit entry and also to record the credit note on the credit side of the receivables ledger.

18 Suspense accounts

18.1 The correct answer is: 1, 2, 3 and 4

All items cause a trial balance imbalance.

18.2 The correct answer is: $2,440 DEBIT

SUSPENSE ACCOUNT

	$		$
Share capital	3,000	Opening balance	3,460
Motor vehicles	9,000	Plant asset (2,800 × 2)	5,600
		Petty cash (TB)	500
		Closing balance	2,440
	12,000		12,000

18.3 The correct answer is: $4,000 received for rent of part of the office has been correctly recorded in the bank general ledger account and debited to the rent account.

This results in a debit to the suspense account therefore reducing the balance.

The first option results in a credit to the suspense account and the third and fourth options do not affect the suspense account at all.

18.4 The correct answer is: 2 and 3 only

1: This entry has been correctly debited but to the wrong account – no effect on trial balance. 4: Double entry has been carried out although the wrong way round – no effect on trial balance

18.5 The correct answer is: DEBIT $210

SUSPENSE ACCOUNT

	$		$
Balance b/d	210	Gas bill[2] (420 – 240)	180
Interest[1]	70	Sales invoice[3] (2 × 50)	100
	280		280

Notes.

1 Error of omission

2 Transposition error

3 Error of commission

18.6 The correct answer is:

	Debit	Credit
	$	$
Plant and machinery	25,000	
Suspense account		25,000

The $25,000 currently held in the Suspense account needs to be posted to Plant and machinery.

18.7 $ 1,500 credit

Suspense account	$	
Opening balance	16,500	CREDIT
Discount received (credit discount received)	(5,100)	DEBIT
Transposition of cash received (credit trade receivables)	(9,900)	DEBIT
Balance remaining	1,500	CREDIT

18.8 The correct answers are:

- $4,600 paid for motor van repairs was correctly treated in the bank general ledger account but was credited to motor vehicles asset account.
- $9,500 paid for rent was debited to the rent account as $5,900.

Only the errors relating to the motor van repairs and the rent involve a suspense account entry to correct them. None of the other errors will cause a trial balance imbalance.

18.9 The correct answer is: Undercasting the purchases account by $100

The first, second and third options will result in a credit balance in the suspense account of $100.

18.10 The correct answer is: Recording a purchase of $130 twice in the purchases account

The third option would have no effect on the general ledger. The first and fourth options would not cause a trial balance imbalance.

18.11 The correct answer is: $840 DEBIT

The initial step in correcting the error of commission would be to make a credit entry of $1,400 in the suspense account as follows:

DEBIT Suspense account	$1,400	
CREDIT Trade receivables		$1,400

The trade receivables account and the suspense account would appear as follows:

TRADE RECEIVABLES

	$		$
Discounts allowed incorrectly debited	700	Suspense account error corrected	1,400
Balance c/d	700		
	1,400		1,400

SUSPENSE ACCOUNT

	$		$
Trade receivables account error corrected	1,400	Balance b/f	560
		(Remaining) Balance c/d	840
	1,400		1,400

The remaining balance on the suspense account is $840.

18.12 The correct answer is: A $1,500 bank balance has been shown in the trial balance as an overdraft of $1,500.

The third option is an error of principle where M Co has incorrectly capitalised an expense by performing the following double entry:

DEBIT Plant and equipment	$3,000	
CREDIT Bank		$3,000

As an equal debit and credit entry has been performed there will be no impact on the suspense account. M Co can correct this error of principle by debiting equipment repairs and crediting plant and equipment.

The first option is an error of commission where M Co has completed the following double entry in error:

DEBIT Bank	$3,000
CREDIT Trade payables	$3,000

The credit entry should have been recorded within the trade receivables account. Again, this error will not impact the suspense account. M Co can fix the error by debiting the trade payables account and crediting the trade receivables account.

The second option is an error of omission where the account is omitted from the trial balance entirely. Interest received is a credit balance and for the trial balance to balance a suspense account on the credit side would be required, not the debit side.

The fourth option will impact the suspense account as a positive bank balance (debit) has incorrectly been recorded as an overdraft (credit) on the trial balance. This will result in debits being understated by $1,500 and credits being overstated by $1,500. The error will have resulted in a debit entry to the suspense account of $3,000 in order for the trial balance to balance.

Therefore, the correct answer is the fourth option.

18.13 The correct answer is: $100,000 CREDIT

To identify the amount that would have been recorded in the suspense account it would be useful to consider how the share issue would have been recorded in the financial statements in full.

On 1 January 20X7 the rights issue would have resulted in a further 80,000 shares being issued (400,000 ordinary shares × 1/5) and would generate cash of $120,000 (80 000 × $1.50). On this date the share issue should have been recorded as follows:

DEBIT Bank	$120,000	
CREDIT Share capital (80,000 × 25c)		$20,000
CREDIT Share premium (80,000 × (1.50 – 0.25)		$100,000

Therefore, the answer is the fourth option as it is a credit to share premium that has been omitted from the financial statements.

Part F: Preparing basic financial statements

19 Shuswap

Exam focus point

This question provides excellent practice of the knowledge and skills required to tackle the longer questions that appear in Section B of the exam.

19.1 The correct answer is: Inventory should be credited with $140,000 at 31.12.20X4.

The sale was made after the year end but provides evidence that inventory was overvalued at the year end.

19.2 **Task 1**

$ 100,000 Loss /Profit

There is $100,000 loss on disposal.

	$'000
Carrying amount	700
Proceeds (5,000,000 – (4,000,000 × $1.10))	(600)
Loss	100

Task 2

$ 350,000

The depreciation adjustment is $350,000 (1,400,000 × 25%).

19.3 **Task 1**

The correct answers are:

- Issued share capital - **Debit**
- Share premium - **Debit**
- Bank - **Neither DEBIT nor CREDIT**
- Plant and equipment – cost - **Neither DEBIT nor CREDIT**
- Plant and equipment – disposal account - **Debit**
- Suspense account - **Credit**

The suspense account had been credited with the proceeds of the share issue. To clear the suspense account, the suspense account will be debited with a corresponding credit to share capital and share premium.

The suspense account also has a debit in respect of the sale of plant. Therefore, a credit is made to the disposal account to correctly record the sale of the plant with the corresponding debit to the suspense account to remove the original entry.

The bank and plant and equipment – cost accounts do not require adjustment.

Task 2

Share capital $ 8,000,000

Share premium $ 2,400,000

Balances after the suspense account has been cleared will be:

Share capital $8,000,000 (6,000,000 + (4,000,000 × 50c))

Share premium $2,400,000 (4,000,000 × 60c)

19.4 The correct answers are:

- Irrecoverable debts - **Debit**
- Depreciation adjustment (Task 2) - **Credit**
- Inventory adjustment (Task 1) - **Debit**

A debit is posted to the irrecoverable debts account in respect of the irrecoverable debts written off at 31 December 20X4.

20 Malright

20.1 The correct answers are:

- Buildings at cost - **On SOFP**
- Buildings, accumulated depreciation, 1 November 20X6 - **Not on SOFP**
- Plant at cost - **On SOFP**
- Plant, accumulated depreciation, 1 November 20X6 - **Not on SOFP**
- Bank balance - **On SOFP**
- Revenue - **Not on SOFP**
- Purchases - **Not on SOFP**
- Inventory at 1 November 20X6 - **Not on SOFP**
- Cash - **On SOFP**
- Trade payables - **On SOFP**
- Trade receivables - **On SOFP**
- Administrative expenses - **Not on SOFP**
- Allowance for receivables, at 1 November 20X6 - **On SOFP**
- Retained earnings at 1 November 20X6 - **Not on SOFP**
- $1 ordinary shares - **On SOFP**
- Share premium account - **On SOFP**

20.2 **Task 1**

The correct answers are:

- Trade receivables - **Neither DEBIT nor CREDIT**
- Administrative expenses - **DEBIT**
- Allowance for receivables - **CREDIT**
- Revenue - **Neither DEBIT nor CREDIT**

The amount included in the statement of profit or loss after the allowance is increased to 5% of trade receivables is $6,000 ((320,000 × 5%) – 10,000).

Task 2

The amount included in the statement of profit or loss after the allowance is increased to 5% of trade receivables is $ 6,000

The amount included in the statement of profit or loss after the allowance is increased to 5% of trade receivables is $6,000. ((320,000 × 5%) – 10,000).

20.3 **Task 1**

The correct answers are:

- Administrative expenses - **Neither DEBIT nor CREDIT**
- Cost of sales - **DEBIT**
- Buildings cost - **Neither DEBIT nor CREDIT**
- Plant costs - **Neither DEBIT nor CREDIT**
- Buildings accumulated depreciation - **CREDIT**
- Plant accumulated depreciation - **CREDIT**

Task 2

Buildings $ 37,000

Plant $ 22,000

Buildings $37,000 (740,000 × 5%)

Plant $22,000 ((220,000 – 110,000) × 20%)

20.4 $ 1,225,000

	$'000
Opening inventory	160
Purchases	1,140
Closing inventory	(75)
	1,225

20.5 **Task 1**

The correct answers are:

- Accrual - **Credit**
- Administrative expenses - **Debit**

Task 2

$ 10,000

The amount to be posted within the year end adjustment double entry above is $10,000 (15,000 × 2/3).

ANSWERS

21 Tonson

21.1 The correct answers are:

- Inventory at 1 November 20X5 - **Not P/L**
- Administrative expenses - **P/L**
- Share premium account - **Not P/L**
- Retained earnings at 1 November 20X5 - **Not P/L**
- Allowance for receivables at 1 November 20X5 - **Not P/L**
- Sales revenue - **P/L**
- Bank - **Not P/L**
- Returns inward - **P/L**
- Trade payables - **Not P/L**
- Loan note interest - **P/L**
- Trade receivables - **Not P/L**
- Purchases - **P/L**
- 7% loan notes - **Not P/L**
- Irrecoverable debts - **P/L**
- $1 ordinary shares - **Not P/L**
- Land at cost - **Not P/L**
- Buildings at cost - **Not P/L**
- Motor vehicles at cost - **Not P/L**
- Furniture and equipment at cost - **Not P/L**
- Accumulated depreciation at 1 November 20X5: Buildings - **Not P/L**
- Accumulated depreciation at 1 November 20X5: Motor vehicles - **Not P/L**
- Accumulated depreciation at 1 November 20X5: Furniture and equipment - **Not P/L**

21.2 Land $ 740,000

Buildings $ 1,065,000

Motor vehicles $ 128,000

Furniture and equipment $ 540,000

Buildings $1,065,000 (1,500 – 360 – (1,500 × 5%))

Motor vehicles $128,000 (240 – 80 – ((240 – 80) × 20%))

Furniture and equipment $540,000 (1,200 – 420 – (1,200 × 20%))

21.3 The correct answers are:

Inventory valuation adjustment	**DEBIT**	
Administrative expenses relating to November 20X6		**CREDIT**
Increase in allowance for receivables	**DEBIT**	
Outstanding wages and salaries	**DEBIT**	

21.4 **Task 1**

The bonus issue will [not affect] Tonson's cash balance.

Task 2

Share capital $ [1,980,000]

Share premium $ [20,000]

Share capital $1,980,000 (1,800 + 180)

Share premium $20,000 (200 – 180)

22 Emma

STATEMENT OF CASH FLOWS FOR THE YEAR ENDED 31 DECEMBER 20X2 (extract)

	$'000	Add/*Subtract*
Cash flows from operating activities		
Profit before tax/Profit after tax	350	
Adjustments for:		
Depreciation	90	Add
Loss on sale for non-current assets	13	Add
Profit on sale of non-current asset investments	(5)	Subtract
Movement in inventories	(48)	Subtract
Movement in receivables	(75)	Subtract
Movement in payables	8	Add
Income taxes paid	(190)	Subtract
Cash flows from investing activities		
Purchase of intangible non-current assets	(50)	Subtract
Purchase of tangible non-current assets	(201)	Subtract
Receipts from sale of non-current assets	62	Add
Cash flows from financing activities		
Proceeds from issue of share capital	60	Add
Dividends paid	(50)	Subtract
Long-term loan	100	Add

Workings

1 ***Depreciation charge***

	$'000	$'000
Depreciation at 31 December 20X2		340
Depreciation 31 December 20X1	290	
Depreciation on assets sold (85 - 45)	40	
		250
Charge for the year		90

2 ***Tax paid***

INCOME TAX

	$'000		$'000
Tax paid	190	1.1.X2 balance b/d	240
31.12.X2 balance c/d	290	Statement of profit or loss	240
	480		480

3 ***Purchase of tangible non-current assets***

TANGIBLE NON-CURRENT ASSETS AT COST

	$'000		$'000
1.1.X2 Balance b/d	595	Disposals	85
Revaluation (100 - 91)	9		
Purchases (balancing figure)	201	31.12.X2 Balance c/d	720
	805		805

4 ***Dividend paid***

RETAINED EARNINGS

	$'000		$'000
Dividends paid (balancing figure)	50	1.1.X2 Balance b/d	100
31.12.X2 Balance c/d	160	Profit for the year	110
	210		210

23 Sioux

STATEMENT OF CASH FLOWS FOR THE YEAR ENDED 31 DECEMBER 20X4

	$'000	*Add/Subtract*
Profit before tax/Profit after tax (indicate 'Before tax' or 'After tax' in right hand column)	2,350	Before tax
Depreciation (W)	1,250	Add
Profit on disposal (500 – 350)	(150)	Subtract
Movement in inventories	400	Add
Movement in receivables	(900)	Subtract
Movement in payables	500	Add
Tax paid	(600)	Subtract
Cash flows from investing activities		
Payments to acquire non-current assets (W)	(3,300)	Subtract
Proceeds from sale of non-current assets	500	Add
Cash flows from financing activities		
Proceeds from issue of loan notes (3,000 – 2,000)	1,000	Add
Dividends paid	(750)	Subtract
Net increase in cash (indicate 'Increase' or 'Decrease' in right hand column)	300	Increase
Cash at 1 January 20X4	100	
Cash at 31 December 20X4	400	

Working

Non-current assets

NON-CURRENT ASSETS AT COST

	$		$
Opening balance	8,000	Disposal	800
Revaluation	500	Closing balance	11,000
Additions (balance figure)	3,300		
	11,800		11,800

NON-CURRENT ASSETS – ACCUMULATED DEPRECIATION

	$		$
Disposal (800 – 350)	450	Opening balance	4,800
Closing balance	5,600	Charge for year (balance figure)	1,250
	6,050		6,050

24 Snowdrop

SNOWDROP LIMITED STATEMENT OF CASH FLOWS FOR THE YEAR ENDED 31 MAY 20X5

	$'000	Add/Subtract
Cash flows from operating activities		
Profit before tax/Profit after tax (indicate 'Before tax' or 'After tax' in right hand column)	1,032	Before tax
Adjustments for		
Depreciation	700	Add
Loss on disposal of non-current assts	20	Add
Movement in inventories	(80)	Subtract
Movement in receivables	(130)	Subtract
Movement in payables	85	Add
Income taxes paid (W1)	(145)	Subtract
Cash flow from investing activities		
Purchase of non-current assets (W2)	(2,800)	
Receipts from sales of tangible non-current assets	180	
Cash flows from financing activities		
Issue of share capital	1,280	Add
Dividends paid	(270)	Subtract
Repayment of long term borrowing	(100)	Subtract
Net increase/(decrease) in cash and cash equivalents (indicate 'Increase' or 'Decrease' in right hand column)	(228)	Decrease
Cash and cash equivalents at the beginning of period	170	
Cash and cash equivalents at end of period	(58)	

Note. Dividends paid should be shown under financing activities.

Workings

1 ***Tax paid***

TAXATION

	$'000		$'000
Tax paid (bal fig)	145	Balance b/fwd	145
Balance c/fwd	180	Statement of profit or loss	180
	325		325

2 ***Payments for tangible non-current assets***

TANGIBLE NON-CURRENT ASSETS

	$'000		$'000
Balance b/fwd	2,700	Depreciation	700
Additions (bal fig)	2,800	Disposals (carrying amount)	200
		Balance c/fwd	4,600
	5,500		5,500

25 Geofrost

Exam focus point

The statement of cash flows questions in this set have required use of the indirect method. Ensure you are also familiar with the direct method, as explained in Chapter 22 of your Workbook.

	$	Add/Subtract
Cash flows from operating activities		
Profit before tax/Profit after tax (indicate 'Before tax' or 'After tax' in right hand column)	15,000	Before tax
Adjustments for		
Depreciation	4,658	Add
Profit on disposal of non-current assets (W1)	(720)	Subtract
Movement in inventory	6,075	Add
Movement in receivables	(1,863)	Subtract
Movement in payables	3,198	Add
Tax paid (W2)	(4,090)	Subtract
Cash flows from investing activities		
Payments to acquire tangible non-current assets	(24,340)	Subtract
Proceeds from sale of non-current assets	2,694	Add
Cash flows from financing activities		
Proceeds from issue of share capital	1,869	Add
Repayment of long term borrowing	(2,300)	Subtract
Net increase/(decrease) in cash in cash and cash equivalents (indicate 'Increase' or 'Decrease' in right hand column)	181	Increase
Cash and cash equivalents at the beginning of period	634	
Cash and cash equivalents at end of period	815	

Workings

1 ***Profit on sale of tangible non-current asset***

	$'000
Sale proceeds	2,694
Carrying amount	1,974
Profit	720

2 ***Tax paid***

TAXATION

	$'000		$'000
Tax paid (bal fig)	4,090	Balance b/f	2,760
Balance c/f	3,020	Statement of profit or loss	4,350
	7,110		7,110

26 Incomplete records

26.1 The correct answer is: $1,587,500

	$
Opening inventory	386,200
Purchases	989,000
Closing inventory	(422,700)
Cost of sales	952,500

952,500 × 100/60 = 1,587,500

26.2 The correct answer is: Closing net assets plus drawings minus capital introduced minus opening net assets

26.3 The correct answer is: $8,400

Cost of sales = $114,000

Therefore, sales should be = $114,000 × 100/60 = $190,000

Theft = $190,000 – 181 600 = $8,400

26.4 $ 744,960

TRADE RECEIVABLES

	$		$
Opening balance	130,000	Bank receipts	687,800
Sales (balancing figure)	744,960	Irrecoverable debts	4,160
		Contra	2,000
		Closing balance	181,000
	874,960		874,960

26.5 The correct answer is: $331,760

TRADE PAYABLES

	$		$
Bank payments	302,800	Opening balance	60,000
Discounts received	2,960	Purchases (balancing figure)	331,760
Contra	2,000		
Closing balance	84,000		
	391,760		391,760

26.6 The correct answer is: $40,700

Cost of sales = $281,250 × 2/3 = $187,500

Loss of inventory = $228,200 – $187,500 = $40,700

26.7 The correct answer is: $57,000

	$
Opening inventory	318,000
Purchases	412,000
Closing inventory	(214,000)
	516,000
Notional cost of sales (612,000 × 75%)	(459,000)
Inventory lost	57,000

26.8 The correct answer is: $1,175,000

	$'000
Profit for the year	1,175
Add back depreciation	100
	1,275
Add: issue of shares	1,000
Less: repayment of loan notes	(750)
Less: purchase of non current assets	(200)
	1,325
Less: increase in working capital	(575)
Increase in bank balance	750

26.9 The correct answer is: $38,930

	$
Capital at 1 April 20X7	6,500
Add: profit (after drawings)	32,500
Less: sales tax element	(70)
Capital at 31 March 20X8	38,930

26.10 $ 937,050

TRADE PAYABLES

	$		$
Payments to suppliers	888,400	Opening balance	130,400
Discounts received	11,200	Goods taken	1,000
Closing balance	171,250	Refunds received	2,400
		Purchases (bal fig)	937,050
	1,070,850		1,070,850

26.11 The correct answer is: $669,375

Cost of sales

	$
Opening inventory	243,000
Purchases	595,400
Less: purchases returns	(41,200)
	797,200
Less: closing inventory	(261,700)
	535,500

Sales = 535,500 × 100/80 = $669,375

26.12 The correct answer is: $508,500

Sales = 381,600 + 6,800 + 112,900 + 7,200 = $508,500

26.13 The correct answer is: $140,000

Cost of sales: $17,000 + $91,000 – $24,000 = $84,000

Sales	100%
Cost of sales	60%
Gross profit	40%

Sales: $84,000/60% = $140,000

26.14 The correct answer is: $32,640

	$
Sales (100%)	64,800
Cost of sales (70%)	45,360
Gross profit (30%)	19,440
Opening inventory	28,400
Purchases	49,600
	78,000
Calculated closing inventory (bal fig)	(32,640)
Cost of sales	45,360
Calculated closing inventory	32,640
Actual closing inventory	
Destroyed by fire	32,640

26.15 The correct answer is: $900,000

	$
Cost of sales	
Opening inventory	38,000
Purchases	637,000
Less: closing inventory	(45,000)
	630,000

Sales 630,000 × 100/70 = $900,000

26.16 The correct answer is: $138,000

Opening net assets + Profit + Capital introduced – Drawings = Closing net assets

210,000 + Profit + 100,000 – 48,000 = 400,000

Profit = $138,000

27 Company financial statements

27.1 The correct answer is: 2, 3 and 4

The revaluation surplus is part of equity. Dividends paid on redeemable preference shares are treated like interest paid on loans, and are therefore accrued for as finance costs in the financial statements.

27.2 The correct answers are:

- Surplus on revaluation of properties
- Issue of share capital

Profit on disposal of properties will be included in profit in the statement of profit or loss and other comprehensive income. Equity dividends proposed after the reporting period are disclosed by note.

27.3 The correct answer is:

Receivables and prepayments	*Payables and accruals*
$	$
22,240	NIL

	$
Receivables and prepayments	
Insurance 9,000 × 8/12 prepayment	6,000
Loan (receivable)	12,000
Interest due 12,000 × 2% (receivable)	240
Rent due (receivable)	4,000
	22,240

27.4 The correct answer is: 1, 2, and 3

All of these items must be disclosed, either on the face of the main financial statements or in the notes. Although dividends proposed are not included in the statement of changes in equity, they must still be disclosed in the notes.

27.5 The correct answers are:

In preparing a statement of cash flows, either the direct or the indirect method may be used. Both lead to the same figure for net cash from operating activities.	**TRUE**	
Loan notes can be classified as current or non-current liabilities.	**TRUE**	
Financial statements must disclose a company's total expense for depreciation, if material.	**TRUE**	
A company must disclose, by note, details of all adjusting events allowed for in the financial statements.		**FALSE**

Adjusting events after the reporting period should be adjusted for, not just disclosed.

27.6 The correct answers are:

- Dividends on equity shares paid during the period
- Proceeds of an issue of ordinary shares

The loss on sale of investments will have been recognised in the statement of profit or loss and other comprehensive income. Dividends proposed after the year end are disclosed in the notes, they are not recognised in the financial statements.

27.7 The correct answer is: Loan stock

Loan stock is a non-current liability.

The other items are presented under equity.

27.8 The correct answer is:

DEBIT Bank	$260,000	
CREDIT Ordinary share capital		$200,000
CREDIT Share premium account		$60,000

The total will be $260,000, of which $60,000 will be credited to share premium.

27.9 The correct answer is: 3 only

A revaluation surplus arises when a non-current asset is **revalued**. Loan notes are not part of share capital.

27.10 $ 22,500

The under provision for the previous year of $2,500 plus the provision for the current year of $20,000 gives a charge to the statement of profit or loss of $22,500.

28 Disclosure notes

28.1 The correct answer is: To provide more detail for the users of financial statements about the information in the statement of financial position and statement of profit or loss and other comprehensive income.

Disclosure notes provide more detail about the information in the main financial statements.

28.2 The correct answer is: 2 and 3 only

A reconciliation of the opening and closing carrying amounts is required by IAS 16 *Property, Plant and Equipment* for tangible non-current assets and by IAS 38 *Intangible Assets* for intangible assets.

28.3 The correct answer is: 2 and 3 only

IAS 2 *Inventories* requires disclosure of the accounting policies adopted in measuring inventories, including the cost formula used, the total carrying amount of inventories and the carrying amount in classifications appropriate to the entity and the carrying amount of inventories carried at net realisable value.

28.4 The correct answer is: 1, 2 and 3 only

IAS 38 *Intangible Assets* does not require the net realisable value of deferred development costs to be disclosed.

28.5 The correct answer is: Both 1 and 2

Both statements are correct.

28.6 The correct answer is: Contingent liabilities

These are the disclosure requirements given in IAS 37 *Provisions, Contingent Liabilities and Contingent Liabilities* for contingent liabilities.

28.7 The correct answer is: 2, 3 and 4 only

IAS 16 *Property, Plant and Equipment* does not require disclosure of the market value of all tangible non-current assets.

28.8 The correct answer is: 1 and 3 only

Inventories must be valued at the lower of cost and net realisable value. The amount of any write-down in the period must be disclosed, and so too must the carrying amount of inventories classified by type and the cost of inventories recognised as an expense in the period. There is no requirement to disclose the original cost of inventories that have been written down in value.

28.9 The correct answer is: An estimate of the financial effect of the event, unless a reasonable estimate cannot be made

IAS 10 requires disclosure of the nature of material non-adjusting events after the reporting period and either an estimate of the financial effect of the event or a statement that a reasonable estimate cannot be made.

29 Events after the reporting period

29.1 The correct answer is: All of them

All of these events are indicative of conditions that existed at the reporting period.

29.2 The correct answers are:

- The bankruptcy of a major customer, with a substantial debt outstanding at the end of the reporting period
- Sale for less than cost of some inventory held at the end of the reporting period

The second and third options do not affect the company's position at the end of the reporting period.

29.3 The correct answer is: 1 and 2 only

These affect the valuation of receivables and inventory at the end of the reporting period.

29.4 The correct answer is: Issue of shares or loan notes, changes in foreign exchange rates, major purchases of non-current assets

These events are adjusting if discovered between the reporting date and the date the financial statements are authorised for issue as they provide evidence about conditions that existed at the reporting date: insolvency of an account receivable which was outstanding at the end of the reporting period, discovery of fraud or error which shows that the financial statements were incorrect, sale of inventory which gives evidence about its value at the end of the reporting period.

29.5 The correct answer is: 2 and 4

2 and 4 both affect the valuation of assets at the end of the reporting period.

29.6 The correct answer is:

Adjust	***Disclose***	***Do nothing***
3	1, 2	

IAS 10 *Events After the Reporting Period* requires the financial statements to be adjusted for events that reflect conditions that existed at the reporting date. Only Event 3 is indicative of conditions at the reporting date – ie the recoverability of the receivable balance. Events 1 and 2 are non-adjusting events, however, they are material so they should be disclosed.

29.7 The correct answer is: None of them

None of these events require adjustment in the financial statements.

29.8 The correct answer is: An event that occurs between the reporting date and the date on which the financial statements are authorised for issue that provides further evidence of conditions that existed at the reporting date

An adjusting event after the reporting date is event that occurs between the reporting date and the date on which the financial statements are authorised for issue that provides further evidence of conditions that existed at the reporting date. The event must occur **after** the reporting period but **before** the date the financial statements are authorised for issue.

29.9 The correct answer is: The nature of the event and an estimate of the financial effect (or a statement that such an estimate cannot be made)

30 Statements of cash flows

30.1 The correct answer is: 2 and 5 only

Only the proceeds of a share issue and dividends received involve the movement of cash.

30.2 The correct answer is: 2, 3 and 4

Loss on sale of non-current assets should be added back to profit before interest and tax, not deducted.

30.3 The correct answer is:

	$
Addition to operating profit	990,000

	$
Add: depreciation charge	980,000
Less: profit on sale of assets	(40,000)
Less: increase in inventories	(130,000)
Add: decrease in receivables	100,000
Add: increase in payables	80,000
Addition to operating profit	990,000

30.4 The correct answer is: 1 and 4 only

Depreciation should be added back as it is not a cash flow and proceeds of sale of non-current assets appears under 'investing' cash flows.

30.5 The correct answer is: None of them

The items will be classified as follows:

(1) Proceeds from sale of premises appears under investing activities.

(2) Dividends received appears under operating or investing activities.

(3) A bonus issue of shares is not a cash flow.

30.6 The correct answer is: 3 only

In respect of the other options:

(1) The direct and indirect methods will give the correct figure.

(2) A rights issue of shares is a cash flow.

(4) The profit on sale of a non-current asset appears as an adjustment to profit in order to reach net cash flow from operations.

30.7 The correct answers are:

- Depreciation charges should have been added, not deducted.
- Increase in payables should have been added, not deducted.

The correct answers are: Depreciation charges should have been added, not deducted. Increase in payables should have been added, not deducted.

30.8 The correct answer is: 2 and 4

Neither a proposed dividend nor a bonus issue of shares involves the movement of cash.

30.9 The correct answer is: Increase in payables, decrease in inventories, profit on sale of plant, depreciation, decrease in receivables

Proceeds from sale of equipment are included in investing activities.

30.10 The correct answer is: $10,000 inflow

		$'000
Cash flows from financing:		
Issue of share capital	(120 + 60) – (80 + 40)	60
Repayment of bank loan	(100 – 150)	(50)
		10

30.11 The correct answer is: 2 and 4

Decrease in inventories should be added, decrease in payables should be deducted.

30.12 The correct answer is: 1 and 3 only

The corrected extract is as follows:

	$'000
Net cash flow from operating activities	
Profit before tax	484
Depreciation charges	327
Profit on sale of property, plant and equipment	(35)
Increase in inventories	(74)
Decrease in trade and other receivables	41
Increase in trade payables	29
Cash generated from operations	772

30.13 The correct answer is: None of them

Interest received and proceeds from the sale of property are cash flows from investing activities; taxation paid is a cash flow from operating activities.

30.14 The correct answer is: A statement of cash flows prepared using the direct method produces the same figure for net cash from operating activities as a statement produced by the indirect method.

The net cash flows from operating activities will be the same using the two methods.

30.15 $ 204,000

	$'000
Carrying amount of assets at beginning of the year	462
Increase in revaluation surplus during the year	50
Carrying amount of assets disposed of (110 – 65)	(45)
Depreciation charge for the year	(38)
	429
Carrying amount of assets at end of the year	633
Purchases of property, plant and equipment during the year	204

30.16 The correct answer is:

Loss on disposal	*Proceeds from sale*
Add as an adjustment in the calculation of cash flows from operating activities	Include in cash flows from investing activities

A loss on disposal of a non-current asset is added back as an adjustment in the calculation of cash flows from operating activities (using the indirect method), and the cash received from the disposal is included within cash flows from investing activities

30.17 $ 3,600

Cash flows from operating activities	$
Cash received from customers ($400 + $33,400 – $900)	32,900
Cash paid to suppliers ($1,000 + $18,500 – $2,550)	(16,950)
Cash paid to employees ($1,500 + $9,500 – $750)	(10,250)
Interest paid	(2,100)
Net cash flow from operating activities	3,600

30.18 The correct answer is: A business may make a profit but have negative cash flow.

30.19 The correct answer is: Jo is correct. A business that does not have cash available to fund operations is likely to fail.

30.20 The correct answer is: There is an opportunity to reclassify some cash outflows that might have been reported in the operating section as investing cash outflows.

30.21 The correct answer is: $729,000

This question is focused around the cash actually received during the financial year ended 31 March 20X7. Therefore, we need to consider (i) the amount owed to the company at the beginning of the year that will be paid during the financial year ie the receivables at 1 April 20X6, (ii) the sales during the year, and (iii) the amounts owed to the company at the end of the year ie receivables at 31 March 20X7.

The calculation can be summarised as follows:

	$
Receivables at 1 April 20X6	163,000
Sales during the year	750,000
Total	913,000
Less receivables at 31 March 20X7	184,000
	729,000

Part G: Preparing simple consolidated financial statements

31 Swing and cat

Exam focus point.

This question provides excellent practice of the knowledge and skills required to tackle long questions that may appear in Section B of the exam.

31.1

	$'000	$'000
Fair value of consideration transferred		120
Plus fair value of non-controlling interest at acquisition		40
Less fair value of net assets acquired as represented by:		
Ordinary share capital	100	
Retained earnings	50	
		(150)
Goodwill		10

31.2 $ 10,000

	$
Profit on intra-group sale (100,000 – 80,000)	20,000
Unrealised profit (50% × 20,000)*	10,000

*50% of the inventories from the intra-group sales remain in inventories at the year end, therefore the unrealised profit is 50% of the overall profit made on the intra-group sales. The rest of the profit from the intra-group sales is now realised as the inventories have been sold outside the group.

31.3 $ 3,410,000

	$'000
Swing	2,900
Cat	600
Intragroup purchases	(100)
Unrealised profit	10
	3,410

31.4 The correct answers are:

- Non-controlling interest describes shares in the subsidiary not held by the parent.
- 20% of Cat's profit for the year will be allocated to the non-controlling interest.

ANSWERS

31.5

	Swing	Cat
	$'000	$'000
Per question	400	200
Adjustment	(10)	
Pre-acquisition retained earnings		(50)
Total		(150)
Group share of Cat	120	
Group retained earnings	510	

Group share of Cat (80% x 150)

32 Black and Bury

32.1 $ 21,000,000

	$'000
Fair value of net assets acquired:	
Share capital	30,000
Retained earnings	2,000
Goodwill acquired	800
Less fair value of NCI	(11,800)
Consideration transferred	21,000

32.2 **Task 1**

The correct answer is: Eliminated on consolidation

This is an intragroup item.

Task 2

The correct answer is: Included in consolidated current liabilities

This is not intragroup, it is owed to third parties. It is not deducted from profit as it is a distribution, not an expense.

32.3 **Task 1**

$ 1,440,000

The unrealised profit is $1,440,000 (12m × 40% × 30%)

Task 2

The correct answers are:

- Inventory - **CREDIT**
- Retained earnings - **DEBIT**

32.4 The correct answers are:

- Payables - **Debit**
- Receivables - **Credit**

This removes the intragroup amount from payables and receivables.

32.5 **Task 1**

$ 4,500,000

Non-controlling interest in the consolidated SPL is $4,500,000 (15,000,000 × 30%)

	$	Add/Subtract
	$'000	
Fair value at acquisition	11,800	
Share of post-acquisition retained earnings (in right hand column, indicate whether to 'Add' or 'Subtract' this)	2,484	Add
Total	14,284	

Non-controlling interest in the consolidated SFP:

	$'000
Fair value at acquisition	11,800
Share of post-acquisition retained earnings ((10,280 – 2,000) × 30%)	2,484
Total	14,284

33 Prestend

33.1

	$	Add/Subtract
	$'000	
Fair value of consideration transferred	3,345	
Fair value of non-controlling interest at acquisition (in right hand column, indicate whether to 'Add' or 'Subtract' this)	1,415	Add
Total A	4,760	
Fair value of net assets acquired:		
Ordinary share capital	4,000	
Retained earnings	60	
Total B	4,060	

33.2 The correct answer is: A minus 100% B

33.3 The correct answer is: $20,000

Unrealised profit on intragroup sales = $20,000 (240,000 × 20/120 × 50%)

33.4 The correct answers are:

- Ownership of more than 50% of equity shares
- Power to appoint or remove the majority of board members

Ownership of preference shares does not give control as they are usually non-voting. Significant influence is not the same as control.

33.5

	Prestend	*Northon*	Add/Subtract
	$'000	$'000	
Per question	525	200	
Adjustment for unrealised profit	(20)		Subtract
Pre-acquisition retained earnings		(60)	Subtract
Total Northon		140	
Group share of Northon	98		
Group retained earnings	603		

34 Liverton and Everpool

34.1

	$
	$'000
Fair value of consideration transferred	3,500
Fair value of non-controlling interest	1,000
Total	4,500
Fair value of net assets acquired:	
Share capital	4,000
Retained earnings	200
Total	4,200
Goodwill	300

34.2 $ 48,000

Unrealised profit: ((200,000 – 120,000) × 60%) = $48,000

34.3

	$
	$'000
Sales revenue	8,800
Cost of sales	(4,998)
Gross profit	3,802
Distribution costs	(1,590)
Administrative expenses	(1,020)

	$
	$'000
Profit before tax	1,192
Income tax expense	(480)
Profit for the year	712
Profit attributable to:	
Owners of the parent	647
Non-controlling interest	65
	712

CONSOLIDATED STATEMENT OF PROFIT OR LOSS FOR THE YEAR ENDED 31 MAY 20X6

	$'000
Sales revenue (6,400 + 2,600 – 200)	8,800
Cost of sales (3,700 + 1,450 – 200 + 48)	(4,998)
Gross profit	3,802
Distribution costs (1,110 + 490)	(1,590)
Administration expenses (700 + 320)	(1,020)
Profit before tax	1,192
Income tax (400 + 80)	(480)
Profit for the year	712
Profit attributable to	
Owners of the parent	647
Non-controlling interest (25% × 260)	65
	712

35 Consolidated financial statements

35.1 The correct answer is: $122,000

	$	$
Fair value of consideration		270,000
Plus fair value of NCI at acquisition		42,000
Less net acquisition-date fair value of identifiable assets acquired and liabilities assumed:		
Share capital	100,000	
Retained earnings at acquisition	90,000	
		190,000
Goodwill in statement of financial position		122,000

ANSWERS

35.2 The correct answer is: $49,000

Non-controlling interest	$
Fair value of NCI at acquisition	42,000
Plus NCI's share of post-acq'n retained earnings (10% × (160 – 90))	7,000
NCI at reporting date	49,000

35.3 $ 273,000

	$
Alpha retained earnings	210,000
Group share post-acq'n ret'd earnings: Beta ((160,000 – 90,000) × 90%)	63,000
	273,000

35.4 The correct answer is: Iota Co and Kappa Co

Iota is a subsidiary as Gamma has power to cast a majority of votes at meetings of the board of directors. Kappa is a subsidiary as Gamma owns >50% of the ordinary shares of Kappa; it doesn't make any difference that Kappa is based overseas or pays tax in that country. Zeta is not a subsidiary of Gamma because Gamma's investment in the non-voting preference shares will not give it the ability to control Zeta.

35.5 The correct answer is: $95,000

	$	$
Fair value of consideration		280,000
Plus fair value of NCI at acquisition		65,000
Less net acquisition-date fair value of identifiable assets acquired and liabilities assumed:		
Share capital	140,000	
Share premium	50,000	
Retained earnings at acquisition	60,000	
		250,000
Goodwill		95,000

35.6 The correct answer is: $73,000

Non-controlling interest	$
Fair value of NCI at acquisition	65,000
Plus NCI's share of post-acq'n retained earnings (20% × (100 – 60))	8,000
NCI at reporting date	73,000

35.7 The correct answer is: $590,000

	$'000
Fair value of net assets acquired:	
Ordinary shares	400
Retained earnings at 1 January 20X7	100
Retained earnings for 9 months to acquisition date (80 × 9/12)	60
	560
Add goodwill	30
	590

35.8 The correct answer is: 35% of the profit for the year of Deciduous should be added to Evergreen's consolidated profit before tax.

Deciduous is an associate of Evergreen. Under equity accounting, the Evergreen group's share of the profit for the year of Deciduous is added to the group profit before tax.

35.9 The correct answer is: $560,000

	$
Mercedes Co retained earnings	450,000
Benz Co retained earnings	120,000
Unrealised profit in closing inventory (50,000 × 25/125)	(10,000)
Consolidated retained earnings at 31 March 20X9	560,000

35.10 The correct answer is: $99,000

	$	$
Fair value of consideration		300,000
Plus fair value of NCI at acquisition		75,000
Less net acquisition-date fair value of identifiable assets acquired and liabilities assumed:		
Share capital	100,000	
Retained earnings at acquisition	156,000	
Fair value adjustment at acquisition	20,000	
		276,000
Goodwill		99,000

35.11 The correct answer is: $627,000

	$'000
Unrealised profit (30,000 × 25% × 40%)	3
Gross profit (330 + 300 – 3)	627

35.12 The correct answers are:

- Aye Co owns 25% of the ordinary share capital of Bee Co, which means that Bee Co is an associate of Aye Co.
- Cee Co can appoint 4 out of 6 directors to the board of Dee Co, which means that Cee Co has control over Dee Co.

An investor must have significant influence over the investee in order for the investee to be classified as an associate. If the investor holds 20% or more of the voting power of the entity, significant influence can be assumed (unless it can clearly be shown that this is not the case). Therefore, the first option is true. For an investee to be classified as a subsidiary, the investor (the parent) must have control over the investee (the subsidiary). Control can be demonstrated if the investor has the power to appoint the majority of board members of the investee, so the second option is true. The third option is incorrect because the power to govern the financial and operating policies of Fef make Fef a subsidiary of Ear. Likewise, the fourth option is incorrect as the power to govern the financial and operating policies of Hay makes Hay a subsidiary of Gee.

35.13 The correct answer is: An amount is shown in the statement of financial position under 'investments' being the original cost paid for the investment, this amount does not change. Dividends received from Tangerine are recognised in the statement of profit or loss of Clementine Co.

Tangerine is an associate of Clementine, however because Clementine has no other investments in other companies, it will not produce consolidated financial statements. Under IAS 27, Tangerine can choose to account for the investment at cost, or the equity method. In this scenario, it has chosen to account for the investment at cost, therefore the investment will appear in the single company financial statements of Clementine as a simple investment. The statement of financial position will show an investment at cost and the statement of profit or loss will show dividends received from Tangerine. If Clementine instead did produce consolidated financial statements, Tangerine would have to be accounted for in the consolidated financial statements using the equity method.

35.14 The correct answer is: 1 and 3 only

A parent may hold less than 50% of the share capital but more than 50% of the voting rights. Goodwill only appears in the **consolidated** statement of financial position. Consolidated financial statements present the substance of the relationship between parent and subsidiaries, rather than the legal form.

35.15 The correct answer is: Q Co and R Co only

S is not a subsidiary as P's shareholdings in S do not give it the power to control S. R is a subsidiary as P has the right to appoint or remove the directors of R, and so control it.

35.16 The correct answer is: 3 only

Investments in associates are accounted for using equity accounting. An investment is an associate if the investor has significant influence over the investee. Significant influence is presumed if the investor owns at least 20% of the voting equity of the investee. Therefore 2 is not an associate. 1 and 4 are subsidiaries as Company A investor has control over them.

35.17 The correct answer is: $620,000

	$'000	$'000
Fair value of consideration (bal fig)		620
Plus fair value of NCI at acquisition		150
Less net acquisition-date fair value of identifiable assets acquired and liabilities assumed:		
Share capital	500	
Retained earnings at acquisition	150	
Revaluation surplus at acquisition	50	
		(700)
Goodwill		70

35.18 The correct answer is: $2,250,000

$950 + $1,250 + $50 = $2,250,000

35.19 The correct answer is: Trade receivables $73,000, Trade payables $55,000

The $30,000 owed by Seven Co to Six Co is included within the receivables of Six Co and the payables of Seven Co. These intra-group balances should be eliminated for the purpose of consolidation.

Trade receivables = $(64,000 + 39,000 – 30,000) = $73,000

Trade payables = $(37,000 + 48,000 – 30,000) = $55,000

The unrealised profit on closing inventory will be an adjustment to inventory on consolidation, and does not affect consolidated receivables and payables.

35.20 $ 27,800

	$
Fair value of NCI at date of acquisition	25,000
NCI share of retained post-acquisition earnings: 20% × $(60,000 – 40,000)	4,000
	29,000
NCI share in unrealised profit: 20% × 50% × $12,000	(1,200)
Non-controlling interest at 31 December 20X4	27,800

35.21 The correct answer is: $668,000

Retained post-acquisition earnings of Lava Co = 4/12 × $(336,000 – 264,000) = $24,000.

	$000
Volcano retained earnings	650
Parent company share of post-acquisition earnings: 75% × $24,000	18
Parent company's share of consolidated retained earnings at 31 Dec 20X3	668

35.22 The correct answer is: $110,500

Post-acquisition earnings of Drum Co = 9/12 ×$60,000 = $45,000.

	$
Tin Co profit for the year	70,000
Parent company share of post-acquisition profit of Drum Co: 90% × $45,000	40,500
Parent company's share of consolidated retained earnings at 31 Dec 20X3	110,500

35.23 The correct answer is: $144,800

The unrealised profit in the closing inventory of Sand Co = 25% × 40% × $40,000 = $4,000.

The NCI share of this is 20% × $4,000 = $800.

	$	$
NCI share of profit of Sun Co: 20% × $35,000		7,000
Less: NCI share of unrealised profit		(800)
		6,200
Combined profits of Sand Co and Sun Co: (120,000 + 35,000)	155,000	
Less: Unrealised profit in closing inventory	(4,000)	
Total consolidated profit for the year		151,000
Attributable to the parent company		144,800

35.24 The correct answer is: $69 million

	$'000
Shares (18m × 2/3 × $5.75)	69,000

35.25 The correct answer is: $1,999,000

	X Co	*Y Co × 2/12*	*Adj*	*Group*
	$'000	$'000	$'000	$'000
Revenue	3,400	400	(10)	3,790
Cost of sales	1,500	300	(10 –1*)	1,791
				1,999

* Unrealised profit

		$
Sale price	125%	10,000
Cost price	100%	(8,000)
Gross profit	25%	2,000
Unrealised profit	(2,000 × 50%)	1,000

35.26 The correct answer is:

Profit attributable to non-controlling interest	***Profit attributable to WX***
decrease by $2,500	decrease by $7,500

The correct answer is: Profit attributable to non-controlling interest decrease by $2,500, Profit attributable to WX decrease by $7,500.

Eliminate unrealised profit on goods in inventory of WX:

		$
Sale price	120%	60,000
Cost price	100%	(50,000)
Gross profit	20%	10,000

Unrealised profit attributable to NCI = $10,000 × 25% = $2,500

Unrealised profit attributable to WX = $10,000 × 75% = $7,500

35.27 The correct answer is: $12 million

	$'000
Profit for the year of S	60,000
NCI share of profit of S (20%)	(12,000)

Because the sale was made from the parent, P to the subsidiary, S, there is no unrealised profit attributable to the non-controlling interest.

Part H: Interpretation of financial statements

36 Binky and Smokey (15 mark question)

Exam focus point

It is unlikely that there would be a 15-mark question solely on interpretation in the exam. However, interpretation could easily form part of a 15-mark question and test the skills covered in this question. Interpretation could also be tested in an objective test question.

36.1 **Required ratios**

Ratio	Binky	Smokey
Gross profit %	(129/284) × 100 = 45.4%	(154/305) × 100 = 50.5%
Net profit %	(61/284) × 100 = 21.5%	(47/305) × 100 = 15.4%
Asset turnover	(284/258) × 100 = 110.1%	(305/477) × 100 = 63.9%
Current ratio	(201/188) = 1.1:1	(383/325) = 1.2:1
Quick ratio	(110/188) = 0.6:1	(90/325) = 0.3:1
Receivables collection period	(46/284) × 365 = 59.1 days	(75/305) × 365 = 89.8 days

36.2 Of the two companies Binky has the higher net profit percentage.

This is due to lower expenses.

Both companies have low quick ratios. In Smokey's case this is because much of its working capital is tied up in inventory. This has given rise to liquidity problems.

Smokey needs to improve credit control.

The asset turnover ratio shows that Binky is making better use of its working capital than Smokey.

37 Interpretation of financial statements

37.1 The correct answer is: Making a rights issue of equity shares

Issuing further loan notes and paying dividends will **increase** gearing. A bonus issue simply capitalises reserves, so has no effect.

37.2 The correct answer is: Understatement of the closing inventory at 31 December 20X1

Understatement of the December 20X1 closing inventory will lead to understatement of December 20X2 opening inventory and therefore understatement of cost of sales.

37.3 The correct answer is: Selling inventory at a profit

Profit will be an addition to owner's capital.

37.4 The correct answer is: 57 days

Purchases = \$(32,500 – 6,000 + 3,800)

= \$30,300

$$\text{Therefore, Accounts payables payment period} = \frac{4,750}{30,300} \times 365 = 57 \text{ days}$$

37.5 Gearing is 13%

Quick ratio is 1.75.

Current ratio is 2.56.

Workings as follows:

$$\text{Gearing} = \frac{\text{Total long term debt}}{\text{Total long term debt + shareholders equity}} = \frac{75}{75+500} = 13\%$$

$$\text{Quick ratio} = \frac{\text{Current assets} - \text{Inventory}}{\text{Current liabilities}} = \frac{205-65}{80} = 1.75$$

$$\text{Current ratio} = \frac{\text{Current assets}}{\text{Current liabilities}} = \frac{205}{80} = 2.56$$

37.6 The correct answer is: Gearing

To get back to the 'real' underlying figures, without the numbers being skewed by the requirements of IFRS Standards.

The gearing ratio is used to assess how much the company owes in relation to its size.

37.7 The correct answer is: 5%

	%	$
Sales	100	2,400
Cost of sales	66 2/3	1,600
Gross profit	33 1/3	800
Expenses	28 1/3	680
Net profit	5	120

37.8 The correct answer is: Liquidity appears to be poorly-controlled as shown by the company's relatively high current ratio.

Current ratio is 2,900: 1,100 = 2.6: 1 ie high compared to the industry norm.

37.9 The correct answer is: So that the significance of financial statements can be better understood through comparisons with historical performance and with other companies

Analysis of financial statements is carried out so that the significance of the financial statements can be better understood. Comparisons through time and with other companies help to show how well the company is doing.

37.10 152 times

$$\text{Interest cover} = \frac{\text{Profit before interest and tax}}{\text{Interest expense}}$$

$$\frac{\$47,000}{\$31,000} = 1.52$$

The interest cover ratio calculates how many times a business can pay its interest expense out of profit for the year.

ANSWERS

Mixed banks

38 Mixed bank 1

38.1 $ 126,000

	$
Increase in net assets	88,000
Capital introduced	(50,000)
Drawings (68,000 + 20,000)	88,000
Profit for the year	126,000

38.2 The correct answer is:

Debit	Bank	$1,100,000
Credit	Share capital	$250,000
Credit	Share premium	$850,000

38.3 The correct answer is: 1 and 2 only

Closing inventory should be valued at the lower of cost and NRV as per IAS 2 *Inventories*.

38.4 The correct answer is:

Share capital	***Share premium account***
$	**$**
687,500	400,000

	Share capital	*Share premium*
	$	$
1 July 20X4	500,000	400,000
1 January 20X5 – bonus issue (250,000 × 50c)	125,000	(125,000)
1 April 20X5 – rights issue	62,500	125,000
	687,500	400,000

38.5 The correct answer is: $135,540

TRADE RECEIVABLES

	$		$
Opening balance	138,400	Receipts from credit customers	78,420
Credit sales	80,660	Payables contra	1,000
Dishonoured cheques	850	Irrecoverable debts written off	4,950
		Closing balance	135,540
	219,910		219,910

38.6 The correct answer is: Debit side of bank general ledger account undercast by $10,000; $6,160 paid for rent correctly entered in the bank general ledger account but entered in the rent account as $1,610.

SUSPENSE ACCOUNT

	$		$
Opening balance	14,550	To bank general ledger account	10,000
		To rent account	4,550

38.7 The correct answers are:

- Repayment of long-term borrowing
- Interest received

A revaluation of a non-current asset and a bonus issue of shares are both non-cash transactions.

38.8 The correct answer is: $1,008,000

	$
Opening inventory	138,600
Purchases	716,100
Closing inventory	(149,100)
Cost of sales	705,600

Sales = 705,600 × 100/70 = 1,008,000

38.9 The correct answer is:

Statement of Profit or Loss	***Statement of Financial Position***
$36,700	Prepayment $9,500

	SPL	*SOFP*
	$	$
Prepaid insurance	8,200	
Payment January 20X5	38,000	
Prepayment July–September 20X5	(9,500)	9,500
	36,700	9,500

38.10 The correct answer is: 1, 2 and 3

All three statements are correct.

38.11 The correct answer is: Beta has issued a credit note for $500 to Alpha which Alpha has not yet received.

38.12 The correct answer is: 2 and 3 only

Research expenditure is never capitalised.

38.13 The correct answer is: 2 and 3

1 and 4 provide information about conditions which existed at the reporting date and are therefore adjusting.

38.14 $ 84,000

RENT RECEIVED

	$		$
Arrears b/f	3,800	In advance b/f	2,400
Rent in advance	3,000	Cash received	83,700
Rental income	84,000	In arrears	4,700
	90,800		90,800

38.15 The correct answer is: $22,000

	$
Allowance for receivables ((517,000 – 37,000) × 5%)	24,000
Previous allowance	(39,000)
Reduction	(15,000)
Debts written off	37,000
Charge to statement of profit or loss	22,000

38.16 The correct answer is: 2 and 3 only

Attributable overheads should be included in finished goods inventories.

38.17 The correct answer is:

Proceeds of sale	***Profit on sale***
Cash inflow under investing activities	Deducted from profit in calculating cash flow from operating activities

The proceeds will appear under **investing activities** and any profit will be deducted under **operating activities**.

38.18 The correct answer is: All four items

All four items will appear in the statement of changes in equity.

38.19 The correct answer is: $43,100 overdrawn

	$
Balance per bank statement	(38,600)
Bank charges	200
Lodgements	14,700
Cheque payments	(27,800)
Cheque payment misposted	8,400
Balance per bank general ledger account	(43,100)

39 Mixed bank 2

39.1 The correct answer is: $64,200

	$
Balance b/f ((280,000 – 14,000) × 20%)	53,200
Addition 1 April (48,000 × 20% × $^9/_{12}$)	7,200
Addition 1 Sept (36,000 × 20% × $^4/_{12}$)	2,400
	62,800
Sale (14,000 × 20% × $^1/_2$)	1,400
	64,200

39.2 The correct answer is: 2, 3 and 4

Item 1 is wrong, as inventory should be valued at the **lower** of cost and net realisable value.

Items 2, 3 and 4 are all correct.

39.3 The correct answer is:

Statement of Profit or Loss	***Statement of Financial Position***
$27,500	$5,000 in deferred income

RENT RECEIVABLE

	$		$
31.1.X6 Statement of profit or loss	27,500	1.2.X5 Balance b/f ($^2/_3$ × $6,000)	4,000
		1.4.X5 Received	6,000
		1.7.X5 Received	7,500
		1.10.X5 Received	7,500
31.1. X6 Balance c/f ($^2/_3$ × $7,500)	5,000	1.1.X6 Received	7,500
	32,500		32,500

39.4 The correct answer is: 20%

ROCE is defined as the profit on ordinary activities before interest and tax divided by capital employed = $300,000/$1.5m = 20%.

39.5 The correct answer is: 1 and 4 only

Items 1 and 4 are adjusting events. Item 2 is a non-adjusting event but might be disclosed by way of note if material. Item 3 is a non-adjusting event that is disclosed by way of note.

39.6 $ 100

	$
Balance per Alta	3,980
Cheque not yet received	(270)
Goods returned	(180)
Contra entry	(3,200)
Revised balance per Alta	330
Balance per Ordan	(230)
Remaining difference	100

39.7 The correct answers are:

- DEBIT: Sales returns $130, Purchase returns $130, CREDIT: Suspense account $260
- DEBIT: Plant and machinery $18,000, CREDIT: Suspense account $18,000

For returns, we need to debit the purchases returns account $130 to reverse the entry and debit the sales returns account $130 to record the entry correctly. The credit of $260 will be to suspense. So the second option is correct.

For machinery, we need to debit plant and machinery $18,000 and credit suspense $18,000. So the fourth option is correct.

39.8 The correct answer is: 3 and 4 only

Item 1, as the plant register is not part of the double entry system, the adjustment does not go through the suspense account.

Item 2, the transaction has been completely omitted from the records.

Therefore, only items 3 and 4 affect the suspense account.

39.9 The correct answer is: $625,240

	$
Initial profit	630,000
Item (1) – increase in depreciation (4,800 – 480)	(4,320)
Item (2) – bank charges	(440)
Item (3) – no effect on P/L	–
Item (4) – no effect on P/L	
Revised profit	625,240

39.10 The correct answer is: 1 and 2

39.11 The correct answer is: 2 and 3

39.12 The correct answer is: $31,500

	$
Closing receivables	458,000
Irrecoverable debts w/off	(28,000)
	430,000
Allowance required (5% × 430,000)	21,500
Existing allowance	(18,000)
Increase required	3,500

Charge to statement of profit or loss (28,000 + 3,500) = $31,500

39.13 The correct answer is: $325,200

TRADE PAYABLES

	$		$
Bank payments to suppliers	988,400	Opening balance	384,600
Discounts received	12,600	Purchases	963,200
Purchases returns	17,400		
Contras	4,200		
Closing balance	325,200		
	1,347,800		1,347,800

39.14 The correct answer is:

DEBIT Drawings
CREDIT Purchases

We need to increase drawings (debit) and reduce purchases (credit). Therefore, the first journal is the correct answer. Remember that we only adjust inventory at the year end.

39.15 The correct answer is: $1,080,000

	$	$
Sales (balancing figure)		1,080,000
Opening inventory	77,000	
Purchases	763,000	
	840,000	
Closing inventory	84,000	
Cost of sales (70%)		756,000
Gross profit (30/70 × 756,000)		324,000

39.16 The correct answer is: 3 and 4

Statements 3 and 4 are correct. Statement 1 is incorrect because land is not usually depreciated. Statement 2 is incorrect as the gain on revaluation for property accounted for in accordance with IAS 16 is shown in the statement of profit or loss and other comprehensive income, under 'other comprehensive income' or in the separate statement of other comprehensive income.

39.17 The correct answer is: $33,630 overdrawn

	$
Balance per bank statement (overdrawn)	(38,640)
Add outstanding lodgements	19,270
	(19,370)
Less unpresented cheques	(14,260)
Balance per bank general ledger account (overdrawn)	(33,630)

39.18 The correct answer is: $50,600

48,000 + 400 + 2,200 = 50,600

39.19 The correct answers are:

- DEBIT: Statement of profit or loss (SPL) $180,000, CREDIT: Inventory account $180,000
- DEBIT: Inventory account $220,000, CREDIT: Statement of profit or loss (SPL) $220,000

Opening inventory: debit statement of profit or loss, credit inventory account

Closing inventory: debit inventory account, credit statement of profit or loss

Remember that inventory is part of cost of sales, which is included in the statement of profit or loss.

39.20 The correct answer is: $1,450,000

	$'000
Fair value of consideration	4,000
Plus fair value of NCI at acquisition	2,200
Less net acquisition-date fair value of identifiable assets acquired and liabilities assumed	(4,750)
Goodwill	1,450

40 Mixed bank 3

40.1 The correct answer is: $185,000

	$
Sales (100%)	650,000
Cost of sales (70%)	455,000
Gross profit (30%)	195,000
Opening inventory	380,000
Purchases	480,000
	860,000
Closing inventory (bal. fig.)	(405,000)
Cost of sales	455,000
Calculated inventory	405,000
Actual inventory	220,000
Lost in fire	185,000

40.2 The correct answer is: 1 and 4 only

Income from investments and dividends paid on redeemable preference shares are recognised in the statement of profit or loss.

40.3 The correct answer is:

SPLOCI for the period	*SOFP liability*
nil	nil

Dividends paid go through the SOCIE, not the statement of profit or loss and other comprehensive income. Also, dividends declared after the end of the reporting period are disclosed by way of note to the financial statements.

40.4 The correct answer is: Partridge Co, Turkey Co and Duck Co

Goose Co has control over all three of these investments, and hence they are all subsidiaries.

40.5 The correct answer is:

Trade receivables	**Allowances for receivables**	**Net balance**
$	**$**	**$**
766,000	60,000	706,000

Trade receivables = 838,000 – 72,000
= 766,000

Allowance for receivables = 60,000

Net balance = 766,000 – 60,000
= 706,000

40.6 The correct answers are:

- According to IAS 2 *Inventories*, average cost and FIFO (first in, first out) are both acceptable methods of arriving at the cost of inventories.
- It may be acceptable for inventories to be valued at selling price less estimated profit margin.

The correct answers are: According to IAS 2 *Inventories*, average cost and FIFO (first in, first out) are both acceptable methods of arriving at the cost of inventories. It may be acceptable for inventories to be valued at selling price less estimated profit margin.

Overheads must be included in the value of finished goods. Inventories should be valued at the lower of cost and net realisable value, not replacement cost.

40.7 The correct answer is: 1 only

Inventory is correctly recorded, so 2 and 4 are incorrect. Purchases are understated, so cost of sales are understated and so profit for 20X6 is overstated. Therefore 1 only is the correct answer.

40.8 The correct answer is: 1.26:1

(Receivables 176,000)/(trade payables 61,000 + overdraft 79,000).

40.9 The correct answer is: All four items

40.10 The correct answer is:

Statement of Profit or Loss	***Statement of Financial position SOFP***
$	**$**
11,100	9,000 prepayment (DEBIT)

INSURANCE

	$		$
Prepayment b/f (3/4 × 10,800)	8,100	SPL	11,100
Paid	12,000	Prepayments c/f (3/4 × 12,000)	9,000
	20,100		20,100

40.11 The correct answer is: 1 and 3

Statement 2 is incorrect. A bounced cheque is credited to the bank general ledger account.

40.12 The correct answer is:

Share capital	***Share premium***
$m	**$m**
210	60

SHARE CAPITAL

	$m		$m
		Bal b/f	100
		Bonus (1/2 × 100m)	50
Bal c/f	210	Rights (2/5 × 150m)	60
	210		210

SHARE PREMIUM

	$m		$m
Bonus	50	Bal b/f	80
Bal c/f	60	Rights	30
	110		110

40.13 The correct answer is: All three statements are correct

40.14 The correct answer is: 1 only

Items 2, 3 and 4 preserve double entry and so would not show up in a trial balance.

40.15 $ 2,850,000

	$'000
Fair value of consideration transferred	8,000
Plus fair value of NCI at acquisition ($1.20 × 3,000,000)	3,600
Less net acquisition-date fair value of identifiable assets acquired and liabilities assumed	(8,750)
Goodwill	2,850

40.16 The correct answer is: 1 and 3

	$
Opening inventory	40,000
Purchases	60,000
	100,000
Closing inventory	(50,000)
Cost of sales	50,000
This implies sales of	100,000 (50,000 × 2)

So either 1 is correct or 3 is correct.

40.17 The correct answer is: $828,700

RENT RECEIVED

	$		$
Arrears b/f	4,800	Prepayments b/f	134,600
Profit or Loss	828,700	Cash received	834,600
Prepayments c/f	144,400	Arrears c/f	8,700
	977,900		977,900

40.18 The correct answer is: $282,830

TRADE RECEIVABLES

	$		$
Opening balance	284,680	Bank receipts from credit customers	179,790
Credit sales	189,120	Irrecoverable debts written off	5,460
		Sales returns	4,920
		Contras	800
		Closing balance	282,830
	473,800		473,800

40.19 The correct answer is: $150,000

	$
Carrying amount at 1 August 20X0	200,000
Less depreciation	(20,000)
	180,000
Proceeds	25,000
Loss	5,000
Carrying amount of asset sold	(30,000)
Therefore, carrying amount	150,000

41 Mixed bank 4

41.1 The correct answer is:

	DEBIT	*CREDIT*
	$	**$**
Sales	1,500,000	
Share capital		1,000,000
Share premium		500,000

Share capital (1m × $1) = 1,000,000

Share premium (1m × 50c) = 500,000

41.2 The correct answer is: Decrease current ratio and decrease quick ratio

Proposed dividends are not accrued for, so the only impact on the financial statements is to decrease cash.

41.3 The correct answer is: $858,600

RENTAL INCOME

	$		$
Arrears b/f	42,300	Prepayments b/f	102,600
Profit or Loss	858,600	Received	838,600
Prepayments c/f	88,700	Arrears c/f	48,400
	989,600		989,600

41.4 The correct answer is:

	Debit	**Credit**
	$	**$**
Sales returns	2,800	
Purchases returns		2,800
Correction of error: sales returns incorrectly debited to purchases returns account		

The first and second journals have their entries reversed and the fourth journal should not include the suspense account at all.

41.5 The correct answer is:

Probable loss	*Probable gain*
Accrued	Disclosed

Per IAS 37 **provide** for probable losses of known amounts and for which there is a constructive obligation, disclose possible losses.

41.6 The correct answer is:

SPLOCI	***SOFP***
$	**$**
136,000	Prepayment 12,000

RENT PAID

	$		$
Prepayment b/f (1/12 × 120,000)	10,000		
Paid – 1/1	30,000	SPL	136,000
– ¼	36,000		
– 1/7	36,000		
– 1/10	36,000	Prepayments c/f ($^1/_3$ × 36,000)	12,000
	148,000		148,000

41.7 The correct answer is: $16,000

	$	$
Trade receivables	863,000	
Irrecoverable debts w/off	(23,000)	
	840,000	
Closing allowance for receivables (5% × 840,000)		42,000
Opening allowance		49,000
Reduction		(7,000)

Charge = 23,000 – 7,000

= 16,000

ANSWERS

41.8 The correct answer is:

Share capital	*Share premium*
$	**$**
2,000,000	1,800,000

SHARE CAPITAL

	$m		$m
		Bal b/f	1.0
		Share issue (note 1)	0.5
Bal c/f	2.0	Bonus (note 2)	0.5
	2.0		2.0

SHARE PREMIUM

	$m		$m
Bonus (note 2)	0.5	Bal b/f	1.4
Bal c/f	1.8	Share issue (note 1)	0.9
	2.3		2.3

Notes.

1 Share issues of 1,000,000 shares raises $1,400,000. Shares are 50c each, so share capital is $500,000 and share premium $900,000.

2 Share capital is $1.5m or 3m shares. Therefore, the bonus issue is 1m shares.

41.9 The correct answer is: 2, 3 and 4 only

Inventory should be valued at the lower of cost and net realisable value, so Statement 1 is incorrect.

41.10 $ 192,600

	$
Held all year ((960,000 – 84,000) × 20%)	175,200
Addition (48,000 × 20% × ½)	4,800
Disposal (84,000 × 20% × ¾)	12,600
	192,600

41.11 The correct answers are:

- The debit side of the wages account had been undercast.
- Sales returns had been credited to the purchases returns account.

The first and fourth options involve completed double entry and so do not go through the suspense account.

41.12 The correct answer is:

	DEBIT	*CREDIT*
	$	*$*
Drawings	2,000	
Purchases		2,000

Debit drawings and credit the cost to purchases.

41.13 The correct answer is: $58,000

Cost + Profit = Selling price

100 + 25 = 125

PUP = $(^{25}/_{125} \times 15{,}000) \times {}^{2}/_{3}$ = $2,000

Inventories = $40,000 + $20,000 – $2,000 = $58,000

41.14 The correct answer is:

Statement of profit or loss and other comprehensive income	*Statement of changes in equity*
Tax on profit and profit for the period	Profit for the period

Tax is separately disclosed in the statement of profit or loss and other comprehensive income only, while profit for the period is shown in the statement of profit or loss and other comprehensive income and in the statement of changes in equity.

41.15 The correct answer is: When the asset is expected to decrease in value less in later years than in the early years of its life

The diminishing balance method charges more depreciation in earlier years.

41.16 The correct answer is: 3 and 4

A decrease in receivables should be added and so should an increase in payables. Therefore 3 and 4 are correct.

41.17 The correct answer is: $47,429

	$	$
Balance per P Johnson		46,747
Add: Whitchurch Co invoice not yet drawn up and therefore omitted from list	267	
Rectofon Co balance, previously omitted from list	2,435	
		2,702
		49,449
Less: Error on posting of Bury Inc's credit note to ledger	20	
P Fox & Son (Swindon) Co's balance included twice	2,000	
		(2,020)
Revised balance per receivables ledger		47,429

ANSWERS

42 Mixed bank 5

42.1 The correct answer is: $1,700

Closing inventory $1,700.

Purchases	*Sales*	*Balance*	*Inventory value*	*Unit cost*
Units	Units	Units	$	$
10		10	3,000	300
12			3,000	250
		22	6,000	
	8		(2,400)	
		14	3,600	
6			1,200	200
		20	4,800	
	12		(3,100)*	
		8	1,700	

Note. * 2 @ $300 + 10 @ $250 = $3,100

42.2 The correct answer is: The IFRS Advisory Council

42.3 The correct answer is: $622 DEBIT

SUSPENSE ACCOUNT

	$		$
Bank	1,512	Balance b/f	759
		Receivables	131
		Balance c/f	622
	1,512		1,512

42.4 The correct answer is: $1,123 CREDIT

	$
Receivables allowance at 30.11.X8 (598,600 × 2%)	11,972
Opening allowance at 1.12.X7	(12,460)
Reduction in allowance (credit to statement of profit or loss)	(488)

Total credit to statement of profit or loss = 488 + 635 = $1,123

42.5 The correct answer is: $1,000 increase

	$
Rent accrual (4/12 × $12,000)	(4,000)
Insurance prepayment (10/12 × $6,000)	5,000
Net increase in profit	1,000

42.6 The correct answer is: $(1,245,000)

	$
Non-current assets at 1 December 20X7	2,500,000
Depreciation charge for the year	(75,000)
Non-current asset disposed of (carrying amount)	(120,000)
Revaluation of non-current assets	500,000
	2,805,000
Non-current assets at 30 November 20X8	4,200,000
Therefore, non-current assets acquired during the year	(1,395,000)
Sales proceeds from disposal of non-current asset	150,000
To be included in 'net cash flows from investing activities'	(1,245,000)

NON-CURRENT ASSETS

	$'000		$'000
Balance b/f	2,500	Depreciation	75
Revaluation	500	Disposal	120
Additions (bal fig)	1,395	Balance c/f	4,200
	4,395		4,395

42.7 The correct answer is: 3 only

A transposition error will not cause an imbalance in the trial balance and therefore does not need to be adjusted through the suspense account. Likewise, an invoice being posted to the wrong general ledger account will not cause an imbalance in the trial balance. The posting of the contra of $400 to receivables only will cause an imbalance and this must be corrected through the suspense account.

42.8 The correct answer is: $2,700

Make sure you read the **dates carefully** as some of the goods are returned after 31 May and we are only concerned with sales returns at that date, which is the goods with a list price of $3,000. The value of the original sale is after the trade discount of 10%, so the actual amount invoiced for those goods is $2,700 ($3,000 × 90%).

42.9 The correct answer is: 1 and 3 only

Only Statement 2 is correct. Development expenditure should be capitalised in accordance with IAS 38 *Intangible Assets*, however, research expenditure should be written off to the statement of profit or loss as incurred. Goodwill arising in a business combination should be capitalised as a non-current asset in the statement of financial position.

42.10 The correct answer is: None of the statements

All of the suggestions are flawed. LIFO is not permitted under IAS 2 *Inventories*. Provisions cannot be created unless a constructive obligation exists, the amount can be reliably estimated and the likelihood of having to pay out cash is probable – none of these conditions are met, therefore a provision cannot be made. Development expenditure must be amortised over its useful life.

42.11 The correct answer is: 3 only

Journal entries 1 and 2 should both be reversed.

42.12 The correct answer is: 1, 3 and 4 only

Carriage outwards is a distribution expense.

42.13 The correct answer is: $665,000

	Frog	*Toad*
	$'000	$'000
Per question	650	160
Pre-acquisition retained earnings		(145)*
		15
Post-acquisition retained earnings of Toad	15	
Group retained earnings	665	

* 100 + (60/12 × 9)

42.14 The correct answer is: $15,000

	$
Profit before tax	36,000
Dividend	(21,000)
Added to retained earnings	15,000

42.15 The correct answer is: A decrease in working capital

It reduces receivables.

42.16 The correct answer is: $2,185

Prepayment b/f $60 (2/3 × 90) + $2,145 – prepayment c/f $60 – accrual b/f $80 + accrual c/f $120 = $2,185.

42.17 The correct answer is: 1, 3 and 5

In Option 2, receivables and drawings are debits but discount received is a credit In Option 4, capital and trade payables are credits but operating expenses are debits.

42.18 $ 205,000

Profit = Drawings + Increase in net assets – Capital introduced

= $77,000 + $173,000 – $45,000

= $205,000

42.19 The correct answer is: $130 loss

Capital = Assets – Liabilities

$50 + $100 + profit for the year = $90 – $70

$150 + profit for the year = $20

Therefore, the profit for the year is in fact a *loss* of $130.

43 Mixed bank 6

43.1 The correct answer is: X owes $1,250 to Y

43.2 The correct answer is: $47,429

TRADE RECEIVABLES

	$		$
Balance b/d	50,241	Returns inwards	41,226
Sales	472,185	Irrecoverable debts written off	4,586
Cheques dishonoured	626	Bank receipts	429,811
		Balance c/d	47,429
	523,052		523,052

43.3 The correct answer is: $2,098 DEBIT

BANK

	$		$
20X3		*20X3*	
31 May Balance b/d	873	31 May Bank charges	630
Error $(936 – 693)	243	Trade journals	52
Balance c/d	2,098	Insurance	360
		Business rates	2,172
	3,214		3,214
		1 May Balance b/d	2,098

43.4 The correct answer is: $87 loss

	$
Carrying amount: 9,000 × 0.7 × 0.7 × 0.7	3,087
Proceeds of sale	(3,000)
Loss on disposal	87

43.5 The correct answer is: The cost of non-current assets is spread over the accounting periods which benefit from their use.

Depreciation is an application of the accruals principle.

ANSWERS

43.6 The correct answer is: $107,500

Original annual depreciation = $(160,000 – 40,000)/8 years = $15,000 per year.

The change in the estimated life of the asset is made on 31 December 20X3, and this means that the change should be applied for the year ending 31 December 20X3.

		$
Cost		160,000
Accumulated depreciation to 31 December 20X2	(2 years × $15,000)	30,000
Carrying amount at 1 January 20X3		130,000
Residual value		40,000
Remaining depreciable amount as at 1 January 20X3		90,000

Remaining life from 1 January 20X3 = 4 years

Annual depreciation = $90,000/4 years = $22,500.

Carrying amount at 31 December 20X3 = $130,000 – $22,500 = $107,500.

43.7 The correct answer is: Purchases returns of $200 were debited to the sales returns account.

$200 debit which should have been credited – correction will bring the trial balance into agreement.

43.8 The correct answer is: Revenue

IAS 1 requires revenue to be disclosed on the face of the statement of profit or loss and other comprehensive income. It does not specify that a company must disclose profit before tax or gross profit on the face of the statement of profit or loss and other comprehensive income, however, most companies choose to do this. Dividends are disclosed in the statement of changes in equity if they are paid or are declared before the period end.

43.9 The correct answer is: $58,440 credit

($73,680) + 102,480 – 87,240 = (58,440) $58,440 overdrawn

43.10 The correct answer is: None of the items

1, 2 and 3 are all incorrect.

43.11 The correct answer is: 1, 2 and 5

Cash received from customers, irrecoverable debts written off, and credits for goods returned by customers are credits to the trade receivables account.

43.12 The correct answer is: $1,587,500

$952,500 × 100/60 = $1,587,500

43.13 The correct answer is: $15,400

	$
Theoretical gross profit ($130,000 × 30%)	39,000
Actual gross profit ($130,000 – $49,800 – $88,600 + $32,000)	23,600
Shortfall – missing inventory	15,400

43.14 The correct answer is: $2,640

	$	$
Sales		240,000
Purchases	134,025	
Therefore, Drawings	(2,640)	
Inventory adjustment	(11,385)	
Cost of sales (50% × 240,000)		120,000
		120,000

43.15 The correct answer is: 1 and 4 only

Incorrect answers: Goods purchased for cash – current assets remain the same, Payables paid out of an overdraft – current liabilities remain the same

43.16 The correct answer is:

Sales	***Cost of sales***
$450,000	$214,000

PUP = 50,000 × 25/125 × 40% = $4,000

	Lexus group
	$'000
Revenue (350 + 150 – 50*)	450
Cost of sales (200 + 60 – 50* + 4)	214

Note. * to remove intragroup sales

43.17 The correct answer is:

Share capital	***Share premium account***
$120,000	$227,000

Share capital 75,000 + 15,000 + 30,000 =	120,000
Share premium 200,000 + 57,000 – 30,000 =	227,000
(Remember shares are 25c)	

43.18 The correct answer is: Decrease in trade receivables, increase in trade payables, loss on sale of non-current assets

44 Mixed bank 7

44.1 The correct answer is: $7,000

PLANT AND EQUIPMENT (CARRYING AMOUNT)

	$'000		$'000
Balance b/d	155	Depreciation charge in year	25
Purchases of plant and equipment	10	Therefore, Carrying amount of sale	15
		Balance c/d	125
	165		165

So:

	$'000
Carrying amount	15
Proceeds	(7)
Loss	8

44.2 The correct answer is: $500,000

(2c + 3c) × 10,000,000. The final ordinary dividend is declared before the year end and so is accrued for. The preference dividend is classified as a finance cost.

44.3 The correct answer is: 1 only

Working capital is increased as the company will receive cash for the share issue Share premium is not reduced as it is not a bonus issue of shares, it will probably increase as the shares are likely to be issued at a premium.

44.4 The correct answer is: 2, 3 and 4

A revaluation surplus will be presented as part of equity, not current liabilities.

44.5 The correct answer is: 3 only

In Statement 1 both sides of the double entry posting from the bank general ledger account would be incorrect but equal in value, so this would not cause a trial balance imbalance. In Statement 2, both expenses and non-current assets are debit balances in the trial balance, so posting to the wrong account in this case would not cause a trial balance imbalance.

44.6 The correct answer is:

SPLOCI for the period	***SOFP liability***
nil	nil

The dividends actually paid will go through the statement of changes in equity. The final proposed dividend of $120,000 is disclosed in the notes to the statement of financial position.

44.7 The correct answer is: None of the statements are correct

Deferred development expenditure should be amortised over its useful life. If the conditions in IAS 38 are met, development expenditure **must** be capitalised. Trade investments are not intangible assets, they should be reported under non-current assets: investments in the SOFP.

44.8 $ 834,600

RENT

	$		$
Balance b/f (rent in arrears)	4,800	Balance b/f (rent in advance)	134,600
SPL	828,700	Bank (bal. fig.)	834,600
Balance c/f (rent in advance)	144,400	Balance c/f (rent in arrears)	8,700
	977,900		977,900

44.9 The correct answer is: Buying shares as an investment

The first, second and third options are all income items reflected in the statement of profit or loss and other comprehensive income. In contrast option four is reflected in the statement of financial position.

44.10 The correct answer is: Expenditure on heat and light

Options one, three and four are all asset items reflected in the statement of financial position.

44.11 The correct answer is: $128,200

TRADE PAYABLES

	$		$
Payment to suppliers	1,364,300	Opening balance	318,600
Discounts received	8,200	Purchases	1,268,600
Purchases returns	41,200	Refunds received from suppliers	2,700
Contras	48,000		
Closing balance	128,200		
	1,589,900		1,589,900

44.12 The correct answer is: DEBIT rent $500, CREDIT accruals $500

We need to increase the rent expenses (debit) and set up a liability to pay this amount (credit accruals).

44.13 The correct answer is: The cake shop has a higher level of wastage of inventory than the electrical store.

Wastage of inventory means that cost of sales is high relative to revenue.

44.14 The correct answer is: $1.5m

Sales: current assets = 5:1

Therefore, current assets ($30m/5) = $6m

Current ratio = 2:1

Therefore, current liabilities ($6m/2) = $3m

Acid test ratio = 1.5:1

Therefore, current assets – inventory ($3m × 1.5) = $4.5m

Hence, Inventory ($6m – $4.5m) = $1.5m

44.15 The correct answer is: All three statements are correct

44.16 The correct answer is: $183,300

485,000 + 48,600 + 18,100 – 368,400

44.17 The correct answer is: $28,600 debit

= 60,000 + ((1,232,000 – 60,000) × 5%) – 90,000

44.18 The correct answer is: To test the accuracy of the double entry bookkeeping records

Although we may use a trial balance as a step in preparing management or financial statements, the main reason is the first option.

Mock Exams

Foundations in Accountancy/ACCA

Financial Accounting (FFA/FA)

Mock Exam 1

Specimen Exam

Questions	
Time allowed	2 hours
This exam is divided into two sections: Section A – ALL 35 questions are compulsory and MUST be attempted Section B – BOTH questions are compulsory and MUST be attempted	

DO NOT OPEN THIS EXAM UNTIL YOU ARE READY TO START UNDER EXAMINATION CONDITIONS

Section A

ALL 35 questions are compulsory and MUST be attempted

1 Which of the following calculates a sole trader's profit for a period?

- O Closing net assets + drawings – capital introduced – opening net assets
- O Closing net assets – drawings + capital introduced – opening net assets
- O Closing net assets – drawings – capital introduced – opening net assets
- O Closing net assets + drawings + capital introduced – opening net assets **(2 marks)**

---

2 Which of the following explains the imprest system of operating petty cash?

- O Weekly expenditure cannot exceed a set amount.
- O The exact amount of expenditure is reimbursed at intervals to maintain a fixed float.
- O All expenditure out of the petty cash must be properly authorised.
- O Regular equal amounts of cash are transferred into petty cash at intervals. **(2 marks)**

---

3 Which of the following statements are **TRUE** of limited liability companies?

(1) The company's exposure to debts and liability is limited.

(2) Financial statements must be produced.

(3) A company continues to exist regardless of the identity of its owners

- O 1 and 2 only
- O 1 and 3 only
- O 2 and 3 only
- O 1, 2 and 3 **(2 marks)**

---

4 Annie is a sole trader who does not keep full accounting records. The following details relate to her transactions with credit customers and suppliers for the year ended 30 June 20X6:

	$
Trade receivables, 1 July 20X5	130,000
Trade payables, 1 July 20X5	60,000
Bank receipts from customers	686,400
Bank payments to suppliers	302,800
Discounts received	2,960
Contra between payables and receivables ledgers	2,000
Trade receivables, 30 June 20X6	181,000
Trade payables, 30 June 20X6	84,000

What figure should appear for purchases in Annie's statement of profit or loss for the year ended 30 June 20X6?

$ [ ] **(2 marks)**

---

5 Which **TWO** of the following errors would cause the total of the debit column and the total of the credit column of a trial balance not to agree?

- ☐ A transposition error was made when creating a sales invoice and entering it into the accounting records.
- ☐ A bank receipt from a customer was credited to bank and correctly recognised in receivables.
- ☐ A purchase of non-current assets was omitted from the accounting records.
- ☐ Rent received was included in the trial balance as a debit balance. **(2 marks)**

---

6 At 31 December 20X5 the following require inclusion in a company's financial statements

(1) On 1 January 20X5 the company made a loan of $12,000 to an employee, repayable on 1 January 20X6, charging interest at 2% per year. On the due date she repaid the loan and paid the whole of the interest due on the loan to that date.

(2) The company paid an annual insurance premium of $9,000 in 20X5, covering the year ending 31 August 20X6.

(3) In January 20X6 the company received rent from a tenant of $4,000 covering the six months to 31 December 20X5.

For these items, what total figures should be included in the company's statement of financial position as at 31 December 20X5?

O Current assets $10,000	Current liabilities $12,240
O Current assets $22,240	Current liabilities $nil
O Current assets $10,240	Current liabilities $nil
O Current assets $16,240	Current liabilities $6,000

(2 marks)

---

7 A company's statement of profit or loss for the year ended 31 December 20X5 showed a profit of $83,600. It was later found that $18,000 paid for the purchase of a motor van had been debited to the motor expenses account. It is the company's policy to depreciate motor vans at 25% per year on the straight line basis, with a full year's charge in the year of acquisition.

What would the profit be after adjusting for this error?

$ ☐ **(2 marks)**

---

8 Xena has the following working capital ratios:

	20X9	*20X8*
Current ratio	1.2:1	1.5:1
Receivables collection period	75 days	50 days
Payables payment period	30 days	45 days
Inventory turnover	42 days	35 days

Which of the following statements is **CORRECT**?

- O Xena's liquidity and working capital has improved in 20X9
- O Xena is receiving cash from customers more quickly in 20X9 than in 20X8.
- O Xena is suffering from a worsening liquidity position in 20X9.
- O Xena is taking longer to pay suppliers in 20X9. **(2 marks)**

---

9 Identify, by selecting the correct boxes in the table below, whether the following statements are true or false.

A statement of cash flows prepared using the direct method produces a different figure to net cash from operating activities from that produced if the indirect method is used.	**TRUE**	**FALSE**
Rights issues of shares do not feature in a statement of cash flows.	**TRUE**	**FALSE**
A surplus on revaluation of a non-current asset will not appear as an item in a statement of cash flows.	**TRUE**	**FALSE**
A profit on the sale of a non-current asset will appear as an item under cash flows from investing activities in the statement of cash flows	**TRUE**	**FALSE**

(2 marks)

---

10 A company receives rent from a large number of properties. The total received in the year ended 30 April 20X6 was $481,200.

The following were the amounts of rent in advance and in arrears at 30 April 20X5 and 20X6:

	30 April 20X5	*30 April 20X6*
	$	$
Rent received in advance	28,700	31,200
Rent in arrears (all subsequently received)	21,200	18,400

What amount of rental income should appear in the company's statement of profit or loss for the year ended 30 April 20X6?

- O $486,500
- O $460,900
- O $501,500
- O $475,900

(2 marks)

---

11 Which **TWO** of the following are differences between sole traders and limited liability companies?

- ☐ A sole trader's financial statements are private; a company's financial statements are sent to shareholders and may be publicly filed.
- ☐ Only companies that have capital invested into the business.
- ☐ A sole trader is fully and personally liable for any losses that the business might make.
- ☐ Revaluations can be carried out in the financial statements of a company, but not in the financial statements of a sole trader.

(2 marks)

---

12 Which of the following statements is **TRUE**?

- O The interpretation of an entity's financial statements using ratios is only useful for potential investors.
- O Ratios based on historical data can predict the future performance of an entity.
- O The analysis of financial statements using ratios provides useful information when compared with previous performance or industry averages
- O An entity's management will not assess an entity's performance using financial ratios

(2 marks)

---

13 A company's motor vehicles (at cost) account at 30 June 20X6 is as follows:

MOTOR VEHICLES (AT COST)

	$		$
Balance b/f	35,800	Disposal	12,000
Additions	12,950	Balance c/f	36,750
	48,750		48,750

What opening balance should be included in the following period's trial balance for Motor vehicles (at cost) at 1 July 20X6?

- O $36,750 DEBIT
- O $48,750 DEBIT
- O $36,750 CREDIT
- O $48,750 CREDIT **(2 marks)**

---

14 Which **TWO** of the following items must be disclosed in the note to the financial statements for intangible assets in accordance with IAS 38 *Intangible Assets*?

- ☐ The useful lives of intangible assets capitalised in the financial statements
- ☐ A description of the development projects that have been undertaken during the period
- ☐ A list of all intangible assets purchased or developed in the period
- ☐ Impairment losses written off intangible assets during the period **(2 marks)**

---

15 Which of the following statements are **CORRECT**?

(1) Capitalised development expenditure must be amortised over a period not exceeding five years.

(2) Capitalised development costs are shown in the statement of financial position under the heading of non-current assets.

(3) If certain criteria are met, research expenditure must be recognised as an intangible asset.

- O 2 only
- O 2 and 3
- O 1 only
- O 1 and 3 **(2 marks)**

---

16 The following transactions relate to Rashid's electricity expense ledger account for the year ended 30 June 20X9:

	$
Prepaid expenses brought forward	550
Cash paid	5,400
Accrued expenses carried forward	650

What amount should be charged to the statement of profit or loss in the year ended 30 June 20X9 for electricity?

- O $6,600
- O $5,400
- O $5,500
- O $5,300

(2 marks)

---

17 At 30 June 20X5 a company's allowance for receivables was $39,000. At 30 June 20X6 trade receivables totalled $517,000. It was decided to write off irrecoverable debts totalling $37,000. The receivables allowance was to be adjusted to an amount equivalent to 5% of the trade receivables based on past events.

What figure should appear in the statement of profit or loss for the year ended 30 June 20X6 for these items?

$ [ ]

(2 marks)

---

18 The total of the list of balances in Valley's payables ledger was $438,900 at 30 June 20X6. The bookkeeper viewed the supplier statements dated 30 June 20X6 and noticed the following discrepancies:

(1) A contra entry of $980 was recorded in the trade payables account, but not entered on the relevant supplier statement.

(2) A purchase return of £1,000 recorded on the supplier statement had not been entered in Valley's payables ledger.

(3) A purchase invoice for $4,344 was posted to the supplier's account in Valley's accounting records as $4,434.

What amount should Valley report in its statement of financial position as trade payables at 30 June 20X6?

- O $436,830
- O $438,010
- O $438,900
- O $437,810

(2 marks)

---

19 According to IAS 2 *Inventories*, which **TWO** of the following costs should be included in valuing the inventories of a manufacturing company?

☐ Carriage inwards

☐ Carriage outwards

☐ Depreciation of factory plant

☐ General administrative overheads **(2 marks)**

---

20 Prisha has not kept accurate accounting records during the financial year. She had opening inventory of $6,700 and purchased goods costing $84,000 during the year. At the year end she had $5,400 left in inventory. All sales are made at a mark up on cost of 20%.

What is Prisha's gross profit for the year?

$ ☐ **(2 marks)**

---

21 At 31 December 20X4 a company's capital structure was as follows:

	$
Ordinary share capital (500,000 shares of 25c each)	125,000
Share premium account	100,000

In the year ended 31 December 20X5 the company made a rights issue of one share for every two held at $1 per share and this was taken up in full. Later in the year the company made a bonus issue of one share for every five held, using the share premium account for the purpose.

What was the company's capital structure at 31 December 20X5?

	Ordinary share capital	***Share premium account***
○	$450,000	$25,000
○	$225,000	$250,000
○	$225,000	$325,000
○	$212,500	$262,500

(2 marks)

---

22 Which of the following should appear in a company's statement of changes in equity?

(1) Total comprehensive income for the year

(2) Amortisation of capitalised development costs

(3) Surplus on revaluation of non-current assets

- O 1, 2 and 3
- O 2 and 3 only
- O 1 and 3 only
- O 1 and 2 only

(2 marks)

---

23 The plant and machinery account (at cost) of a business for the year ended 31 December 20X5 was as follows

PLANT AND MACHINERY (AT COST)

20X5	$	20X5	$
1 Jan Balance b/f	240,000	31 Mar Transfer to disposal account	60,000
30 Jun Cash purchase of plant	160,000	31 Dec Balance c/f	340,000
	400,000		400,000

The company's policy is to charge depreciation at 20% per year on the straight line basis, with proportionate depreciation in the years of purchase and disposal.

What should be the depreciation charge for the year ended 31 December 20X5?

- O $68,000
- O $64,000
- O $61,000
- O $55,000

(2 marks)

---

24 The following extracts are from Hassan's financial statements:

	$
Profit before interest and tax	10,200
Interest	(1,600)
Tax	(3,300)
Profit for the year	5,300
Share capital	20,000
Retained earnings	15,600
	35,600
Loan liability	6,900
	42,500

What is Hassan's return on capital employed?

[ ] %

(2 marks)

25 Identify, by selecting the relevant boxes in the table below, whether each of the following statements about sales tax is true or false.

Sales tax is an expense to the ultimate consumer of the goods purchased.	**TRUE**	**FALSE**
Sales tax is recorded as income in the accounts of the entity selling the goods	**TRUE**	**FALSE**

(2 marks)

26 Q's trial balance failed to agree and a suspense account was opened for the difference. The following errors were found in Q's accounting records.

(1) In recording an issue of shares at par, cash received of $333,000 was credited to the ordinary share capital account as $330,000.

(2) Cash of $2,800 paid for plant repairs was correctly accounted for in the bank general ledger account but was credited to the plant asset account

(3) The petty cash balance of $500 had been omitted from the trial balance.

(4) A bank payment for $78,400 paid for the purchase of a motor car was debited to the motor vehicles account as $87,400.

Which of the errors will require an entry to the suspense account to correct them?

- O 1, 2 and 4 only
- O 1, 2, 3 and 4
- O 1 and 4 only
- O 2 and 3 only

(2 marks)

27 Prior to the financial year end of 31 July 20X9, Cannon Co has received a claim of $100,000 from a customer for providing poor quality goods which have damaged the customer's plant and equipment. Cannon Co's lawyers have stated that there is a 20% chance that Cannon will successfully defend the claim.

Which of the following is the correct accounting treatment for the claim in the financial statements for the year ended 31 July 20X9?

- O Cannon should neither provide for nor disclose the claim.
- O Cannon should disclose a contingent liability of $100,000.
- O Cannon should provide for the expected cost of the claim of $100,000.
- O Cannon should provide for an expected cost of $20,000. **(2 marks)**

---

28 Gareth, a sales tax registered trader purchased a computer for use in his business. The invoice for the computer showed the following costs related to the purchase:

	$
Computer	890
Additional memory	95
Delivery	10
Installation	20
Maintenance (one year)	25
	1,040
Sales tax (17.5%)	182
Total	1,222

How much should Gareth capitalise as a non-current asset in relation to the purchase?

$ [ ] **(2 marks)**

---

29 The following bank reconciliation statement has been prepared by a trainee accountant:

	$
Overdraft per bank statement	3,860
Less: Unpresented cheques	9,160
	5,300
Add: Outstanding lodgements	16,690
Bank general ledger account balance	21,990

What should be the correct balance per the bank general ledger account?

- O $21,990 balance at bank as stated
- O $3,670 balance at bank
- O $11,390 balance at bank
- O $3,670 overdrawn **(2 marks)**

---

30 The IASB's *Conceptual Framework* identifies characteristics which make financial information faithfully represent what it purports to represent.

Which **TWO** of the following are examples of those qualitative characteristics?

☐ Accruals

☐ Completeness

☐ Going concern

☐ Neutrality **(2 marks)**

---

31 The following general ledger account has been prepared by a trainee accountant:

TRADE RECEIVABLES

	$		$
Opening balance	308,600	Bank receipts	148,600
Credit sales	154,200	Interest charged on overdue accounts	2,400
Cash sales	88,100	Irrecoverable debts	4,900
Contras against credit balances in payables ledger	4,600	Allowance for receivables	2,800
		Closing balance	396,800
	555,500		555,500

What should the closing balance be when all the errors made in preparing the trade receivables account have been corrected?

○ $395,200

○ $304,300

○ $309,500

○ $307,100 **(2 marks)**

---

32 Identify, by selecting the relevant boxes in the table below, whether the following material events, which occurred after the reporting date and before the financial statements are approved, are adjusting or non-adjusting events.

A valuation of property providing evidence of impairment in value at the reporting date	**ADJUSTING**	**NON-ADJUSTING**
Sale of inventory held at the reporting date for less than cost	**ADJUSTING**	**NON-ADJUSTING**
Discovery of fraud or error affecting the financial statements	**ADJUSTING**	**NON-ADJUSTING**
The insolvency of a customer with a debt owing at the reporting date which is still outstanding	**ADJUSTING**	**NON-ADJUSTING**

(2 marks)

---

33 A company values its inventory using the FIFO method. At 1 May 20X5 the company had 700 engines in inventory, valued at $190 each. During the year ended 30 April 20X6 the following transactions took place:

20X5	
1 July	Purchased 500 engines at $220 each
1 November	Sold 400 engines for $160,000
20X6	
1 February	Purchased 300 engines at $230 each
15 April	Sold 250 engines for $125,000

What is the value of the company's closing inventory of engines at 30 April 20X6?

- $188,500
- $195,500
- $166,000
- $106,000

(2 marks)

---

34 Amy is a sole trader and had assets of $569,400 and liabilities of $412,840 on 1 January 20X8. During the year ended 31 December 20X8 she paid $65,000 capital into the business and she paid herself wages of $800 per month.

At 31 December 20X8, Amy had assets of $614,130 and liabilities of $369,770.

What is Amy's profit for the year ended 31 December 20X8?

$ [ ]

(2 marks)

---

35 Bumbly Co extracted the trial balance for the year ended 31 December 20X7. The total of the debits exceeded the credits by $300.

Which of the following could explain the imbalance?

- Sales of $300 were omitted from the receivables ledger.
- Returns inward of $150 were extracted to the debit column of the trial balance.
- Discounts received of $150 were extracted to the debit column of the trial balance.
- The bank general ledger account did not agree with the bank statement by a debit of $300.

(2 marks)

Section B

BOTH questions are compulsory and MUST be attempted

36 **Background**

Keswick Co acquired 80% of the share capital of Derwent Co on 1 June 20X5. The summarised draft statements of profit or loss for Keswick Co and Derwent Co for the year ended 31 May 20X6 are shown below:

	Keswick Co	*Derwent Co*
	$'000	$'000
Revenue	8,400	3,200
Cost of sales	(4,600)	(1,700)
Gross profit	3,800	1,500
Distribution costs	(1,500)	(510)
Administrative costs	(700)	(450)
Profit before tax	1,600	540
Tax	(600)	(140)
Profit of the year	1,000	400

During the year Keswick Co sold goods costing $1,000,000 to Derwent Co for $1,500,000. At 31 May 20X6, 30% of these goods remained in Derwent Co's inventory.

Task 1

Use the information above to complete the following financial statement. **(11 marks)**

Keswick Co

	$'000
Revenue	
Less: Cost of sales	
Gross profit	
Less:	
Distribution costs	
Administrative costs	
Profit before tax	
Less: Tax	
Profit for the year	
Attributable to:	
Equity owners of Keswick Co	
Non-controlling interest	

Task 2

Identify, by selecting the relevant boxes in the table below, whether each of the following factors indicate the existence of a parent – subsidiary relationship?

50% of all shares and debt being held by an investor	**YES**	**NO**
Greater than 50% of the preference shares being held by an investor	**YES**	**NO**
Control	**YES**	**NO**
Greater than 50% of the equity shares being held by an investor	**YES**	**NO**
100% of the equity shares being held by an investor	**YES**	**NO**
Significant influence	**YES**	**NO**
Non-controlling interest	**YES**	**NO**
Greater than 50% of preference shares and debt being held by an investor	**YES**	**NO**

(4 marks)

(Total = 15 marks)

---

37 Malright, a limited liability company, has an accounting year end of 31 October. The accountant is preparing the financial statements as at 31 October 20X7. A trial balance has been prepared.

Task 1

Do each of the following items belong on the statement of financial position (SOFP) as at 31 October 20X7? **(4 marks)**

	DEBIT	CREDIT	Belongs on SOFP as at 31 October 20X7
Buildings at cost	740		
Buildings accumulated depreciation at 1 November 20X6		60	
Plant at cost	220		
Plant accumulated depreciation at 1 November 20X6		110	
Bank balance		70	
Revenue		1,800	
Net purchases	1,140		
Inventory at 1 November 20X6	160		
Cash	20		
Trade payables		250	
Trade receivables	320		

	DEBIT	CREDIT	Belongs on SOFP as at 31 October 20X7
Administrative expenses	325		
Allowance for receivables at 1 November 20X6		10	
Retained earnings at 1 November 20X6		130	
Equity shares, $1		415	
Share premium account		80	
	2,925	2,925	

Task 2

The allowance for receivables is to be increased to 5% of trade receivables. The allowance for receivables is treated as an administrative expense.

The year end journal for allowance for receivables is given below. Prepare the double entry by selecting the correct option for each row.

Trade receivable	**DEBIT**	**CREDIT**	**NO DEBIT OR CREDIT**
Administrative expenses	**DEBIT**	**CREDIT**	**NO DEBIT OR CREDIT**
Allowance for receivables	**DEBIT**	**CREDIT**	**NO DEBIT OR CREDIT**
Revenue	**DEBIT**	**CREDIT**	**NO DEBIT OR CREDIT**

(3 marks)

Task 3

Complete the following:

The amount included in the statement of profit or loss after the allowance is increased to 5% of trade receivables is $ ________ . **(2 marks)**

Task 4

Plant is depreciated at 20% per annum using the diminishing balance method and buildings are depreciated at 5% per annum on their original cost. Depreciation is treated as a cost of sales expense.

The year end journal for buildings and plant depreciation is given below. Using the information above, prepare the double entry by selecting the correct option for each row.

Administrative expenses	**DEBIT**	**CREDIT**	**NO DEBIT OR CREDIT**
Cost of sales	**DEBIT**	**CREDIT**	**NO DEBIT OR CREDIT**
Buildings cost	**DEBIT**	**CREDIT**	**NO DEBIT OR CREDIT**
Plant cost	**DEBIT**	**CREDIT**	**NO DEBIT OR CREDIT**
Buildings accumulated depreciation	**DEBIT**	**CREDIT**	**NO DEBIT OR CREDIT**
Plant accumulated depreciation	**DEBIT**	**CREDIT**	**NO DEBIT OR CREDIT**

(3 marks)

Task 5

Calculate the depreciation charge for the below for the year ended 31 October 20X7. Use the information above to help you.

Buildings: $ [ ]

Plant: $ [ ] **(1 mark)**

Task 6

Closing inventory has been counted and is valued at $75,000.

Ignoring the depreciation charge calculated earlier, what is the cost of sales for the year?

$ [ ] **(1 mark)**

Task 7

An invoice of $15,000 for energy costs relating to the quarter ended 30 November 20X7 was received on 2 December 20X7. Energy costs are included in administrative expenses.

Complete the following statements:

The double entry to post the year end adjustment for energy costs is:

Debit: [ ]

Credit: [ ]

The amount to be posted within the year end adjustment double entry above:

$ [ ] **(1 mark)**

(Total = 15 marks)

Answers

DO NOT TURN THIS PAGE UNTIL YOU HAVE COMPLETED THE MOCK EXAM

Section A

1 The correct answer is: Closing net assets + drawings – capital introduced – opening net assets

Remember that: closing net assets = opening net assets + capital introduced + profit – drawings.

2 The correct answer is: The exact amount of expenditure is reimbursed at intervals to maintain a fixed float.

Under the imprest system, a reimbursement which equals the total of expense vouchers paid out, is made at intervals to maintain the petty cash balance at a certain amount.

3 The correct answer is: 2 and 3 only

The shareholder's exposure to debts is limited, not the company's

4 $ 331,760

TRADE PAYABLES

	$		$
Bank payments to suppliers	302,800	Balance b/f	60,000
Discounts received	2,960	**Purchases (bal fig)**	**331,760**
Contra	2,000		
Balance c/f	84,000		
	391,760		391,760

5 The correct answers are:

- A bank receipt from a customer was credited to bank and correctly recognised in receivables.
- Rent received was included in the trial balance as a debit balance.

Errors (1) and (3) will not cause a trial balance imbalance. In error (1), the incorrect amount will be posted to both sales and receivables (Dr receivables, Cr sales). In error (3), the complete omission of the transaction will have no effect on the trial balance.

6 The correct answer is:

Current assets $22,240 Current liabilities $nil

Current assets	$
Loan asset	12,000
Interest (12,000 × 12%)	240
Prepayment (8/12 × 9,000)	6,000
Accrued rent	4,000
	22,240

7 $ 97,100

	$
Profit	83,600
Purchase of van	18,000
Depreciation (18,000 × 25%)	(4,500)
	97,100

8 The correct answer is: Xena is suffering from a worsening liquidity position in 20X9.

The ratios given relate to working capital and liquidity. The ratios have all worsened from 20X8 to 20X9, suggesting a worsening liquidity position. Receivables days have gone up, meaning that customers are taking longer to pay. Payables days have gone down, meaning that Xena is paying suppliers more quickly. Inventory turnover days have gone up, meaning inventories are being held for longer.

9 The correct answers are:

A statement of cash flows prepared using the direct method produces a different figure to net cash from operating activities from that produced if the indirect method is used.		**FALSE**
Rights issues of shares do not feature in a statement of cash flows.		**FALSE**
A surplus on revaluation of a non-current asset will not appear as an item in a statement of cash flows.	**TRUE**	
A profit on the sale of a non-current asset will appear as an item under cash flows from investing activities in the statement of cash flows		**FALSE**

The direct and indirect method both produce the same figure for cash from operating activities. A rights issue of shares does feature in a statement of cash flows as cash is received for the issue, a bonus issue, however, would not feature as no cash is received. A profit on the sale of a non-current asset would not appear as an investing cash flow, rather the cash received from the sale would appear as an investing cash flow and the profit on the sale would be added back to profit before tax under the indirect method of calculating cash from operating activities

10 The correct answer is: $475,900

	$
Balance b/f (advance)	28,700
Balance b/f (arrears)	(21,200)
Cash received	481,200
Balance c/f (advance)	(31,200)
Balance c/f (arrears)	18,400
	475,900

11 The correct answers are:

- A sole trader's financial statements are private; a company's financial statements are sent to shareholders and may be publicly filed.
- A sole trader is fully and personally liable for any losses that the business might make.

A sole trader's financial statements are not publicly available, but they might be made available to some third parties, for example, the tax authorities.

12 The correct answer is: The analysis of financial statements using ratios provides useful information when compared with previous performance or industry averages

Ratio analysis is useful for different users of financial statements, including management, potential investors, the government, employees and so on. Historical performance can give an indication of what might occur in the future, especially if a trend is shown, but it cannot be used to accurately predict the future.

13 The correct answer is: $36,750 DEBIT

Motor vehicles – cost account is an asset and so the balance brought forward must be a debit. It is $36,750 as this is the figure that balances the account.

14 The correct answers are:

- The useful lives of intangible assets capitalised in the financial statements
- Impairment losses written off intangible assets during the period

An entity is **not** required to disclose a description of the development projects undertaken in the period, or a list of all intangible assets purchased or developed in the period. It is however, required to: disclose a description, the carrying amount and remaining amortisation period of any individual intangible asset that is **material** to the entity's financial statements, and distinguish between internally generated intangible assets capitalised in the period and those acquired in the period.

15 The correct answer is: 2 only

Statement 2 is the only correct statement. Statement 1 is incorrect because capitalised development expenditure is amortised over its useful life. Statement 3 is incorrect because research expenditure is never capitalised.

16 The correct answer is: $6,600

	$
Prepaid expenses brought forward	550
Expense incurred (cash)	5,400
Accrued expenses carried forward	650
	6,600

ANSWERS

17 $ 22,000

	$	$
Debts written off		37,000
Movement in allowance:		
(517 – 37) × 5%	24,000	
Less opening allowance	39,000	
		(15,000)
Receivables expense		22,000

18 The correct answer is: $437,810

	$
Balance per ledger	438,900
Less purchase return	(1,000)
Posting error	(90)
Corrected balance	437,830

The contra entry of $980 has already been entered into the accounting records. The purchase return of $1,000 must be recorded in the accounting records, thereby reducing trade payables. The invoice has been overstated by $90 and must also be deducted.

19 The correct answers are:

- Carriage inwards
- Depreciation of factory plant

Carriage outwards is a distribution expense. General administrative overheads should not be included per IAS 2.

20 $ 17,060

(6,700 + 84,000 – 5,400) × 20% = $17,060.

21 The correct answer is:

Ordinary share capital	***Share premium account***
$225,000	$250,000

Share capital = 125,000 + 62,500 rights issue of 250,000 25c shares (500,000/2) + 37,500 bonus issue of 150,000 25c shares (750,000/5) = 225,000

Share premium = 100,000 + 187,500 rights issue (250,000 × 75c) – 37,500 bonus issue (150,000 × 25c) = 250,000

22 The correct answer is: 1 and 3 only

Amortisation of development costs will appear in the statement of profit or loss, not the statement of changes in equity.

23 The correct answer is: $55,000

	$
Depreciation:	
Jan–Mar 240,000 × 20% × 3/12	9,000
Apr–Jun (240,000 – 60,000) × 20% × 3/12	34,000
Jul–Dec (180,000 + 160,000) × 20% × 6/12	12,000
	55,000

24 [24] %

The correct answer is: 10,200/42,500 = 24%.

25 The correct answers are:

Sales tax is an expense to the ultimate consumer of the goods purchased.	**TRUE**	
Sales tax is recorded as income in the accounts of the entity selling the goods		**FALSE**

Sales tax is merely collected by the business, the ultimate consumer bears the expense.

26 The correct answer is: 1, 2, 3 and 4

All of the errors would require an entry to the suspense account to correct them.

27 The correct answer is: Cannon should provide for the expected cost of the claim of $100,000.

It is probable that Canon will have to pay $100,000 for the claim, therefore a provision is required.

28 $ [1,015]

1,040 – 25 = $1,015. The maintenance costs should not be capitalised. The sales tax is recoverable as Gareth is registered for sales tax, therefore, it should not be capitalised.

29 The correct answer is: $3,670 balance at bank

	$
Overdraft per bank statement	(3,860)
Less Unpresented cheques	(9,160)
Add: Outstanding lodgements	16,690
Bank general ledger account balance	3,670

30 The correct answers are:

- Completeness
- Neutrality

Completeness and neutrality are two characteristics given in the *Conceptual Framework*. Going concern is the underlying assumption and accruals is not a stated characteristic.

31 The correct answer is: $307,100

TRADE RECEIVABLES

	$		$
Opening balance	308,600	Bank receipts	148,600
Credit sales	154,200	Contras	4,600
Interest charged on overdue accounts	2,400	Irrecoverable debts	4,900
		Closing balance	**307,100**
	465,200		465,200

32 The correct answers are:

A valuation of property providing evidence of impairment in value at the reporting date	**ADJUSTING**	
Sale of inventory held at the reporting date for less than cost	**ADJUSTING**	
Discovery of fraud or error affecting the financial statements	**ADJUSTING**	
The insolvency of a customer with a debt owing at the reporting date which is still outstanding	**ADJUSTING**	

All of the events are adjusting events.

33 The correct answer is: $188,500

Closing inventory:

	$
50 × $190	9,500
500 × $220	110,000
300 × $230	69,000
	188,500

34 $ 32,400

Closing net assets = opening net assets + capital introduced + profit – drawings

	$
Opening assets	569,400
Opening liabilities	(412,840)
Capital introduced	65,000
Drawings (800 × 12)	(9,600)
	211,960
Profit (bal fig)	**32,400**
Closing net assets (614,130 – 369,770)	244,360

35 The correct answer is: Discounts received of $150 were extracted to the debit column of the trial balance.

Discounts received are recorded as a credit balance and appear as other income in the statement of profit or loss: DEBIT payables, CREDIT discounts received.

Section B

36 **Task 1**

Keswick Co

	$'000
Revenue	10,100
Less: Cost of sales	(4,950)
Gross profit	5,150
Less:	
Distribution costs	(2,010)
Administrative costs	(1,150)
Profit before tax	1,990
Less: Tax	(740)
Profit for the year	1,250
Attributable to:	
Equity owners of Keswick Co	1,170
Non-controlling interest	80

KESWICK GROUP

CONSOLIDATED STATEMENT OF PROFIT OR LOSS FOR THE YEAR ENDED 31 MAY 20X6

	$'000
Revenue (8,400 + 3,200 – 1,500)	10,100
Less: Cost of sales (4,600 + 1,700 – 1,500 + 150)	(4,950)
Gross profit	5,150
Less:	
Distribution costs	(2,010)
Administration costs	(1,150)
Profit before tax	1,990
Less: Tax (600 + 140)	(740)
Profit of the year	1,250
Attributable to:	
Equity owners of Keswick Co	1,170
Non-controlling interest ($400,000 × 20%)	80

Task 2

The correct answers are:

50% of all shares and debt being held by an investor		**NO**
Greater than 50% of the preference shares being held by an investor	**YES**	
Control	**YES**	
Greater than 50% of the equity shares being held by an investor	**YES**	
100% of the equity shares being held by an investor	**YES**	
Significant influence		**NO**
Non-controlling interest		**NO**
Greater than 50% of preference shares and debt being held by an investor		**NO**

37 **Task 1**

	DEBIT	CREDIT	Belongs on SOFP as at 31 October 20X7
Buildings at cost	740		Yes
Buildings accumulated depreciation at 1 November 20X6		60	No
Plant at cost	220		Yes
Plant accumulated depreciation at 1 November 20X6		110	No
Bank balance		70	Yes
Revenue		1,800	No
Net purchases	1,140		No
Inventory at 1 November 20X6	160		No
Cash	20		Yes
Trade payables		250	Yes
Trade receivables	320		Yes
Administrative expenses	325		No
Allowance for receivables at 1 November 20X6		10	No
Retained earnings at 1 November 20X6		130	No
Equity shares, $1		415	Yes
Share premium account		80	Yes
	2,925	2,925	

Task 2

The correct answers are:

Trade receivable			**NO DEBIT OR CREDIT**
Administrative expenses	**DEBIT**		
Allowance for receivables		**CREDIT**	
Revenue			**NO DEBIT OR CREDIT**

Task 3

The amount included in the statement of profit or loss after the allowance is increased to 5% of trade receivables is $ 6,000 .

Working

Required end allowance is 320,000 × 5% = $16,000

As the allowance for receivables has an existing balance of $10,000, the allowance must be increased by $6,000.

Task 4

The correct answers are:

Administrative expenses			**NO DEBIT OR CREDIT**
Cost of sales	**DEBIT**		
Buildings cost			**NO DEBIT OR CREDIT**
Plant cost			**NO DEBIT OR CREDIT**
Buildings accumulated depreciation		**CREDIT**	
Plant accumulated depreciation		**CREDIT**	

Task 5

Buildings: $ 37,000

Plant: $ 22,000

Working

740 × 5%

(220 –110) × 20%

Task 6

$ 1,225,000

Working

	$'000
Opening inventory	160
Purchases	1,140
Closing inventory	(75)
	1,225

Task 7

The double entry to post the year end adjustment for energy costs is:

Debit: Administrative expenses

Credit: Accrual

The amount to be posted within the year end adjustment double entry above:

$ 10,000

Energy cost accrual

15,000 × 2/3 = $10,000

ANSWERS

Foundations in Accountancy/ACCA

Financial Accounting (FFA/FA)

Mock Exam 2

Questions	
Time allowed	2 hours
This exam is divided into two sections: Section A – ALL 35 questions are compulsory and MUST be attempted Section B – BOTH questions are compulsory and MUST be attempted	

DO NOT OPEN THIS EXAM UNTIL YOU ARE READY TO START UNDER EXAMINATION CONDITIONS

Section A

ALL 35 questions are compulsory and MUST be attempted

1 In accordance with IAS 37 *Provisions, Contingent Liabilities and Contingent Assets*, which of the following criteria must be present in order for a company to recognise a provision?

(1) There is a present obligation as a result of past events.

(2) It is probable that a transfer of economic benefits will be required to settle the obligation.

(3) A reliable estimate of the obligation can be made.

- O All three criteria must be present
- O 1 and 2 only
- O 1 and 3 only
- O 2 and 3 only **(2 marks)**

---

2 Which of the following types of error is never indicated when a trial balance is extracted?

- O Errors of commission
- O Errors of omission
- O Errors of principle
- O Transposition errors **(2 marks)**

---

3 Nooma Co owns 55% of the ordinary shares of Matic Co. What is the correct accounting treatment of the revenues and costs of Matic Co in the consolidated statement of profit or loss of the Nooma Group?

- O The revenues and costs of Matic Co are added to the revenues and costs of Nooma Co on a line by line basis.
- O 55% of the profit for the year of Matic Co should be added to Nooma Co's consolidated profit for the year.
- O 55% of the revenues and costs of Matic Co are added to the revenues and costs of Nooma Co on a line by line basis.
- O Only dividends received from Matic Co are shown in the consolidated statement of profit or loss of Nooma Co. **(2 marks)**

---

4 Your firm's accounting records at 30 April 20X8 shows a bank general ledger account balance of $2,490. Comparison with the bank statement at the same date reveals the following differences:

	$
Unpresented cheques	840
Bank charges not in bank general ledger account	50
Receipts not yet credited by the bank	470
Dishonoured cheque not in bank general ledger account	140

What is the adjusted bank balance per the bank general ledger account at 30 April 20X8?

$ [ ] **(2 marks)**

---

5 W Co, a sales tax registered trader, bought a new printing machine. The cost of the machine was $80,000, excluding sales tax at 17.5%. The delivery costs were $2,000 and installation costs were $5,000. Before using the machine to print customers' orders, a test was undertaken and the paper and ink cost $1,000.

What should be the cost of the machine in the company's statement of financial position?

$ [ ] **(2 marks)**

---

6 Which of the following correctly defines 'equity' according to the IASB's *Conceptual Framework*?

- O Equity is a present obligation of the entity arising from past events, the settlement of which is expected to result in an outflow from the entity of resources embodying economic benefit.
- O Equity is a resource controlled by an entity as a result of past events and from which future economic benefits are expected to flow to the entity.
- O Equity is the residual interest in the assets of the entity after deducting all its liabilities.
- O Equity is increases in economic benefits during the accounting period in the form of inflows or enhancements of assets or decreases of liabilities. **(2 marks)**

---

7 Which of the following is a qualitative characteristic of financial information included in the IASB's *Conceptual Framework*?

- O Relevance
- O Materiality
- O Consistency
- O Accruals **(2 marks)**

---

8 S & Co sells three products – A, B and C. The following information was available at the year end.

	Basic	*Super*	*Luxury*
	$ per unit	$ per unit	$ per unit
Original cost	10	9	20
Estimated selling price	9	12	26
Selling and distribution costs	1	4	5
	units	*units*	*units*
Units of inventory	500	1,250	850

In accordance with IAS 2 *Inventories*, what is the value of inventory at the year end?

$ [ ] **(2 marks)**

---

9 A car was purchased by a business in May 20X1 for:

	$
Cost	10,000
Road fund licence	150
Total	10,150

The business adopts a date of 31 December as its year end.

The car was traded in for a replacement vehicle in August 20X4 at an agreed value of $5,000.

It has been depreciated at 25% per annum using the diminishing balance method, charging a full year's depreciation in the year of purchase and none in the year of sale.

What was the profit or loss on disposal of the vehicle during the year ended December 20X4?

- O Loss of $2,890
- O Profit of $781
- O Profit of $2,500
- O Profit of $3,750 **(2 marks)**

---

10 At 1 January 20X3, Attila Co had an allowance for receivables of $35,000. At 31 December 20X3, the trade receivables of the company were $620,000. It was decided to:

(1) Write off (as uncollectable) receivables totalling $30,000; and

(2) Adjust the allowance for receivables to an amount equivalent to 5% of receivables.

What is the combined expense that should appear in the company's statement of profit or loss for the year, for irrecoverable debts and the allowance for receivables?

- O $24,500
- O $26,000
- O $34,000
- O $35,500 **(2 marks)**

---

11 The annual sales of a company are $235,000 including sales tax at 17.5%. Half of the sales are on credit terms, half are cash sales. The receivables in the statement of financial position are $23,500.

What is the output tax?

$ [ ] **(2 marks)**

---

12 Beta purchased some plant and equipment on 1 July 20X1 for $40,000. The scrap value of the plant in ten years' time is estimated to be $4,000. Beta's policy is to charge depreciation on the straight line basis, with a proportionate charge in the period of acquisition.

What is the depreciation charge on the plant in Beta's financial statements for the year ended 30 September 20X1?

- O $900
- O $1,000
- O $3,600
- O $4,000

(2 marks)

---

13 The following figures are taken from the statement of financial position of GEN Co.

	$m
Inventory	2
Receivables	3
Cash	1
Payables	3
Bank loan repayable in 5 years time	3

What is GEN Co's current ratio?

- O 1.33
- O 2.00
- O 1.00
- O 0.33

(2 marks)

---

14 A particular source of finance has the following characteristics: fixed payments, a fixed repayment date, it is secured on the assets of the company and the payments are class fied as an expense.

Which of the following best describes this source of finance?

- O A redeemable preference share
- O An irredeemable preference share
- O A loan note
- O An overdraft

(2 marks)

---

15 Tong Co acquired 100% of the $100,000 ordinary share capital of Cheek Co for $1,200,000 on 1 January 20X5 when the retained earnings of Cheek Co were $550,000 and the balance on the revaluation surplus was $150,000. At the date of acquisition, the fair value of plant held by Cheek Co was $80,000 higher than its carrying amount.

What is the goodwill arising on the acquisition of Cheek Co?

- O $320,000
- O $400,000
- O $470,000
- O $550,000

(2 marks)

---

16 During the year ended 31 December 20X1, Alpha Rescue had the following transactions on the trade receivables ledger.

	$
Receivables at 1 January 20X1	100,000
Receivables at 31 December 20X1	107,250
Goods returned	12,750
Amounts paid into the bank from receivables	230,000
Discount received	75,000

What were the sales for the year?

- O $107,250
- O $240,000
- O $250,000
- O $320,000

(2 marks)

---

17 Financial analysts calculate ratios from the published financial statements of large companies. Which one of the following reasons is **UNLIKELY** to be a reason why they calculate and analyse financial ratios?

- O Ratios can reduce lengthy or complex financial statements into a fairly small number of more easily-understood indicators.
- O Ratios can predict a company's future performance.
- O Ratios can help with comparisons between businesses in the same industry.
- O Ratios can indicate changes in the financial performance and financial position of a business over time.

(2 marks)

---

18 Cat Co has held 85% of the share capital of Dog Co for many years. During the current year Cat Co sold goods to Dog Co for $15,000, including a mark up of 25% on cost. 60% of these goods were still in inventory at the year end.

The following extract was taken from the accounting records of Cat Co and Dog Co at 31 March 20X8.

	Cat Co	*Dog Co*
	$'000	$'000
Opening inventory	650	275
Closing Inventory	750	400

What is the figure for inventory to be included in the statement of financial position of the Cat Group at 31 March 20X8?

- O $1,151,800
- O $1,152,250
- O $1,197,750
- O $1,148,200

(2 marks)

---

19 A company's quick ratio has increased from 0.9:1 at 31 December 20X1 to 1.5:1 at 31 December 20X2. Which of the following events could explain this increase?

- O Improved inventory control
- O The refinancing of a long-term loan
- O A reduction in payables
- O An increase in payables

(2 marks)

---

20 Which of the following represents an error of original entry?

- O The purchase of goods for resale using cash was debited to the purchases account and credited to the bank general ledger account using the incorrect amount in both cases.
- O The purchase of goods for resale using cash was debited to the motor vehicles account and credited to the bank general ledger account using the correct amount in both cases.
- O The purchase of goods for resale using cash was debited to the purchases account and credited to the sales account using the correct amount in both cases.
- O The purchase of goods for resale using cash was debited to the purchases account but no credit entry was made.

(2 marks)

---

21 A machine was purchased for $100,000 on 1 January 20X1 and was expected to have a useful life of 10 years. After three years, management revised their expectation of the remaining useful life to 20 years. The business depreciates machines using the straight line method.

What is the carrying amount of the machine at 31 December 20X5?

$ [ ]

(2 marks)

---

22 Your organisation has received a statement of account from one of its suppliers, showing an outstanding balance due to them of $1,350. On comparison with your ledger account, the following is determined:

- Your ledger account shows a credit balance of $260.
- The supplier has disallowed a settlement discount of $80 due to late payment of an invoice.
- The supplier has not yet allowed for goods returned at the end of the period of $270.
- Cash in transit of $830 has not been received by the supplier.

Following consideration of these items, what is the unreconciled difference between the two records?

O $nil

O $10

O $90

O $180 **(2 marks)**

---

23 A company is preparing its statement of cash flows for the year ended 31 December 20X2. Relevant extracts from the accounts are as follows.

Statement of profit or loss	$
Depreciation	15,000
Profit on sale of non-current assets	40,000

Statement of financial position	*20X2*	*20X1*
	$	$
Plant and machinery – cost	185,000	250,000
Plant and machinery – depreciation	45,000	50,000

Plant and machinery additions during the year were $35,000. What is the cash flow arising from the sale of non-current assets?

O $40,000

O $100,000

O $120,000

O $135,000 **(2 marks)**

---

24 Which body is responsible for issuing IFRS Standards?

O IFRS Interpretations Committee

O IFRS Advisory Council

O International Accounting Standards Board (the Board)

O The United Nations **(2 marks)**

---

25 Teo Co acquired 95% of the ordinary share capital of Mat Co 31 December 20X0. The following information relates to Mat Co:

	20X0	*20X1*
	$'000	$'000
Retained earnings	700	800
Revaluation surplus	–	100
	700	900

The fair value of the non-controlling interest in Mat Co at the date of acquisition was $45,000.

What is the amount reported for non-controlling interest in the statement of financial position of the Teo Group as at 31 December 20X1?

$ [ ]

(2 marks)

---

26 Identify, by selecting the relevant boxes in the table below, whether each of the following statements is correct or incorrect.

AZ owns 25% of the preferred (non-voting) share capital of BX, which means that BX is an associate of AZ.	CORRECT	INCORRECT
CW has a 10% shareholding in DY and can appoint 4 out of 6 directors to the board of DY, so DY is classified as a subsidiary of CW.	CORRECT	INCORRECT
ES has significant influence over FT, which means that FT is an associate of ES.	CORRECT	INCORRECT
GR owns 55% of the share capital of HU, but by agreement with the minority shareholder, does not have control or significant influence over the financial and operating policies of HU, so HU is a simple investment of GR.	CORRECT	INCORRECT

(2 marks)

---

27 Which, if any, of the following journal entries is correct according to their narratives?

		DEBIT $	CREDIT $
1	B receivables ledger account Irrecoverable debts account Irrecoverable debt of B written off	450	 450
2	Investments: Q ordinary shares Share capital 80,000 shares of 50c each issued at $1.25 in exchange for shares in Q.	100,000	 100,000
3	Suspense account Motor vehicles account Correction of error – debit side of motor vehicles account undercast by $1,000	1,000	 1,000

- O None of them
- O 1 only
- O 2 only
- O 3 only

(2 marks)

---

28 Jay Co values inventories on the first in first out (FIFO) basis. Jay Co has 120 items of product A valued at $8 each in inventory at 1 October 20X9. During October 20X9, the following transactions in product A took place.

3 October	Purchases	180 items at $9 each
4 October	Sales	150 items at $12 each
8 October	Sales	80 items at $15 each
18 October	Purchases	300 items at $10 each
22 October	Sales	100 items at $15 each

What is the closing balance on the inventory account at 31 October 20X9?

$ [ ]

(2 marks)

---

29 Fred's trial balance did not balance so he opened a suspense account with a debit balance of $346.

Fred discovered the following:

(1) A purchase credit note for $400 had been omitted from the accounting records.

(2) Credit purchases of $520 have only been recorded in the trade payables account.

(3) Profit on sale of non-current assets of $670 had been recorded in the sundry income account as $760.

What is the remaining balance on Fred's suspense account after these errors have been corrected?

- O $264 CREDIT
- O $136 DEBIT
- O $956 DEBIT
- O $1,266 DEBIT

(2 marks)

---

30 Charles Co entered into the following transactions:

(1) He made a credit sale to Mary allowing a 5% trade discount on the list price of $640, and a further 5% discount for immediate cash payment.

(2) He purchased goods with a list price of $600 and received a 10% trade discount and further 2% discount for payment within seven days. He paid three days later.

How much discount should be recorded in the discounts received account as a result of the above transactions?

- O $10.80
- O $30.40
- O $62.40
- O $70.80

(2 marks)

---

31 Where, in a company's financial statements complying with IFRS Standards, should you find the proceeds of non-current assets sold during the period?

- O Statement of cash flows and statement of financial position
- O Statement of changes in equity and statement of financial position
- O Statement of profit or loss and other comprehensive income and statement of cash flows
- O Statement of cash flows only

(2 marks)

---

32 If the current ratio for a company is equal to its quick ratio, which of the following statements is true?

- O The current ratio must be greater than one.
- O The company does not carry any inventory.
- O Receivables plus cash is greater than payables minus inventories.
- O Working capital is positive

(2 marks)

---

33 The closing inventory of Epsilon amounted to $284,000 at 30 September 20X1, the reporting date. This total includes two inventory lines about which the inventory taker is uncertain.

(1) 500 items which had cost $15 each and which were included at $7,500. These items were found to have been defective at the end of the reporting period. Remedial work after the reporting period cost $1,800 and they were then sold for $20 each. Selling expenses were $400.

(2) 100 items which had cost $10 each. After the reporting period they were sold for $8 each, with selling expenses of $150.

What figure should appear in Epsilon's statement of financial position for inventory?

- O $283,650
- O $283,800
- O $284,000
- O $284,450

(2 marks)

---

34 Which **TWO** of these statements about research and development expenditure are correct in accordance with IAS 38 *Intangible Assets*?

- ☐ If certain conditions are satisfied, research and development expenditure must be capitalised.
- ☐ One of the conditions to be satisfied if development expenditure is to be capitalised is that the technical feasibility of the project is reasonably assured.
- ☐ The amount of capitalised development expenditure for each project should be reviewed each year. If circumstances no longer justify the capitalisation, the balance should be written off over a period not exceeding five years.
- ☐ Development expenditure may only be capitalised if it can be shown that adequate resources will be available to finance the completion of the project

(2 marks)

---

35 A company measures the average time to collect receivables as:

[Receivables at end of financial year/Annual credit sales] × 365 days

Accounting ratios have just been calculated from the financial statements for the financial year that has just ended. These show an abnormally high average time to collect receivables, compared with ratios calculated for the previous financial year.

Which of the following may help to explain this unusually high turnover period for trade receivables?

- O There was an unusually large sale on credit close to the end of the financial year.
- O The company has seasonal trade, and sales in the final quarter of the year are always higher than in the other quarters.
- O However, sales in the final quarter of the year that has just ended were lower than in the previous year.
- O The company improved its credit control processes during the year.

(2 marks)

Section B

BOTH questions are compulsory and MUST be attempted

36 You have been given the following information relating to a limited liability company called Nobrie. This company is preparing financial statements for the year ended 31 May 20X4.

NOBRIE

STATEMENT OF PROFIT OR LOSS FOR THE YEAR ENDED 31 MAY 20X4

	$'000
Revenue	66,600
Cost of sales	(13,785)
Gross profit	52,815
Distribution costs	(7,530)
Administrative expenses	(2,516)
Investment income	146
Finance cost	(1,177)
Profit before tax	41,738
Tax	(9,857)
Profit for the year	31,881
Retained earnings brought forward at 1 June 20X3	28,063
Retained earnings carried forward at 31 May 20X4	59,944

NOBRIE

STATEMENTS OF FINANCIAL POSITION AS AT 31 MAY

		20X4		*20X3*
	$'000	$'000	$'000	$'000
Assets				
Non-current assets				
Cost		144,844		114,785
Accumulated depreciation		(27,433)		(26,319)
		117,411		88,466
Current assets				
Inventory	24,931		24,065	
Trade receivables	18,922		13,238	
Cash	3,689		2,224	
		47,542		39,527
Total assets		164,953		127,993

	$'000	20X4 $'000	$'000	20X3 $'000
Equity and liabilities				
Equity				
Ordinary share capital	27,000		23,331	
Share premium	14,569		10,788	
Revaluation surplus	15,395		7,123	
Retained earnings	59,944		28,063	
		116,908		69,305
Non current liabilities				
6% loan note		17,824		24,068
Current liabilities				
Bank overdraft	5,533		6,973	
Trade payables	16,699		20,324	
Taxation	7,989		7,323	
		30,221		34,620
Total equity and liabilities		164,953		127,993

Additional information

(1) During the year ended 31 May 20X4, the company sold a piece of equipment for $3,053,000, realising a profit of $1,540,000. There were no other disposals of non-current assets during the year.

(2) Depreciation of $5,862,000 has been charged.

(3) There were no amounts outstanding in respect of interest payable or receivable as at 31 May 20X3 or 20X4.

(4) There were no dividends paid or declared during the year.

Task 1

Complete the following cash flows from operating activities section in the statement of cash flows for Nobrie for the year ended 31 May 20X4. **(8 marks)**

NOBRIE

STATEMENT OF CASH FLOWS FOR THE YEAR ENDED 30 MAY 20X4

	$'000	$'000
Cash flow from operating activities		
Profit before tax		
Adjustments for		
Depreciation		
Profit on equipment disposal		
Investment income		
Interest paid		
Operating profit before working capital changes		

	$'000	$'000
Increase in inventory	[ ]	
Increase in receivables	[ ]	
Decrease in payables	[ ]	
Cash generated from operations	[ ]	
Interest paid*	[ ]	
Tax paid [ ]	[ ]	
Net cash flows from operating activities		[ ]

Task 2

Complete the following sentences.

The carrying amount of property, plant and equipment disposals:

$ [ ]

The cash purchases of property, plant and equipment for the year ended 31 May 20X4:

$ [ ] **(5 marks)**

Task 3

Which **TWO** of the following increases in equity accounts are shown as cash inflows in the cash flows from financing section of the statement of cash flows?

☐ Increase in share capital

☐ Increase in share premium

☐ Increase in revaluation surplus

☐ Increase in retained earnings **(2 marks)**

(Total = 15 marks)

---

37 The draft statements of financial position of Spyder and its subsidiary company Phly at 31 October 20X5 are as follows.

	Spyder	*Phly*
	$'000	$'000
Assets		
Non-current assets		
Tangible assets		
Land and buildings	315,000	278,000
Plant	285,000	220,000
	600,000	498,000
Investment		
Shares in Phly at cost	660,000	–

	Spyder	Phly
	$'000	$'000
Current assets		
Inventory	357,000	252,000
Receivables	525,000	126,000
Bank	158,000	30,000
	1,040,000	408,000
	2,300,000	906,000
Equity and liabilities		
Equity		
$1 ordinary shares	1,500,000	600,000
Retained earnings	580,000	212,000
	2,080,000	812,000
Current liabilities		
Payables	220,000	94,000
Total equity and liabilities	2,300,000	906,000

The following information is also available

(1) Spyder purchased 480 million shares in Phly some years ago, when Phly had a credit balance of $95 million in retained earnings. The fair value of the non-controlling interest at the date of acquisition was $165 million.

(2) At the date of acquisition the freehold land of Phly was valued at $70 million in excess of its carrying amount. The revaluation was not recorded in the accounts of Phly.

(3) Phly's inventory includes goods purchased from Spyder at a price that includes a profit to Spyder of $12 million.

(4) At 31 October 20X5 Phly owes Spyder $25 million for goods purchased during the year.

Task 1

Calculate the total goodwill on acquisition by completing the table below. **(5 marks)**

Calculation of goodwill

	$'000	$'000
Fair value of consideration transferred		
Fair value of NCI at acquisition		
Less Net acquisition-date fair value of identifiable assets acquired and liabilities assumed:		
Share capital	600,000	
Retained earnings at acquisition	95,000	
Fair value adjustment at acquisition	70,000	
		(765,000)
Goodwill		

Task 2

Complete the following consolidated statement of financial position for Spyder as at 31 October 20X5. **(10 marks)**

SPYDER GROUP

CONSOLIDATED STATEMENT OF FINANCIAL POSITION AS AT 31 OCTOBER 20X5

		$'000
Assets		
Non-current assets		
Goodwill		
Land and buildings		
Plant		
Current assets		
Inventory		
Receivables		
Bank		
Total assets		
Equity and liabilities		
Equity attributable to owners of the parent		
$1 ordinary shares		
Retained earnings		
Non-controlling interest		
Current liabilities		
Payables		
Total equity and liabilities		

(Total = 15 marks)

Answers

DO NOT TURN THIS PAGE UNTIL YOU HAVE COMPLETED THE MOCK EXAM

Section A

1 The correct answer is: All three criteria must be present

2 The correct answer is: Errors of principle

The existence of a transposition error should always be revealed by a trial balance. Errors of omission and commission may or may not be revealed, depending on the nature of the error and whether the error has resulted in a mismatch between debt and credit entries in the general ledger accounts. An error of omission is never revealed, because there have been no entries in the general ledger for the omitted item.

3 The correct answer is: The revenues and costs of Matic Co are added to the revenues and costs of Nooma Co on a line by line basis.

Matic Co is a subsidiary of Nooma Co, so the results of Matic Co should be consolidated on a line by line basis with the results of Nooma Co.

4 $ 2,300

	$
Original bank general ledger account figure	2,490
Adjustment re bank charges	(50)
Adjustment re dishonoured cheque	(140)
Adjusted bank general ledger account figure	2,300

5 $ 88,000

	$
Cost of machine	80,000
Installation	5,000
Delivery	2,000
Testing	1,000
	88,000

6 The correct answer is: Equity is the residual interest in the assets of the entity after deducting all its liabilities.

The first option is the definition of a liability, the second option is the definition of an asset and the fourth option is the definition of income according to the IASB's *Conceptual Framework*.

7 The correct answer is: Relevance

Relevance is a qualitative characteristic. The other options are accounting concepts.

8 $ 31,000

	Cost	Net realisable value	Lower of cost & NRV	Units	Value
	$	$	$		$
A	10	8	8	500	4,000
B	9	8	8	1,250	10,000
C	20	21	20	850	17,000
					31,000

9 The correct answer is: Profit of $781

	$
Cost	10,000
20X1 Depreciation	2,500
	7,500
20X2 Depreciation	1,875
	5,625
20X3 Depreciation	1,406
	4,219
20X4 Part exchange	5,000
Profit	781

10 The correct answer is: $24,500

	$	$
Amount written off		30,000
Allowance for receivables at 31 December 20X3 5% × $(620,000 – 30,000)	29,500	
Allowance for receivables at 1 January 20X3	35,000	
Reduction in allowance for receivables		(5,500)
Combined expense		24,500

11 $ 35,000

Output tax = $^{235,000}/_{117.5}$ × 17.5

12 The correct answer is: $900

($36,000/10) × 3/12

13 The correct answer is: 2.00

This is the ratio of current assets to current liabilities. The third option is wrong as the five-year bank loan would not normally be included with current liabilities. The first option is the quick ratio (excludes inventory).

14 The correct answer is: A loan note

It is a loan note. It is not a preference share because it is secured. An overdraft does not have a fixed return or a fixed repayment date and is not secured.

15 The correct answer is: $320,000

	$	$
Fair value of consideration		1,200,000
Net assets at acquisition as represented by		
Share capital	100,000	
Retained earnings	550,000	
Revaluation surplus	150,000	
Fair value adjustment	80,000	
		(880,000)
Goodwill		320,000

16 The correct answer is: $250,000

TRADE RECEIVABLES

	$		$
Balance b/f	100,000	Bank	230,000
Sales (balancing figure)	250,000	Returns	12,750
		Balance c/f	107,250
	350,000		350,000

Discounts received refer to purchases and are posted to the trade payables account.

17 The correct answer is: Ratios can predict a company's future performance.

Ratios can be used to analyse financial performance, and to make comparisons of performance over time and between different businesses in the same industry, but they cannot usually provide a reliable indicator of insolvency, especially if they are prepared only once a year.

18 The correct answer is: $1,148,200

	$'000
Unrealised profit (15,000 × 25/125 × 60%)	1.8
Inventory (750 + 400 – 1.8)	1,148.2

ANSWERS

19 The correct answer is: A reduction in payables

Quick ratio = current assets excluding inventories/current liabilities.

The quick ratio does not include inventories or long term loans, so the first and second options will have no effect. An increase in payables would reduce the quick ratio.

20 The correct answer is: The purchase of goods for resale using cash was debited to the purchases account and credited to the bank general ledger account using the incorrect amount in both cases.

The second and third options are errors of principle, the fourth option is an error of omission.

21 $ 63,000

Carrying amount at the end of year 3: 100,000 – (100,000 × 3/10) = $70,000

Carrying amount at the end of year 5: 70,000 – (70,000 × 2/20) = $63,000

22 The correct answer is: $90

	$
Ledger balance	260
Add back:	
disallowed discount	80
returns goods	270
cash in transit	830
Total balance	1,440
As stated by the supplier	1,350
Unreconciled difference	90

23 The correct answer is: $120,000

	$
Sale proceeds (balancing figure)	120,000
Carrying amount (see below)	80,000
Profit on sale	40,000
Carrying amount at 31 December 20X1 (250,000 – 50,000)	200,000
Additions	35,000
	235,000
Carrying amount of disposals (balancing figure)	(80,000)
Depreciation	(15,000)
Carrying amount at 31 December 20X2 (185,000 – 45,000)	140,000

24 The correct answer is: International Accounting Standards Board (the Board)

The Board is responsible for issuing IFRS Standards.

25 $ 55,000

	$
Fair value of NCI at acquisition	45,000
Plus NCI's share of post-acquisition retained earnings (and other reserves) ((800 – 100) × 5% + 100 × 5%)	10,000
NCI at reporting date (31 December 20X1)	55,000

26 The correct answers are:

AZ owns 25% of the preferred (non-voting) share capital of BX, which means that BX is an associate of AZ.		INCORRECT
CW has a 10% shareholding in DY and can appoint 4 out of 6 directors to the board of DY, so DY is classified as a subsidiary of CW.	CORRECT	
ES has significant influence over FT, which means that FT is an associate of ES.	CORRECT	
GR owns 55% of the share capital of HU, but by agreement with the minority shareholder, does not have control or significant influence over the financial and operating policies of HU, so HU is a simple investment of GR.	CORRECT	

The correct answer is: An investor must have significant influence over the investee in order for the investee to be classified as an associate, therefore (3) is correct.

If the investor owns between 20% and <50% of the **ordinary shares (voting)** of the investee, significant influence can be assumed. (1) is not true as the shares held do not have voting rights. For an investee to be classified as a subsidiary, the investor must have control over the investee. Control can be demonstrated if the investor can appoint the majority of board members of the investee, so (2) is correct. (4) is also correct as despite its 55% shareholding, GR does not have control or significant influence over HU and as such is not classified as a subsidiary or as an associate, but as a simple trade investment

27 The correct answer is: None of them

All three are incorrect. In 1 and 3 the debit and credit entries should be reversed and 2 should show a credit of $60,000 to the share premium account.

ANSWERS

28 $ 2,700

Date		No. of items	Unit price $	Value $
1.10.X9	Balance	120	8	960
3.10.X9	Purchases	180	9	1,620
	Balance	300		2,580
4.10.X9	Sales	(120)	8	(960)
	Sales	(30)	9	(270)
	Balance	150		1,350
8.10.X9	Sales	(80)	9	(720)
	Balance	70		630
18.10.X9	Purchases	300	10	3,000
	Balance	370		3,630
22.10.X9	Sales	(70)	9	(630)
	Sales	(30)	10	(300)
	Balance	270		2,700

29 The correct answer is: $264 CREDIT

SUSPENSE ACCOUNT

	$		$
Balance b/f	346	Purchases (2)	520
Balance c/f	264	Sundry income (3)	90
	610		610

30 The correct answer is: $10.80

Discounts received account for cash/settlement discounts received from suppliers on purchases. Transaction 1 relates to discounts on sales so does not impact the discounts received account. Therefore, in transaction 2, purchase net of trade discount = $600 × 90% = $540 (trade discounts are not accounted for separately). Early settlement discount = 2% × $540 = $10.80.

31 The correct answer is: Statement of cash flows only

Proceeds of a sale of non-current assets will only be presented in the statement of cash flows.

32 The correct answer is: The company does not carry any inventory.

The company does not carry any inventory. The calculation for the quick ratio excludes inventory. So, if the current ratio (including inventory) and the quick ratio (excluding inventory) are the same, this must mean that 'inventory' is zero.

33 The correct answer is: $283,650

	$	
	284,000	
Item 1	–	No change as NRV exceeds cost
Item 2	(350)	Reduce to NRV (1,000 – 650)
	283,650	

34 The correct answers are:

- One of the conditions to be satisfied if development expenditure is to be capitalised is that the technical feasibility of the project is reasonably assured.
- Development expenditure may only be capitalised if it can be shown that adequate resources will be available to finance the completion of the project

Statements (1) and (3) are incorrect.

35 The correct answer is: There was an unusually large sale on credit close to the end of the financial year.

If there has been a large credit sale near the end of the financial year, the amount owed will be included within receivables at the year end and trade receivables may be unusually high. If so, the average time for receivables to pay may be distorted, because year-end receivables are used to calculate the turnover ratio.

A large volume of sales in the final quarter of every year may explain why the measurement of the average collection period is long every year, but not why the collection period should be unusually long compared with the previous year.

Comparatively low sales in the final quarter would be more likely to result in a shorter-than-normal measurement of the average collection period.

Tighter credit control processes should result in a more efficient receivables collection period and therefore trade receivables being lower at the end of the current year, relative to the previous year.

ANSWERS

Section B

36 **Task 1**

NOBRIE

STATEMENT OF CASH FLOWS FOR THE YEAR ENDED 30 MAY 20X4

	$'000	$'000
Cash flow from operating activities		
Profit before tax	41,738	
Adjustments for		
Depreciation	5,862	
Profit on equipment disposal	(1,540)	
Investment income	(146)	
Interest paid	1,177	
	47,091	
Operating profit before working capital changes		
Increase in inventory	(866)	
Increase in receivables	(5,684)	
Decrease in payables	(3,625)	
Cash generated from operations	36,916	
Interest paid*	(1,177)	
Tax paid (W1)	(9,191)	
Net cash flows from operating activities		26,548

Working

Tax paid

TAXATION

	$'000		$'000
Tax paid (bal fig)	9,191	Balance b/fwd	7,323
Balance c/fwd	7,989	Statement of profit or loss	9,857
	17,180		17,180

Task 2

The carrying amount of property, plant and equipment disposals:

$ 1,513,000

The cash purchases of property, plant and equipment for the year ended 31 May 20X4:

$ 28,048,000

Workings

1 ***PROPERTY, PLANT AND EQUIPMENT***

	$'000		$'000
Balance b/fwd (carrying amount)	88,466	Disposals (carrying amount) (see working below)	1,513
Revaluation (15,395 – 7,123)	8,272	Depreciation	5,862
Purchases (bal fig)	28,048	Balance c/fwd (carrying amount)	117,411
	124,786		124,786

2 ***Disposals***

	$'000
Proceeds	3,053
Profit	1,540
Carrying amount of disposals	1,513

Task 3

The correct answers are:

- Increase in share capital
- Increase in share premium

Only the increase in share capital and share premium from the cash issue of shares is shown as a cash inflow on the statement of cash flows.

The increase in the revaluation surplus is a non-cash transaction and therefore is not included in the statement of cash flows.

The increase in retained earnings is shown as profit before tax in cash flows from operating activities in the statement of cash flows.

37 **Task 1**

Calculation of goodwill

	$'000	$'000
Fair value of consideration transferred		660,000
Fair value of NCI at acquisition		165,000
Less Net acquisition-date fair value of identifiable assets acquired and liabilities assumed:		
Share capital	600,000	
Retained earnings at acquisition	95,000	
Fair value adjustment at acquisition	70,000	
		(765,000)
Goodwill		60,000

Task 2

SPYDER GROUP

CONSOLIDATED STATEMENT OF FINANCIAL POSITION AS AT 31 OCTOBER 20X5

	$'000
Assets	
Non-current assets	
Goodwill	60,000
Land and buildings (315 + 278 + 70)	663,000
Plant (285 + 220)	505,000
	1,228,000
Current assets	
Inventory (357 + 252 - 12)	597,000
Receivables (525 + 126 - 25)	626,000
Bank (158 + 30)	188,000
	1,411,000
Total assets	2,639,000
Equity and liabilities	
Equity attributable to owners of the parent	
$1 ordinary shares	1,500,000
Retained earnings (W2)	661,600
Non-controlling interest (W3)	188,400
Current liabilities	
Payables (220 + 94 - 25)	289,000
Total equity and liabilities	2,639,000

Workings

1 ***Group structure***

480m/600m = 80%

2 ***Retained earnings***

	Spyder	*Phly*
	$m	$m
Per question	580.0	212
Adjustment (unrealised profit)	(12.0)	
Pre-acquisition retained earnings		(95)
		117
Group share of post-acquisition retained earnings: Phly (80% × 117)	93.6	
Group retained earnings	661.6	

3 ***Non-controlling interest***

	$m
Fair value of NCI at acquisition	165.0
Plus NCI's share of post-acquisition retained earnings (20% × 117)	23.4
NCI at reporting date	188.4

ANSWERS

Foundations in Accountancy/ACCA

Financial Accounting (FFA/FA)

Mock Exam 3

Questions	
Time allowed	2 hours
This exam is divided into two sections: Section A – ALL 35 questions are compulsory and MUST be attempted Section B – BOTH questions are compulsory and MUST be attempted	

DO NOT OPEN THIS EXAM UNTIL YOU ARE READY TO START UNDER EXAMINATION CONDITIONS

Section A

ALL 35 questions are compulsory and MUST be attempted

1 What is the role of the IFRS Interpretations Committee?

- O To oversee the standard setting process.
- O To monitor company's compliance with current IFRS Standards.
- O To issue new IFRS Standards to keep up to date with current environmental conditions.
- O To provide guidance on specific practical issues in the application of IFRS Standards.

(2 marks)

---

2 A company receives a cash discount of $35 from a supplier. The amount is debited to the discount received account.

What is the effect on profit for the year?

- O Understated by $35
- O Understated by $70
- O Overstated by $70
- O Overstated by $35

(2 marks)

---

3 The allowance for receivables brought forward from 20X6 was $1,200. During 20X7 an irrecoverable debt of $75 required writing off. At the end of the year closing receivables were $100,000 and an allowance of 1.5% is required for receivables.

What is the charge to the statement of profit and loss for receivables expense for the year? (Do not enter numbers as minus and do not enter commas.)

$ [ ]

(2 marks)

---

4 Which groups of people are most likely to be interested in the financial statements of a large supermarket with shares listed on the stock exchange?

(1) The general public

(2) The company's suppliers

(3) The company's bank

(4) Stockbrokers

- O 1 and 2 only
- O 2 and 3 only
- O 2, 3 and 4 only
- O 1, 2, 3 and 4

(2 marks)

---

5 Which **TWO** of the following sets of items all appear on the same side of the trial balance?

☐ Sales; interest received; and accruals

☐ Receivables; drawings; and discount received

☐ Capital; trade payables; and other operating expenses

☐ Sundry expenses; prepayments; and purchases **(2 marks)**

---

6 Which **TWO** of the following formulae are correct?

☐ Credit sales = closing receivables + receipts from trade receivables – opening receivables

☐ Payments to trade payables + opening payables – closing payables = credit purchases

☐ Cost of goods sold = closing inventories + purchases – opening inventories

☐ Cost of goods sold + closing inventories – opening inventories = purchases **(2 marks)**

---

7 Clanger's trial balance did not balance and a suspense account was opened to restore equality. The following errors were discovered:

(1) Telephone expenses of $673 had been entered in the telephone account as $763.

(2) A purchase invoice of $2,340 had been entered in the accounting records as $3,240

(3) Discounts received of $264 had been debited to the purchases account.

What is the balance required in the suspense account to balance the trial balance? (Do not enter sums as minus and do not enter commas.)

$ [   ] credit **(2 marks)**

---

8 Identify, by selecting the correct box in the table below, which, if any, of the following items could form part of the calculation of cash flow from financing activities in accordance with IAS 7 *Statement of Cash Flows*.

Item	**Part of cash flow from financing activities**	**Not part of cash flow from financing activities**
Proceeds of sale of premises	○	○
Dividends received	○	○
Bonus issue of shares	○	○

(2 marks)

---

9 Identify, by selecting the correct box in the table below, whether the following statements about bank reconciliations are correct or incorrect.

Statement	Correct	Incorrect
A difference between the bank general ledger account and the bank statement must be corrected by means of a journal entry	O	O
In preparing a bank reconciliation, lodgements recorded before date in the bank general ledger account but credited by the bank after date should reduce an overdrawn balance in the bank statement	O	O
Bank charges not yet entered in the bank general ledger account should be dealt with by an adjustment in the bank reconciliation statement	O	O
If a cheque received from a customer is dishonoured, a credit entry in the bank general ledger account is required	O	O

(2 marks)

10 The acid test ratio and the current ratio are frequently calculated ratios.

Which of the following do these ratios give information about?

- O Long-term solvency
- O Profitability
- O Liquidity
- O Gearing

(2 marks)

11 Tollan Co has the following intangible assets in its statement of financial position at 31 October 20X4:

	$
Patent relating to new chair design (useful life 5 years)	510,000
Development project A (complete, useful life 10 years)	250,000
Development project B (incomplete, expected to complete in 20X5, expected useful life 10 years)	160,000
Total intangible assets	920,000

Tollan calculates amortisation on a straight line basis.

In accordance with IAS 38 *Intangible Assets*, what amount for amortisation of intangible assets should be included in Tollan's statement of profit or loss for the year ended 31 October 20X4?

- O $102,000
- O $127,000
- O $25,000
- O $143,000

(2 marks)

12 Which of the following statements concerning the receivables ledger is not correct?

- O In a computerised accounting system, the total sum of the individual credit customer accounts will equal the balance per the trade receivables account.
- O In a computerised accounting system, key details from the sales invoice raised by the bookkeeper are automatically posted to the sales account and trade receivables account in the general ledger.
- O The trade receivables account shows the amount due to the business from individual credit customers.
- O The receivables ledger shows the total amount due to a business from its receivables.

(2 marks)

---

13 A bank statement shows a balance of funds in the account of $1,200. An examination of the bank statement shows a $500 cheque paid in per the bank general ledger account but not yet on the bank statement and a $1,250 cheque paid out but not yet on the statement. In addition, the bank statement shows deposit interest received of $50 but this has not yet been recorded in the bank general ledger account.

What is the balance per the bank general ledger account?

- O $400 in hand
- O $500 overdrawn
- O $1,900 in hand
- O $1,900 overdrawn

(2 marks)

---

14 An ordinary dividend is declared prior to the year end.

Identify, by selecting the correct box in the table below, what the accounting treatment relating to the ordinary dividend in the financial statements is.

	Debit	Credit	No effect
Share capital (SOFP)	O	O	O
Retained earnings (SOFP)	O	O	O
Finance cost (SPL)	O	O	O
Dividend payable (SOFP)	O	O	O

(2 marks)

---

15 The rent expense in the statement of profit and loss for the year was $4,000. $200 was prepaid at the start of the year and $400 was owing at the end of year.

What was the bank general ledger account figure for rent paid?

- O $4,000
- O $4,200
- O $3,400
- O $3,800

(2 marks)

---

16 Which of the following errors could explain a suspense account balance of $50 (debit) on a preliminary trial balance?

- A purchase invoice for $50 had only been recorded in the trade payables account
- Discounts received of $50 had been omitted from the trial balance
- An sales invoice for $550 was recorded as $500 in the accounting records
- A bank payment of $50 in respect of an electricity expense was only recorded in the electricity expense account **(2 marks)**

---

17 A company incurs the following expenditure: $86,000 in attempting to convert seaweed into a cure for muscular injuries; $192,000 developing a painkiller whose commercial production commenced on 1 April 20X1; the painkiller is expected to be a market leader for ten years.

Amortisation is charged proportionality in the year of acquisition and the year of disposal.

What is the carrying amount of development expenditure in the statement of financial position as at year end 31 July 20X1?

- $135,600
- $278,000
- $271,600
- $192,000 **(2 marks)**

---

18 Identify, by selecting the correct box in the table below, whether the following statements are true or false in accordance with IAS 37 *Provisions, Contingent Liabilities and Contingent Assets*

	True	False
Remote contingent liabilities should be disclosed	O	O
Possible contingent liabilities should be disclosed	O	O
Possible contingent assets should be disclosed	O	O
Probable contingent liabilities should be disclosed	O	O

(2 marks)

---

19 McIntosh has opening inventory of 100 units valued at $2.50 each. During February, the following movements of inventory occurred.

Date	Movement	Quantity	$
4th	Receipts	400	2.60
7th	Issues	150	
14th	Issues	50	
17th	Receipts	100	2.70
23rd	Issues	250	

McIntosh uses the FIFO method to value inventory.

According to IAS 2 *Inventories*, what is the value of inventory at the end of February?

- O $380
- O $400
- O $360
- O $350

(2 marks)

---

20 Hartley Co wishes to increase its return on capital employed (ROCE).

Identify, by selecting the correct boxes in the table below, whether the following courses of action increase or decrease ROCE in the short term.

	Increase ROCE	**Decrease ROCE**
Revalue land and buildings upwards	O	O
Reduce overhead expenses	O	O
Issue ordinary shares	O	O
Increase revenue	O	O

(2 marks)

---

21 Which of the following will appear on the debit side of a trade payables account?

- O Invoices to customers
- O Invoices from suppliers
- O Discounts received
- O Irrecoverable debts written off

(2 marks)

---

22 An inexperienced bookkeeper has drawn up the following trade receivables account:

TRADE RECEIVABLES

	$		$
Opening balance	180,000	Credit sales	190,000
Bank receipts from credit customers	228,000	Irrecoverable debts written off	1,500
Sales returns	12,200	Contras against payables	2,400
Cash refunds to credit customers	3,300	Closing balance (balancing figure)	229,600
	423,500		423,500

What should the closing balance be after correcting the errors made in preparing the account?

- O $130,600
- O $129,200
- O $142,400
- O $412,600

(2 marks)

---

23 Ranjit Singh started a business on 1 November. On that date, he opened a bank account for the business by paying in $4,000. During November, the following transactions took place.

Purchased goods on credit	$1,500
Cash sales banked	$650
Drawings	$800
Payments to suppliers	$750

What balance should Ranjit's trial balance show for the bank account at 30 November?

- O $3,100 debit
- O $3,100 credit
- O $1,600 debit
- O $1,600 credit

(2 marks)

---

24 The net assets of Kate's business were $16,100 at 1 January 20X3 and $27,600 at 31 December 20X3. During the year Kate paid lottery winnings of $2,950 into the business bank account and withdrew $1,450.

What was the profit for the year ended 31 December 20X3? (Do not enter numbers as minus and do not enter commas.)

$ [ ]

(2 marks)

---

25 A Co has the following year end balances as at 31 December 20X5.

	$'000
Ordinary share capital	1,000
Redeemable preference share capital (redeemable in 31.12.Y9)	500
Bank overdraft	680
Bank loan (repayable 31.12.X8)	500
Tax payable	250

What is the total of the non-current liabilities on the statement of financial position as at 31 December 20X5?

- O $500
- O $1,000
- O $1,680
- O $1,930

(2 marks)

---

26 Which groups of people are most likely to be interested in the financial statements of a sole trader?

(1) Shareholders of the company
(2) The business's bank manager
(3) The tax authorities
(4) Financial analysts

- O 1 and 2 only
- O 2 and 3 only
- O 2, 3 and 4 only
- O 1, 2 and 3 only

(2 marks)

---

27 A bookkeeper has recorded the following totals of the transactions which took place during May:

	$
Discount received	750
Irrecoverable debt expense	150
Returns inwards	310
Bank payments to suppliers	59,650
Purchases	40,750
Returns outwards	270

If the trade payables opening balance was $55,750, what was the closing balance? (Do not enter numbers as minus and do not enter commas.)

$ [ ]

(2 marks)

---

28 Which **TWO** of the items below would not appear in the statement of cash flows?

- ☐ A bonus issue of shares
- ☐ Dividend paid to preference shareholders in the year
- ☐ Repayment of a bank loan
- ☐ The statement of profit and loss charge for taxation for the current period

(2 marks)

---

29 Lydd Co purchases production machinery costing $100,000 and having an estimated useful life of 20 years and a residual value of $2,000. After being in use for six years the remaining useful life of the machinery is revised and estimated to be 25 years, with an unchanged residual value.

The company's depreciation policy for production machinery is to depreciate on a straight line basis.

What is the annual depreciation charge on the machinery in year 7?

$ ☐ **(2 marks)**

---

30 Identify, by selecting the relevant boxes in the table below, whether the following items could form part of the calculation of cash flow from operating activities in accordance with IAS 7 *Statement of Cash Flows*.

	Part of cash flow from operating activities	**Not part of cash flow from operating activities**
Proceeds from a rights issue of shares	○	○
Dividends paid	○	○
Interest paid	○	○
Interest received	○	○

(2 marks)

---

31 During its financial period, a business has the following transactions.

	$
Sales	50,000
Purchases	33,000
Sales returns	3,500
Purchase returns	2,000
Closing inventory	3,500

Gross profit was $14,000. What was the figure for opening inventory? (Do not enter numbers as minus and do not enter commas.)

$ ☐ **(2 marks)**

---

32 At 01.04.X8, PRH Co has 1 million shares in issue (par value $1).

During the year ended 31.03.X9, the following share transactions took place:

On 01.08.X8, PRH Co makes a 1 for 4 bonus issue.

On 01.12.X8, PRH Co makes a 1 for 5 rights issue at $1.20 which was fully subscribed.

What is PRH Co's ordinary share capital balance at 31.03.X9?

- O $1,500,000
- O $1,550,000
- O $1,440,000
- O $1,450,000

(2 marks)

---

33 Extracts from the preliminary trial balance of Jessie and Co as at 30 September 20X2 are included in the table. Further adjustments are to be made as follows:

(1) No entries have been made in respect of cash of $920 received from Kieran whose balance had been written off last year; and

(2) At 30 September 20X2 an allowance is for 1.5% of the receivables balance.

	Debit	*Credit*
Trade receivables account	$90,350	
Allowance for receivables (brought forward as at 1 October 20X1)		$2,490
Irrecoverable debts and allowance for receivables expense	$1,860	

What is the total charge or credit in the statement of profit or loss for receivables? (Do not enter numbers as minus and do not enter commas.)

$ [ ] credit

(2 marks)

---

34 Which **TWO** of the following describe consistency?

- ☐ The effects of transactions should be reflected in the financial statements for the accounting period in which they occur and not necessarily in the period where any cash involved is received or paid.
- ☐ Using the same treatment for the same items from one period to the next.
- ☐ In situations where there is uncertainty, appropriate caution must be exercised in recognising transactions in financial records.
- ☐ Similar items within a single set of financial accounts should be given similar accounting treatment

(2 marks)

---

35 A Co has issued share capital of 300,000 ordinary shares of $0.10 each. It declares and pays a dividend of 1c per share. What is the journal entry to account for the dividend?

- O Dr Dividends $30,000, Cr Cash $30,000
- O Dr Finance Cost $30,000, Cr Cash $30,000
- O Dr Dividends $3,000, Cr Cash $3,000
- O Dr Finance Cost $3,000, Cr Cash $3,000

(2 marks)

Section B

BOTH questions are compulsory and MUST be attempted

36 The following information has been extracted from the accounting records of Monsoon, a limited liability company, as at 31 October 20X6.

	DR	CR
	$'000	$'000
Cash in hand	10	
Inventory at 1 November 20X5	300	
General expenses	330	
Marketing expenses	50	
Wages and salaries	675	
Share premium account		250
Retained earnings at 1 November 20X5		524
Allowance for receivables at 1 November 20X5		40
Sales revenue		5,685
Bank		94
Trade payables		290
Loan note interest	28	
Trade receivables	900	
Purchases	3,520	
7% loan notes		400
Irrecoverable debts	150	
$1 ordinary shares		1,500
Land at cost	740	
Buildings at cost	1,500	
Furniture and equipment at cost	1,200	
Motor vehicles at cost	240	
Accumulated depreciation at 1 November 20X5:		
Buildings		360
Motor vehicles		80
Furniture and equipment		420
	9,643	9,643

You have also been provided with the following information:

- Inventory at 31 October 20X6 was valued at $275,000 based on its original cost. However, $45,000 of this inventory has been in the warehouse for over two years and the directors have agreed to sell it in November 20X6 for a cash price of $15,000.
- The marketing expenses include $5,000 which relates to November 20X6.
- The allowance for receivables is to be increased to 8% of trade receivables.
- There are wages and salaries outstanding of $40,000 for the year ended 31 October 20X6.
- Depreciation is to be charged as follows:
  - Building at 5% of cost.
  - Motor vehicles at 20% of carrying amount.
  - Furniture and equipment at 20% of cost.
- No dividends have been paid or declared.
- Tax of $150,000 is to be provided for the year.

Task 1

Complete the following statement of profit or loss for the year ended 31 October 20X6, prepared for internal purposes. **(2 marks)**

Statement of profit or loss

	$'000
Sales revenue	5,685
Cost of sales	

Task 2

Complete the following:

	$'000
(1) ▼	(2) ▼

Pull down list 1

- Gross profit
- Gross profit margin
- Mark up
- Operating profit

Pull down list 2

- Cost of sales divided by revenue
- Revenue add cost of sales
- Revenue less cost of sales

(2 marks)

Task 3

Complete the following: **(9 marks)**

	$'000	$'000
Expenses		
Marketing expenses	[ ]	
Wages and salaries	[ ]	
General expenses	[ ]	
Loan note interest	[ ]	
Irrecoverable debt expense	[ ]	
Depreciation	[ ]	
		[ ]
Profit before taxation		[ ]
Taxation		[ ]
Profit for the year		[ ]

Task 4

Identify, by selecting the relevant boxes in the table below, where the following balances are presented in the statement of financial position.

	Assets	**Liabilities**	**Equity**
Share premium account	O	O	O
Trade receivables	O	O	O
7% loan notes	O	O	O

(2 marks)

(Total = 15 marks)

---

37 On 1 July 20X6, Matlock Co acquired 150,000 $1 ordinary shares in Rugby Co at a cost of $300,000. The fair value of the non-controlling interest at acquisition was $100,000. Rugby Co's financial statements at the date of acquisition showed equity of:

	$
Ordinary share capital	200,000
Retained earnings	36,200
	236,000

At 30 June 20X8, Rugby Co had retained earnings of $16,000.

Task 1

What is the goodwill arising on consolidation?

$ [ ] **(3 marks)**

Task 2

In the year to 30 June 20X8, Matlock Co had revenue of $350,000 and Rugby Co had revenue of $125,000. Included in Matlock's revenue are goods sold to Rugby for $25,000 that cost Matlock $20,000 to buy. Half of these goods are still in Rugby's inventory at the year end.

On 30 June 20X8, the inventory figures shown in the statements of financial position of each company were: Matlock $200,000 and Rugby $100,000.

What is the consolidated revenue figure for the year ended 30 June 20X8?

- O $475,000
- O $450,000
- O $465,000
- O $455,000

(3 marks)

Task 3

What amount of inventory will be shown in the consolidated statement of financial position at 30 June 20X8?

$ ☐

(3 marks)

Task 4

Sapphire's profit for the year was $45,500. During the year, Matlock sold goods to Sapphire. As a result, inventories in the consolidated statement of financial position have been reduced to reflect unrealised profit of $5,000.

How much of the non-controlling interests (NCI) figure that appears in the consolidated statement of profit or loss for the year relates to NCI in Sapphire Co, for the year ended 30 June 20X9?

$ ☐

(3 marks)

Task 5

Identify, by selecting the relevant boxes in the table below, what type of investment P has in S in the following situations.

P owns 49% of the voting rights of S and can appoint 2 out of 5 directors to its board.	**SUBSIDIARY**	**ASSOCIATE**	**INVESTMENT**
P has a 25% interest in S and exercises significant influence over S's operating and financial policy.	**SUBSIDIARY**	**ASSOCIATE**	**INVESTMENT**
P owns 49% of the voting rights of S and controls its board.	**SUBSIDIARY**	**ASSOCIATE**	**INVESTMENT**
P has power to govern the financial and operating policies of S under an agreement.	**SUBSIDIARY**	**ASSOCIATE**	**INVESTMENT**

(3 marks)

(Total = 15 marks)

Answers

DO NOT TURN THIS PAGE UNTIL YOU HAVE COMPLETED THE MOCK EXAM

Section A

1 The correct answer is: To provide guidance on specific practical issues in the application of IFRS Standards.

2 The correct answer is: Understated by $70

Discounts received should have been credited. To correct the error we need to credit discounts received twice, once to reverse the error and once to post the correct entry. Therefore, profit is understated by $70.

3 $ 375

The T-account for receivables expense looks like this:

RECEIVABLES EXPENSE

	$		$
Debt written off	75	Opening balance b/f	1,200
Closing balance c/f	1,500	Statement of profit or loss	375
	1,575		1,575

4 The correct answer is: 1, 2, 3 and 4

The general public may be interested to see how the supermarket can contribute to the local economy and create jobs, as well as the affect it has on the environment.

The supermarket's suppliers will want to know about the supermarkets ability to pay them in a reasonable timeframe.

The company's bank will want to know about the supermarkets ability to repay any debts, or the likelihood of being in breach of any debt agreement.

Stockbrokers will want to examine if the supermarket is a sound investment for investors to buy shares in.

5 The correct answers are:

- Sales; interest received; and accruals
- Sundry expenses; prepayments; and purchases

Sales, interest received and accruals are all credit balances

Sundry expenses, prepayments and other operating expenses are all debit balances.

6 The correct answers are:

- Credit sales = closing receivables + receipts from trade receivables – opening receivables
- Cost of goods sold + closing inventories – opening inventories = purchases

The remaining two formulae should read:

Payments to trade payables + closing payables - opening payables = credit purchases

Cost of goods sold = opening inventories + purchases – closing inventories

7 $ 618 credit

Item 1 means that total debits were overstated by $90. Item 2 leads to compensating errors in the purchases and payables accounts. 3 means that total debits were overstated by 2 × $264 = $528

8 The correct answers are:

- Proceeds of sale of premises - **Not part of cash flow from financing activities**
- Dividends received - **Not part of cash flow from financing activities**
- Bonus issue of shares - **Not part of cash flow from financing activities**

Item	Part of cash flow from financing activities	Not part of cash flow from financing activities
Proceeds of sale of premises		✔ (presented under investing activities)
Dividends received		✔ (presented under operating or investing activities)
Bonus issue of shares		✔ (a bonus issue is not a cash flow)

9 The correct answers are:

- A difference between the bank general ledger account and the bank statement must be corrected by means of a journal entry - **Incorrect**
- In preparing a bank reconciliation, lodgements recorded before date in the bank general ledger account but credited by the bank after date should reduce an overdrawn balance in the bank statement - **Correct**
- Bank charges not yet entered in the bank general ledger account should be dealt with by an adjustment in the bank reconciliation statement - **Incorrect**
- If a cheque received from a customer is dishonoured, a credit entry in the bank general ledger account is required - **Correct**

Statement	Correct	Incorrect
A difference between the bank general ledger account and the bank statement must be corrected by means of a journal entry.		✔ (a journal entry is only required if the bank general ledger account is incomplete or incorrect)
In preparing a bank reconciliation, lodgements recorded before date in the bank general ledger account but credited by the bank after date should reduce an overdrawn balance in the bank statement.	✔	
Bank charges not yet entered in the bank general ledger account should be dealt with by an adjustment in the bank reconciliation statement.		✔ (they should be entered into the bank general ledger account and the bank general ledger account balance adjusted)
If a cheque received from a customer is dishonoured, a credit entry in the bank general ledger account is required.	✔	

10 The correct answer is: Liquidity

Information about long-term solvency is obtained through calculating gearing and debt ratios. Information about profitability is obtained through the use of ROCE, ROE and gross and net profit margins

11 The correct answer is: $127,000

	$
Patent (510/5)	102,000
Development project A (250/10)	25,000
Total amortisation	127,000

The balance relating to development project B should not be amortised until the project is finished and the asset is available for use.

12 The correct answer is: The trade receivables account shows the amount due to the business from individual credit customers.

The trade receivables account shows the total amount due to the business from credit customers but not the individual amounts owed by each customer.

13 The correct answer is: $400 in hand

Working

	$
Balance per bank statement	1,200
Add: outstanding deposits	500
Less	
Unpresented cheques	(1,250)
Deposit interest not yet recorded in bank general ledger account	(50)
Balance per bank general ledger account	400

14 The correct answers are:

- Share capital (SOFP) - **No effect**
- Retained earnings (SOFP) - **Debit**
- Finance cost (SPL) - **Credit**
- Dividend payable (SOFP) - **Credit**

15 The correct answer is: $3,400

Rent paid will be: $4,000 – $200 (prepaid) – $400 (owing) = $3,400

16 The correct answer is: A purchase invoice for $50 had only been recorded in the trade payables account

Discounts received of $50 had been omitted from the trial balance which does not cause an imbalance in the trial balance. The error in recording the sales invoice will not result in a suspense account balance as this affects both trade receivables and the sales account. The single entry of the electricity expense in the electricity expense account only would produce a credit balance on the suspense account.

17 The correct answer is: $185,600

The $192,000 relates to a specific project and is technically and economically viable. Assuming that the costs will be amortised on a straight line basis 4 months amortisation should be provided ($192,000/10 × 4/12 = $6,400).

18 The correct answers are:

- Remote contingent liabilities should be disclosed - **False**
- Possible contingent liabilities should be disclosed - **True**
- Possible contingent assets should be disclosed - **False**
- Probable contingent liabilities should be disclosed - **True**

If the chance of occurrence is probable, contingent assets should be disclosed (IAS 37: para. 89).

It is only when probability is remote that contingent liabilities are ignored altogether (IAS 37: para. 86).

If a contingent liability becomes probable, then it is no longer a contingent liability and should be provided for (IAS 37: para. 30).

19 The correct answer is: $400

The value of closing inventory after each transaction is as follows:

Date	Quantity	$
4th	500	250 + 1,040 = 1,290
7th	350	910
14th	300	780
17th	400	780 + 270 = 1,050
23rd	150	130 + 270 = 400

20 The correct answers are:

- Revalue land and buildings upwards - **Decrease ROCE**
- Reduce overhead expenses - **Increase ROCE**
- Issue ordinary shares - **Decrease ROCE**
- Increase revenue - **Increase ROCE**

ROCE is likely to increase if the company increases revenue or reduces overhead expenses as these will both increase operating profit.

Revaluing land and buildings upwards and issuing ordinary shares will increase capital employed and decrease ROCE in the short term. (The issue of shares may lead to an increase in profits and ROCE in the longer term because more cash will be available to invest in the business to generate more sales.)

21 The correct answer is: Discounts received

Invoices from suppliers will be credited to the trade payables account. Invoices to customers and irrecoverable debts written off will both appear in the trade receivables account.

22 The correct answer is: $129,200

TRADE RECEIVABLES

	$		$
Opening balance	180,000	Bank receipts from credit customers	228,000
Credit sales	190,000	Irrecoverable debts written off	1,500
Cash refund	3,300	Sales returns	12,200
		Contras	2,400
		Closing balance	129,200
	373,300		373,300

23 The correct answer is: $3,100 debit

	$
Opening balance	4,000 debit
Add: Bankings	650
	4,650
Less payments:	
Drawings	800
To suppliers	750
	1,550
Balance c/f	3,100 debit

Remember that the goods purchased on credit do not affect the bank account until payments are made to suppliers.

24 $ 10,000

(Capital c/f – capital b/f – capital introduced + drawings = profit for the year)

	$
Closing net assets	27,600
Less: opening net assets	(16,100)
Less: capital introduced	(2,950)
Add: drawings	1,450
Profit for the year	10,000

Working

Proof

Opening capital + capital introduced + profit for the year – drawings = closing capital

16,100 + 2,950 + 10,000 – 1,450 = 27,600

25 The correct answer is: $1,000

	$'000
Redeemable preference share capital (redeemable in 31.12.Y9)	500
Bank loan (repayable 31.12.X8)	500
	1,000

Because the preference share capital is redeemable, it is classified as a liability in accordance with IAS 32 *Financial Instrument: Presentation*. The bank overdraft and tax payable are current liabilities. Ordinary share capital is equity.

26 The correct answer is: 2 and 3 only

A sole trader does not have any shareholders. The accounts are unlikely to be of interest to a financial analyst, they are usually interested in the accounts of public companies

27 $ 35,830

TRADE PAYABLES

	$		$
Bank payments to suppliers	59,650	Balance b/f	55,750
Returns outwards	270	Purchases	40,750
Discount received	750		
Balance c/f	35,830		
	96,500		96,500

28 The correct answers are:

- A bonus issue of shares
- The statement of profit and loss charge for taxation for the current period

The statement of profit and loss charge for taxation for the current period is not shown in the statement of cash flows.

The cash flow will show the actual tax paid.

There is no cash received or paid when a bonus issue of shares is made, so the bonus issue will not appear in the statement of cash flows.

29 $ 2,744

Depreciation to date = (100,000 – 2,000)/20 × 6 = 29,400

Carrying amount = 100,000 – 29,400 = 70,600

New depreciation = (70,600 – 2,000)/25 = 2,744

30 The correct answers are:

- Proceeds from a rights issue of shares - **Not part of cash flow from operating activities**
- Dividends paid - **Part of cash flow from operating activities**
- Interest paid - **Part of cash flow from operating activities**
- Interest received - **Not part of cash flow from operating activities**

31 $ 5,000

	$	$
Net sales		46,500
Opening inventory	5,000	
Net purchases	31,000	
	36,000	
Closing inventory	3,500	
		32,500
Gross profit		14,000

32 The correct answer is: $1,500,000

1 million shares at $1	$1,000,000
Plus bonus issue 1 for 4	$250,000
Plus rights issue 1 for 5	$250,000
(The 20c premium would be in the share premium account)	$1,500,000

33 $ 195 credit

Irrecoverable debts and allowance for receivables expense per TB	$1,860
Less: Irrecoverable debt recovered	$920
Less: Decrease in allowance	$1,135
	$195 credit

Allowance required = 1.5% × 90,350	$1,355
Allowance b/f	$2,490
Therefore decrease	$1,135

34 The correct answers are:

- Using the same treatment for the same items from one period to the next.
- Similar items within a single set of financial accounts should be given similar accounting treatment

The correct answers are: Using the same treatment for the same items from one period to the next. Similar items within a single set of financial accounts should be given similar accounting treatment.

These statements describe consistency.

Under the accruals concept, the effects of transactions should be reflected in the financial statements for the accounting period in which they occur and not necessarily in the period where any cash involved is received or paid.

Prudence states that in situations where there is uncertainty, appropriate caution must be exercised in recognising transactions in financial records.

35 The correct answer is: Dr Dividends $3,000, Cr Cash $3,000

The dividend is shown in the statement of changes in equity and is calculated as $0.01 × $300,000 = $3,000.

Section B

36 **Task 1**

Statement of profit or loss

	$'000
Sales revenue	5,685
Cost of sales	-3,575

Task 2

	$'000
Gross profit	Revenue less cost of sales

Task 3

	$'000	$'000
Expenses		
Marketing expenses	45	
Wages and salaries	715	
General expenses	330	
Loan note interest	28	
Irrecoverable debt expense	182	
Depreciation	347	
		-1,647
Profit before taxation		463
Taxation		-150
Profit for the year		313

MONSOON

STATEMENT OF PROFIT OR LOSS FOR THE YEAR ENDED 31 OCTOBER 20X6

	$'000	$'000
Sales revenue		5,685
		5,685
Cost of sales (W1)		–3,575
Gross profit		Revenue less cost of sales
Expenses		
Marketing expenses (50 – 5)	45	
Wages and salaries (675 + 40)	715	
General expenses	330	
Loan note interest	28	
Irrecoverable debt expense (W2)	182	

	$'000		$'000
Depreciation (W3)	347		
			−1,647
Profit before taxation			463
Taxation			−150
Profit for the year			313

Workings

1 ***Cost of sales***

	$'000	$'000
Opening inventory		300
Purchases		3,520
Closing inventory		
Per question	275	
Less write-down to NRV (45 – 15)	−30	
		−245
		3,575

2 ***Irrecoverable debt expense***

		$
Receivables per trial balance	900	
Allowance required 900,000 × 8%	72	
Allowance per trial balance	(40)	
Increase		32
Irrecoverable debt written off		150
Total irrecoverable debt expense		182

3 ***Depreciation***

	Land	*Buildings*	*Motor vehicles*	*Furniture and equipment*
	$'000	$'000	$'000	$'000
Cost	740	1,500	240	1,200
Depreciation at 1.11.X5	0	360	80	420
Charge for the year 1,500 × 5%		75		
(240 – 80) × 20%			32	
1,200 × 20%				240
Total depreciation charge: 75 + 32 + 240 =				347

Task 4

The correct answers are:

- Share premium account - **Equity**
- Trade receivables - **Assets**
- 7% loan notes - **Liabilities**

37 **Task 1**

$ 164,000

Goodwill calculation	$
Consideration transferred	300,000
Fair value of NCI	100,000
Net assets acquired (200 + 36)	(236,000)
Goodwill	164,000

The reduction in net assets since acquisition is not relevant for the purposes of determining goodwill.

Task 2

The correct answer is: $450,000

Matlock 350,000 + Rugby 125,000 – intragroup sales 25,000 = $450,000

Task 3

$ 297,500

Inventory = Matlock $200,000 + Rugby $100,000 – unrealised profit $2,500 ($5,000 × 50%) = $297,500

Task 4

$ 13,650

NCI = 45,500 × 9/12 × 40% = $13,650.

The intragroup sales were from the parent to the subsidiary and so the unrealised profit is in the parent, which does not affect the NCI.

Task 5

The correct answers are:

P owns 49% of the voting rights of S and can appoint 2 out of 5 directors to its board.		**ASSOCIATE**	
P has a 25% interest in S and exercises significant influence over S's operating and financial policy.		**ASSOCIATE**	
P owns 49% of the voting rights of S and controls its board.	**SUBSIDIARY**		
P has power to govern the financial and operating policies of S under an agreement.	**SUBSIDIARY**		

Tell us what you think

Got comments or feedback on this book? Let us know.
Use your QR code reader:

Or, visit:
https://bppgroup.fra1.qualtrics.com/jfe/form/SV_9TrxTtw8jSvO7Pv

Need to get in touch with customer service?

www.bpp.com/request-support

Spotted an error?

www.bpp.com/learningmedia/Errata